President

You

Keith —
Johnson's County
Gazette. Enjoy
the read and thanks
for the published
article.
Tom Williams
#30
2019

President You

How a Thoughtful

Ordinary Citizen

Could Change

the Most Complex

Government on Earth

Tom Williams

To Mom and Dad

Table of Contents

A Note to the Reader

Americans today are inundated with discussions about politics and government. Television programs, talk radio shows, podcasts, blogs, and publications both print and digital offer nonstop commentary. Amid abundant news stories and copious reactions to them, encouragement to study the nuances of complex issues and think through the challenges of national policy is sorely lacking.

I wrote *President You* in part to provide that encouragement. As my fictional chief executive, head of state, and commander in chief grapples with difficult problems and complex policy tradeoffs, I hope you will reflect on those matters yourself. You may agree or disagree with his conclusions; you may find yourself fascinated by some of the issues he addresses and less compelled by others. My goal is never to tell you what to think or to suggest that there is a single valid answer.

Instead, my hope is simply that this book will inspire you to think more deeply about the issues that face us today and become more active in shaping our American future in whatever way feels most authentic to you.

My fictional President Augustus Lincoln Treatise demonstrates something that numerous real-life figures, including our Founding Fathers, prove: "ordinary" citizens can have a transformative impact on the life of our nation and, by extension, the world. We do not need wealth, pre-existing power, or extensive training to effect change. We just need a willingness to question, learn, think, and commit to taking action. Influencing the future of one of the world's largest and most complex nations is undeniably hard work. Nevertheless, it can be done using capacities that are inherent in and tools that are available to all of us, no matter what our situation.

Two logistical notes before the story starts. First, you will find questions for further reflection at the close of the narrative. Second, I hope it goes without saying that no single book can accurately encompass all of America's policies. I have attempted to address some of the issues that feel both most central and most urgent to me, but *President You* makes no claim to be comprehensive.

President Treatise's namesake, Abraham Lincoln, famously called ours a "government of the people, by the people, for the people." I champion the same idea with the (admittedly less euphonious) phrase "President YOU." In our American enterprise, there are no mere consumers or recipients. We are all involved; we are all influential; and we are all essential.

Thank you for allowing Augustus and me to be part of your own American journey.

Tom Williams
July 2019

"All issues are political issues,
and politics itself is a mass of lies, evasions, folly,
hatred and schizophrenia."

George Orwell

"Politics and the English Language," *Horizon,* London monthly, April 1946.

Chapter 1

Discussion

discussion *n.* A debate; argument pro and con.

"Are you out of your ever-loving mind?" Angelica's shocked voice rose above the *Macy's Thanksgiving Day Parade* broadcast. Her normally soft brown eyes, now intently focused on her husband, contained a hint of anger. "We were discussing retiring, traveling, doting on our grandchildren, enjoying life, reducing stress, making time for each other. You want to do what?"

"Run for president," Augustus' dry, chapped, downward-arched lips, with bits of skin starting to peel off, calmly reiterated.

"I think the cold weather has frozen your brain."

That wintery Thursday had been excessively cold. Overnight a heavy frost had attached to everything in sight as though thousands of graffiti artisans had spray-painted white on all that could be seen. The muted light of dawn exposed an overcast sky, providing the snow-covered landscape a grayish hue. The air was laden with moisture; dampness soaked clear to the bone. A brisk north wind penetrated even the thickest clothing. Augustus had just completed shoveling the sidewalk and driveway when he uttered those three fateful words. This was the day their lives were about to metamorphose.

"Do you actually want to put our lives under the microscopes of government agencies, incessant intrusions by the press, and misrepresentations from political adversaries? Seriously?"

"Well, not really. But the country needs to change. And I think I'm the guy to do it. Besides, with my employment in government and your career in law enforcement, our lives are an open book as far as government is concerned. Plus, I have had media relations training and interactions with the press, and so have you. We both have had dealings with more demanding and better people than any number of politicians. And, in your case, some very not-so-nice people."

Angelica was personable, outgoing, and extroverted—a stark contrast to her reserved husband—a bubbly woman who made friends easily. Thoughtful and caring, she would light up a room with her effervescent joy and laughter. She could banter and take a joke, was quick-witted, and often provided a clever retort before jokesters knew what hit them. An intuitive woman, she loved the "game" of verbal dueling and readily picked up on slights, undertone innuendo, and the subtle thoughts that eyes expressed and facial features told. Moreover, she had a "look." That look that every man and husband knows. The "you went too far" and "don't go there" look. She was in rare form that day.

"Augustus, if you want something to keep you busy in retirement, run for city council, town mayor, or the county board. Hell, even take a shot at the state legislature. But president—you've got to be kidding. Be realistic."

"Look. You keep nagging me to stop yelling at the newspaper, talk radio, television, internet, and social media blogs."

"Yes, but talking in your sleep or mumbling around the house about what you would do if you were made king is a far cry from actually being ruler."

"I can do this. I have to try."

Augustus' receding light brown hair with noticeable streaks of gray; mussed by the north wind before he entered their home. He made no effort to repair the uncombed fibers. His clean-shaven face was pale, more from genetics than anemia. At his core, Augustus was judgmental, introverted, and hard to get to know. He was a serious man; one could become his friend — or enemy — for life. Not vindictive, he just had a strong sense of right and wrong, of fair play, of duty. Yet light blue eyes beneath his scowling brow intimated a hidden inner softness. Raised mostly by his mother while his overworked absent father kept the family out of the poorhouse, Augustus found it easier to converse with and had a greater affinity for women than for men.

"I like our house and home," countered Angelica.

"Living in the White House is every woman's dream. You won't have to clean, cook, do laundry; you'll have a chauffeur and other servants. And you love to entertain. You're a wonderful hostess and have assembled some great parties."

"It'll be like living in a glass prison. Strangers watching and reporting my every move, what I wear, what I say — or don't say when they think I should. Restrictions on when and where I can go. I like my retail therapy, getting out on my own to shop. I'll lose my freedom."

"Other first ladies have been able to sneak — I mean, get out — and shop."

"What about our eclectic museum of stuff from around the world? I'm enjoying all the things we have collected. They remind me of our travels and life together."

"We'll take it with us. And acquire more."

"We have great neighbors. I adore the two girls who

kitty-sit. Speaking of the neighbors, we don't live in a gated community. Suppose you carry this out. Are you willing to alienate our friends? Media trucks will surely block driveways. Supporters and opponents will likely clog the streets. Local police will be diverted from responsibilities that are more important. Private security, bodyguards, or the Secret Service walking around our house and through the neighbors' yards at all hours of the day and night."

"Only a temporary necessary evil. Besides, I can no longer tolerate my America heading for catastrophe."

"Just what makes you think you can change the country? That you are the guy to do it? And that what you do won't lead America into the calamity you're afraid she is heading toward?"

"You know me. I'm disciplined, honest, unwavering..."

"Stubborn, you mean."

"...and an average, good citizen with integrity who thinks and feels the way millions of Americans do. All I have to do is relate to them and get them to relate to..."

"Vote for..."

"...me."

"I think you're being a little naïve," pressed Angelica. "Everything you've said up to now has been personal. Nothing has been national, much less global."

"Look, both of us have a lot of experience in a wide variety of disciplines. We can use many of those things we learned. We've lived in ten states, traveled to all the rest, and have family and friends in most of them. Plus, we have lived, worked, vacationed, and traveled throughout sixty or more countries."

"We? Do you have a mouse in your pocket?"

"Several aspects of our lives can be readily applied to government. To make it function better. More efficiently. More effectively. To better the lives of all Americans."

"I'm not convinced. You'll have to do a lot more. For example, how will you get a dysfunctional Congress to ignore all the special interest groups with which they are already familiar and have a working relationship? Not to mention the millions of voters who are devoted and dedicated to their particular party?"

"It'll be a lot of work," acknowledged Augustus.

"What party will you represent? We're registered voters, but tend to vote independently. We don't donate to any party or any politician. We haven't joined any political clubs and don't know officials of any party."

"I thought I'd run as a private citizen. Perhaps as a write-in candidate."

"Which means starting from scratch. Before I sign on for this, you'd better do your research, find folks who will support you and know the laws, help with your campaign, and create the organization. Then figure out how to pay for all that. And NOT with OUR savings!"

"I've already begun making a list of relatives, long-time friends like Forrestor Addums, neighbors, and associates all across the country in nearly every state. There are more than two thousand; contacts from my military service, corporate and small business employment, charity work, time in government, high school, college, and graduate school classmates, and other activities. Your sources include people in credit unions, banks, law enforcement, pharmaceutical companies and chemical manufacturers, as well as defense attorneys, U.S. attorneys, federal judges, and health-care providers. It's taken me two months. Thank goodness for high school yearbooks, directories of college alumni, our collection of business cards, Christmas and birthday card lists, e-mail addresses, and social media accounts."

"Then there is your vision and platform and ideas and…"

"Too many other things to mention," lamented Augustus.

"What about the children? Are you going to seek their advice, comments, ideas, thoughts, and feelings?"

"Of course."

"What if they say no?"

"What if they say yes?"

Chapter 2

Inauguration

Before he enter on the Execution of his Office, he shall take the following Oath or Affirmation:—"I do solemnly swear (or affirm) that I will faithfully execute the Office of President of the United States, and will to the best of my Ability, preserve, protect and defend the Constitution of the United States."

(Article II, Section I, United States Constitution)

"America's decline on the world's stage ends now!" began his speech and presidency.

Unlike those of most of his predecessors, Augustus' inauguration was held at Independence Hall and its Assembly Room, in the nation's first capital city of Philadelphia, Pennsylvania; much to the delight of the residents of the "City of Brotherly Love" and to the consternation of Washington, D.C. elitists, lobbyists, political hacks, power brokers, ruling classes, and the like. Convening the instatement at a site other than the Capitol was not precedent setting, as many attempted to make the public believe. George Washington's first inauguration was conducted at Federal Hall in New York City. John Adams took his oath of office in Philadelphia at Congress Hall, which is conjoined with Independence Hall. Other presidents' inaugurations were held in the White House.

Independence Hall was purposely selected. Here were held the Continental Congress' formal discussions regarding revolution and independence from English monarchy rule; the subsequent drafting, signing, and presenting of the Declaration of Independence; and many heated debates leading to the creation of a constitutional republic called the United States of America. What better location to introduce the next president, whose election was itself a kind of independence declaration and revolution—a revolution in which voters had declared independence from politics as usual.

Different from previous inaugurations, it was entirely open to the public. The green spaces north of Independence Hall to the National Constitution Center and between 5th and 6th Streets were designated first come first enter. Applicable portions of Chestnut, Market, and Arch Streets were closed to vehicle traffic. Members of Congress, the Supreme Court, Cabinet secretaries, Joint Chiefs, governors, mayors, press and media, and other so-called VIPs, if attending, got in line with everyone else. Reserved seating inside and in front of Independence Hall was restricted to the newly elected president, his wife and children, the outgoing president and spouse, the chief justice of the United States (now a widow), governor of the common-wealth of Pennsylvania, mayor of the city of Philadelphia, and their spouses.

The ceremony itself took place at street level directly in front of the main entrance to Independence Hall. Nearly every previous inauguration had the distinguished party and guests elevated high above the populace as if they were monarchs positioned behind the battlements of their castle walls or dictators situated on the balconies of their palaces. In times past, standing aloft was a necessity in order for the assemblage to see and hear their leaders. With existing technologies, altitude was no longer required. At this event the president-elect, pending first lady, and guests were on the same level as the men, women, and children observers. This was a predetermined symbolic gesture made by Augustus as a visual demonstration he was the citizens' chief executive, head of state, and commander in chief, and not a self-proclaimed political ruling class member.

The White House communications office employed every type of technology to broadcast the ceremony and his speech across the globe. Live feeds provided access for the world's media, located wherever they could obtain permission and permits, blocks away. Constructed and positioned around Philadelphia Independence Mall and Independence National Historic Park were several gigantic screens and sound systems for viewing, listening, and participating by the public in attendance.

The inauguration location and ceremony were designed to instill a new sense of patriotism and nationalism and continue to build on the anti-establishment mood that had gotten the candidate elected in the first place. The event was scripted from beginning to end with the music, sequence, and activities chosen and approved by the president-in-waiting. Ceremony music was provided by "The President's Own," the United States Marine Corps Band. They played, in order of admission into the Union, each state's or commonwealths official song, from Delaware's *Our Delaware* to Hawaii's *Hawai'i Pono'ī*, as well as the official songs of America's five territories and the District of Columbia.

As the last melodious notes subsided, the chief justice, governor of Pennsylvania and his wife, and mayor of Philadelphia and her husband, came from inside the hall and sat in their assigned chairs.

The mayor commenced the official ceremony. Standing at the centered lectern, she first welcomed the large audience before her and those listening and watching from around the world. She then introduced the three dignitaries who had just arrived with her by reading a short biography of each; followed by a recognition of her husband's presence. The mayor called everyone's attention to the several jumbo-trons positioned around the area. On those screens, words of songs, pledges, and speeches would be displayed. She asked everyone present, those watching or listening at home, at work, and around the globe, to join her as she led the singing of *God Bless America*.

Upon its conclusion, Pennsylvania's governor, replacing the mayor at the podium, announced, "Ladies, and gentleman, the President and First Lady of the United States." To the sound of *Ruffles and Flourishes*, the outgoing commander in chief and soon-to-be former first lady joined the five dignitaries already outside. After they had taken their designated places, the band played *Hail to the Chief*.

Musical acknowledgement finished, the chief justice, now at the podium, addressed the crowd. While she introduced the next president and first lady, and their family, and before exiting the Hall, Augustus turned to Angelica, their children, and daughter-in-law and said their family prayer: "Here's to God and all His little Saints. Angelica, Cooper, Bailey, Morgan, and Dorthy included." They then walked out of the building to appear before the mass of people. After waving to the crowd and publicly greeting the dignitaries with handshakes, embraces, and thankful words, Augustus approached the dais while his family seated themselves next to the country's departing leader and spouse.

Before taking his Oath of Office, Augustus stepped up to the microphone, "As my last act as a private citizen, I ask everyone to join me in reciting the *Pledge of Allegiance*." He turned, faced the Stars and Stripes, placed his right hand over his heart, and began to recite, leading the people in their pledge. When it was finished, the band struck up the tune *You're a Grand Old Flag* and Augustus led the country in singing this homage to America's national colors.

Immediately following, the chief justice administered the Oath of Office. Upon completing his affirmation, the president thanked the mayor, governor, chief justice, his predecessor, and their spouses. According to his plan, all dignitaries except Augustus and Angelica were escorted back into Independence Hall while the band played and the crowd sang *America the Beautiful*. With Angelica standing by his side, Augustus prefaced his inaugural address.

"Before I begin the formal portion of my speech, I take this opportunity to thank all Americans for bestowing upon me the honor and privilege of becoming your President of the United States. Thank you."

After an enthusiastic ovation by the multitude that lasted three minutes, he continued, "And for making Angelica, my bride of many years, your next First Lady of America."

An inspiring and adoring round of cheers and applause greeted Angelica as she smiled and waved to the legion of supporters.

Even though protocol dictated that the first lady sit down, she remained at Augustus' side during his entire oration. This was a planned signal that women have an equal partnership and a rightful and just role with men.

Augustus initiated his historic remarks.

"America's decline on the world's stage ends now!"

That forcefully delivered exclamation was followed by another resounding couple of minutes of acclamation. Once the multitudes quieted, the new leader of the free world continued,

My remarks today are, first and foremost, for the citizens of the United States of America; second, for the leaders of the world's nations; and third, for the people of the earth.

Americans, there are three instruments of national power: the will of the people, military might, and economic stability. I shall remark on those self-evident truths.

Fellow citizens, for only the second time in the United States' long history, since George Washington's election, we elected a chief executive NOT affiliated with any political party. As voters, we rejected the status quo of today's environment and sent positive shock waves throughout our country. We citizens demonstrated to freedom loving individuals everywhere that politics as usual could be defeated when people implement their willpower. Collectively, we shall use our potent voices to unite Congress, and together we shall accomplish what is best for America and each other.

Regarding the might of our Armed Forces, as commander in chief and with your support, we shall establish our Active-duty personnel numbers at one percent of the population based on the latest census. We citizens have seen our military grow and shrink at the whim of politicians' campaign promises. If we are to maintain our position as the mightiest nation on the face of the earth, we must support our Armed Forces with consistent personnel strengths and budgets.

Economically, people recognize that a country's financial stability enables its head of state to negotiate from a position of power. As individuals, we are responsible for and must pay our own debts. We shall effect the programs necessary, pay our government's bills, balance our budget, shed the shackles of debt, and create a new era of prosperity free from monetary yokes of politicians, lobbyists, the elite, other nations, or international financial entities.

God bless America and her citizens.

To the leaders of the nations of the globe, I extend to you my hand in friendship and offer all that is America in the hopes that your homeland and its inhabitants will prosper. Many of you have accepted this offer from previous presidents, and our joint efforts have been advantageous to our countries and our citizens. Some of you were former enemies and now reap the rewards of our long-standing amity. We will continue to sustain and build upon those relationships.

On the other hand, some leaders do not see how the United States can be of significant benefit to either their lands or its people. Many decline offers of goodwill and peace and continue to foment hatred and malice. Therefore, let me provide notice to any leader or government: We reserve the right to implement our instruments of national power, if and when necessary.

That said, America shall continue her efforts to reach a shared and mutually positive understanding.

To the peoples of the world, the first lady and I greet you. Up to this point in our lives, we lived, worked, vacationed, visited, or traveled through more than sixty of your homelands. In every encounter with your fellow citizens, we were treated with courtesy and respect and were assisted by good, ever-helpful citizen-ambassadors. We learned from our interactions with your cultures, your heritages, your histories, and your languages, that, as individual human beings, you are no different from Americans.

We work, play, learn, live, love, laugh, and cry. We celebrate good times and lament bad days. We live our lives as best we can and aspire to do what is best for our elders, children, grandchildren, and families. This should come as no surprise since the United States is the land of immigrants from all nations. Our only real difference is the type of government we choose or are required to support.

America, the first lady, and I will continue to be your acquaintances and do everything we can to maintain existing cordiality and establish new relationships. Angelica and I hope to visit every one of your great homelands and meet more of you wonderful people.

In conclusion, may the citizens of the United States use this, our third revolution, to the benefit of all Americans and to the greater good of all humankind. Thank you.

The ceremony ended with the president and first lady leading the nation in singing *My Country 'Tis of Thee.*

At its conclusion, all members of the inauguration party remained at Independence Hall. The public, who had observed the event, were afforded the first opportunity to leave the area without the snarl of traffic that routinely accompanies presidential motorcades. After a couple hours, the dignitaries departed for their respective residences. Air Force Two transported the former president and first lady to their hometown. By separate government aircraft, the chief justice returned to the nation's capital. Augustus, Angelica, their children, and grandchildren began a new chapter in their lives on Air Force One as they flew to Washington, D.C. and their temporary White House home.

President You

Chapter 3

Mr. President

No Person except a natural born Citizen, or a Citizen of the United States...shall be eligible to the Office of President...who shall not have attained to the Age of thirty five years, and been fourteen Years a Resident within the United States.

(Article II, Section 1, United States Constitution)

...no religious Test shall ever be required as a Qualification to any Office or public Trust under the United States.

(Article VI, United States Constitution)

Each State shall appoint, in such Manner as the Legislature thereof may direct, a Number of Electors, equal to the whole Number of Senators and Representatives to which the State may be entitled in the Congress...

(Article II, Section 1, United States Constitution)

The Electors shall meet in their respective States, and vote by Ballot for President...they shall name in their ballots the person voted for as President...and transmit sealed...directed to the President of the Senate...The Person having the greatest Number of Votes shall be the President...

(Amendment XII, United States Constitution)

Just how, in God's name, did Augustus rise from obscurity to become one of four dozen senior occupants of 1600 Pennsylvania Avenue? It started in earnest after Angelica assented.

> From 1775 to 1783, liberty revering, independent minded, ordinary people accomplished an unheard of, unimaginable feat—a revolution which defeated the globe's mightiest army and forced that world's greatest empire to negotiate.
>
> Then, in 1787, many of those same revolutionaries created something exceptional: a Constitution that rejected violence as a means to change government and codified the most important four-letter word in all humanity—VOTE.
>
> Much like the long-ago English Parliament that retained power, controlled policies, and ignored British colonial subjects, America's current Congress holds power, controls the agenda, and ignores the will of the people.
>
> Therefore, I ask America's freedom loving, independent thinking, everyday citizens to conduct an extraordinary deed—a voter revolution to defeat mighty politicians and force political parties to negotiate on behalf of the people instead of retaining their own self-interests.
>
> To succeed, Americans must not only vote, but also VOTE AGAINST every incumbent

and VOTE FOR every challenger.

At the very least, go the polls on Election Day and in that booth write down your own name or mine.

Augustus Lincoln Treatise

That appeal was primarily directed at two groups: the 30% who did not usually vote, and those who identified as Independents. In recent years, successive government statistics and private polling revealed a continued reduction in the membership of major political parties and a corresponding increase in voters who claimed independent status. By the time of his election, 40% of registered voters were Independents, 30% Democrats, 25% Republicans, and the remaining 5% were categorized as Others. Augustus correctly concluded the waning of traditional party membership and lackadaisical public interest was the direct result of citizen frustration with years of politics as usual. His whirlwind campaign focused on that emotion.

It was a hot, muggy July afternoon in the upper level of a nondescript office building. Room air conditioning was set at a bone-chilling 60 degrees. Ecru colored walls, referred to locally as Johnson County beige, the standard paint applied to every newly constructed building, were bare. Flooring was typical builder-grade linoleum tiles. A wall of windows looked directly into uninteresting offices next door. Little natural lighting shone into the cavern, and illumination was supplemented by milky white globes dangling from the ceiling. Black, molded plastic chairs were arranged in neat rows and columns. Along one wall, five flagpoles inserted into separate pedestals displayed the Stars and Stripes to enhance the effect for the pending photo shoot. Opposite were positioned several still and video cameras with which news photographers and campaign staff would record every millisecond of activity.

The novice politician specifically requested this date and time to pronounce his candidacy. He chose the first Tuesday after the 4th of July at one o'clock in the afternoon to maximize media coverage that night and the remainder of the week. Augustus had toyed with the idea ever since his Thanksgiving discussion with Angelica and had planned in earnest for this moment. He researched, and then wrote several concepts—stances, really—on the issues of the day. Refinements to policy were now finalized and ready for public consumption. Technologies had been installed and operational procedures instituted. Hiring a longtime friend of Angelica's, the as-yet-unknown candidate had purchased a server, established a website, registered his domain name, created e-mail and assorted social media accounts, and prepared to unleash his platform. Everything was planned, positioned, and timed to activate immediately after his pronouncement.

At the appointed time, Augustus and Angelica stood in front of the five American flags. She was better dressed than he was. Keenly aware—as were all women in politics, including political wives—that her fashion choice would be significantly critiqued, she wore a dark gray skirt suit accented with a single strand of pearls. He wore dark slacks, a white open-collared shirt, and a navy sports jacket with an American flag lapel pin. His only reflection of personal taste was a bicentennial belt buckle celebrating the Constitution. Both appeared an average couple, an image that would lead them to the White House.

After obligatory introductions, Augustus announced, "I am proclaiming my intent to become the next President of the United States."

The room erupted with laugher as if he had just told the biggest and best fish tale ever heard.

The volunteer candidate continued, "My campaign slogan is 'A Vote for Me is a Vote for We.'"

Gut-busting jocularity filled the room a second time.

With a sheepish grin and demonstrating an ability to go along with what he knew they would take as a joke, he raised his hands, palms forward, and continued, "Go to my website and social media and read my vision for America." At that precise moment, all Augustus' electronic means of communications, which contained his platform and ideas from A to Z on national and international policies, were activated.

As the throng eventually quieted, the newbie pressed forth in all seriousness:

> What I want all Americans to know is that a vote for me is a vote for every person. I do not have any political party affiliation. I am an ordinary citizen disgusted with politics as usual in Washington. I am disheartened at the direction America has been taken by the past few presidents and congresses. I, like many of you, have written to members of Congress in an effort to address important issues. Too often, our ideas have been ignored by those in power who are overly influenced by lobbyists, special interests, and their major donors. The only way to effect real change is to elect an outsider. I am that outsider!
>
> I want your vote. I want that little bit of time it takes, about the same amount of time

as driving through a fast food restaurant or getting your morning coffee or latte. If you do not like the traditional slate of party nominees, or their policies, not voting only continues the status quo. Instead, vote for me as the symbol of your protest. Should I not be your preferred candidate, go to the polls anyway and write your own name on the ballot. You can do that! You are not limited to the names printed or digitally displayed. Remember, a "Vote for Me is a Vote for We."
I am your write-in solution for president.

As with many previous unknowns who had made similar claims, media asked the most basic of questions. Augustus definitely had his own ideas about government and the meaning of forming a more perfect union, establishing justice, insuring domestic tranquility, providing for the common defense, promoting the general welfare, and securing the blessings of liberty. His answers, although serious in his mind, were not given much attention, and almost everything was edited out in the newsroom or ended up in the digital trash.

A fortnight later, his longtime friend and vice president candidate, Forrestor Addums, conducted his own announcement. That event was newsworthy, since he was a former Congressman. At the end of July, the two appeared together and fielded greater inquiries from a more observant press. In that and subsequent appearances, questions of party affiliation, qualification, experience, religion, and policy were asked.

Augustus and Forrestor had decided to run as write-in candidates independent of political parties. Throughout America's history, there had been many such attempts. Any successes were limited to a few states during primary elections. No write-in candidates had ever won a general election for president and vice president. Augustus and Forrestor had a mind to change that.

The ballot access requirements were daunting, but not impossible. Eight states and the District of Columbia had no preconditions and allowed voters to write names directly on the ballot. Thirty-three states had regulations that ranged from as simple as placing a notice in the newspaper or completing an affidavit, certificate, nomination form, or registration, to as burdensome as filing a declaration of intent with every county election board. That process ensured votes would be counted whether their names were printed on the ballot or not. Nine states did not allow write-in candidates whatsoever, so Augustus and Forrestor had to submit a petition as independent candidates. In most cases, that petition included a fee as well as a number of signatures based on a percentage of the state's registered voters or eligible population. They had several months to accomplish those prerequisites in addition to the more traditional campaign challenges.

In previous presidential election cycles, opposing candidates, with ever increasing vitriolic attacks, accused each other of not being "qualified." One claimed his opponent was a crook and a liar and therefore not qualified. Another professed her opponent was racist and not competent, which disqualified him. Others were just as adamant when touting their success in life or jobs in government qualified them. An Independent spoke of his life's work in business as qualification enough to lead the nation, while his opposition offered her experience in Congress and the Cabinet qualified her to command the country. The media, too, asked for candidates' qualifications. Qualified, or not qualified, were the most misused words and phrases in election years.

The Founding Fathers decided on only three qualifications to become president: place of birth, a minimum age, and length of residency. Many debaters of the Constitution rejected the notions only the wealthy, highly educated, successful people or those who worked in government were qualified to become president. They came to that conclusion because in their time, the prevailing forms of sovereignty of other countries were kingdoms in which a single family ruled the land for generations and lawmakers consisted of the rich and powerful. Average, poor commoners were subject to the whims of kings and queens and had little to no voice. That was not to be the case in the newly formed United States of America.

In their freshly created democracy, citizens, regardless of occupation, experience, or wealth, would have the opportunity to lead this great country. Five, including George Washington, were considered educated at home or by some family relative. President Andrew Jackson had a sporadic education, engaged in fights, and killed a man in a duel. It is said Abraham Lincoln taught himself to read and write. Others came from humble beginnings, dire financial situations, and broken homes to succeed through perseverance.

Augustus was constantly asked, "What qualifies you to be president?" In response, he referred to Article II, Section 1 of the Constitution, "I am a natural born citizen, have attained and exceeded the age of thirty-five years, and have been a resident of the United States more than fourteen years. I am exercising my constitutional right to seek the presidency and, like George Washington, I am not a member of any political party. That, ladies and gentlemen, is all that is required. If you want to label me, call me the 'Citizen's Candidate,' as I have repeatedly stated."

Asked for his résumé or curriculum vitae, he provided a brief history lesson of previous chief executives, heads of state, and commanders in chief lives before they assumed the highest office in the land. Just over half were lawyers; the rest held other jobs with varying degrees of success. Several dabbled in many fields of endeavor, but the primary careers included one actor, two authors, two businessmen, one editor-publisher, one engineer, two farmers, two planters, three professors, one public official, four soldiers, and one tailor. More than thirty served in the Armed Forces on active duty, in the National Guard, as a volunteer soldier, in a state militia or the Continental Army. Three never served in any elected government capacity whatsoever. One had neither military service nor political expertise.

Experience aside, nearly every former president stated in some form or another that nothing in their lives fully prepared them for the challenges as President of the United States. History has revealed that events during their terms in office defined each leader to a greater degree than education, military service, private career, or previous public service.

When pressed, Augustus provided details of his education, business, local and state government, Army, and nonprofit experiences, and then diverted attention by lambasting opponents.

> Just what are my opponents' experiences?
> They proudly catalog and enumerate their
> achievements, as a member of a soon-to-be-
> forgotten Cabinet, when all they really
> accomplished was to march, lock step, in
> tune with their political patron like lemmings
> or a herd of cows following the noisy

clanging of the bell around the lead bovine's neck.

They regale the voter with tall tales of years of service to the country in a divisive, do-nothing, gridlocked, partisan Congress where favors are bought and paid for by special interests at the expense of the taxpayer. In open forum public spectacles, orating in politic-speak, they preach "do as I say, not as I do"—all the while in secret, closed door, back rooms patting themselves on the back for pulling the wool over people's eyes. They use their political positions to enrich their own coffers at the expense of citizens; for that is all they know.

That, ladies and gentlemen, is a summation of my opponents' experiences as career politicians.

During Augustus' run for the Oval Office, Americans read, heard, saw, and learned about former presidents and determined experience in business, government, law, military, nonprofit, politics, or other professions, vocations, or avocations did not guarantee the success or failure of a presidency. How world or national events and challenges were managed were the key factors. Sometimes, individual moral character ultimately strengthened or failed the nation. The voters sensed Augustus had the attributes to lead America.

As with past attacks on Catholic President Kennedy, Mormon candidate for president Romney and Christian President Obama accused of being a Muslim, the influence of Augustus' religion on government policy was questioned.

Agnostics, atheists, cult leaders, death penalty opponents, pro-choice and pro-life advocates, as well as any other entity that could tie its public policy agenda to some religion or faith, or lack thereof, clamored for answers.

Augustus responded on three fronts. First, he quoted Article VI of the Constitution: "No religious Test shall ever be required as a Qualification to any Office or Public Trust under the United States." Second, he lectured on the importance of education. "If people would make a little more effort in study of a given subject before expending a lot of energy gossiping, more knowledge would be gained and less ignorance would be spread. Former presidents were Baptist, Disciples of Christ, Dutch Reformed, Episcopalian, Methodist, Presbyterian, Quaker, Unitarian, and United Church of Christ. Thomas Jefferson and Abraham Lincoln did not identify with a specific religion or attend a specific church; they did, however, have faith."

His third answer was usually a combination of, "My and millions of Americans' ancestors came to America to escape religious intolerance. We should all think about that before asking any candidate about his or her religious beliefs. That being said, my first recollection of church was a 'Hell, Fire, and Brimstone' sermon right out of the Old Testament. Later sermons, Sunday school, and Catechism were New Testament oriented. The key point is my parents felt it important my intellectual growth as a human being included religion. My library contains a Bible, the Quran, the Book of Mormon, and the Torah. I have been exposed to Buddhism, Hinduism, Jainism, Methodism, Mormonism, Shintoism, and Sikhism, and I have read about others. In my experience, all religions, faiths and beliefs—renowned, organized, individual, or otherwise—have one overriding and similar factor: They all believe in the creation of humankind by a single and unique entity, whatever or whoever that might be called."

As his popularity grew, Augustus eventually became a newsworthy story. Pundits quickly labeled him a "Third Party Candidate" and discussed the potential historical impact of his candidacy on the two major parties and their respective nominees. The volleys of questions were like a fusillade, to which he calmly and succinctly, if not curtly, responded.

"In actuality and technically, I am a seventh or eighth party candidate. Nearly every ballot in every state during a presidential election lists candidates representing the four major parties: Communist, Democrat, Libertarian, and Republican. Then there is the Independent, Green, or others."

The press and pundits attempted to correct him. Augustus *was* a third party candidate because he could potentially come in third place behind the two leading opponents based on total popular votes cast. He may likely receive enough votes to sway the election in favor of one party's nominee by taking votes away from the other. That placement made Augustus a viable, and therefore, third party candidate.

Mr. Treatise countered, "You members of the press are performing a disservice to America, her voters, candidates of other parties and their supporters, and the democratic election process. By espousing that I am the third party candidate, regardless the criterion utilized, you are, in essence, dismissing other citizens running for president as irrelevant to America's political processes and thus, disenfranchising their constituents. You, the media, by both your exclusionary actions and proclivity for labeling, are not providing people the information they need to perform their civic duty of voting with knowledge. I want every citizen engaged in America's election process."

Using multiple forms of social media, Augustus was able to

get his anti-status quo, anti-politics-as-usual, anti-establishment message to his targeted audience in particular and to the public at large. Every week, from his initial announcement up to Election Day, he communicated to blog followers and voters, via every means available, policy initiatives for which he stood. Some concepts were new, but most were his own ideas on how to correct or eliminate existing failed government programs. His messages were easily understood, short on platitudes, and long on detailed remedies supported by facts and appropriate historical references. The people, tired of political party promise after promise and turned off by the constant sniping of traditional candidates, listened intently to Augustus' practical, common sense, kitchen table, homegrown solutions. Citizens may not have agreed with all he stated, but at least his proposals provided a basis upon which rational discussion could occur.

As public interest in him continued to gather strength, Augustus received more and more invitations to appear on network television and cable news, talk, pundit, and late night programs, as well as social media podcasts. That provided a larger audience of viewers, listeners, and voters to attach his name to a face and voice. From his point of view, it was free advertising. During those broadcasts, Augustus was able to stay on message and held his own under some tough and often satirical questioning. His preparation and rehearsals, in which questions asked of him were turned back for the inquisitor asking the question to answer, served him well during these verbal duels. The intimidators, not used to being politely and publicly questioned on their own programs, seldom asked him for a return engagement.

A political outsider and still considered a third party candidate, he was not invited to join that election year's nationally televised debates. Those debates also denied participation to the Communist, Green, Independent, Libertarian, and other parties who had citizens running for president. That action was blatantly unfair to those individuals and their supporters. Augustus used the snubs to his advantage. Once again, he told voters about the inherent unfairness to them and their candidate of choice because of media and major party exclusionary policies.

He repeatedly asked, "Shouldn't Americans be equally exposed to all citizens seeking the presidency at the same time and in the same forums?" "Shouldn't all candidates have their day in court—the public debates?" "In a country that believes in fairness, shouldn't all persons wanting the highest office in the land be allowed equal opportunity to present their ideas to every voter and rightfully defend those thoughts against opponents?" The people agreed. The Democratic and Republican parties did not. The debates were held without the minor, insignificant-labeled participants.

Undeterred, the newcomer approached the other lesser-known Oval Office seekers with the idea of conducting their own debate; they wholeheartedly agreed. All met with the executives of the major television and cable networks—to no avail. The turndown responses were many and varied. "We have already established our programming line-up." "Our advertisers won't buy the air time." "It's not part of our business model." "Cost-benefit analysis doesn't support the effort." "Polling indicates a lack of viewership." One executive lamented, "Our ratings are too low. We were hoping another network would agree so we could entice their viewers to watch our programs."

In a third and final effort, as unique as the forward pass was more than one hundred years before, Augustus tossed the debate concept to the professional and collegiate sports networks. After all, several players, many coaches, a few owners, and at least one commissioner had either injected or allowed politics full display on fields, courts, diamonds, and rinks.

Augustus argued, "Speaking on behalf of the other minor party candidates, why not lure viewers with a political debate? Each of us will talk about the sports we played in our youth, life's lessons participating in those sports taught, which teams we follow today, and why we do or do not support a particular sport or team. Interspersed, of course, with policy initiatives and requests for votes." While it was a novel idea, the desperate candidates did not score. Clearly, sports fans were interested in politics—but not in sports venues.

For most of Election Day, media reported on the vast numbers of citizens who showed up to vote. Long lines, hours of waiting, and extended poll hours were news. In recent election memory, of 250 million voting age (18 years and older) people in the U.S., an estimated 200 million citizens were registered to vote—and only 70% to 80% of those regularly voted. Augustus' election year percentage greatly increased. News reports estimated the number who voted at 187 million. The actual percentage of voter turnout was just over 95.3%, a figure not seen since the 1964 presidential election.

Regardless of whether Augustus and Forrestor's names were on the ballot, as the first polls closed on the East Coast, entrance and exit interviews showed a trend. Party favorites were locked in a virtual tie with the write-in novices. Voters, whose anger was directed towards the House of Representatives and the United States Senate, decided a regular person, not the politician, would provide America with leadership yearned for by its people. Thousands of citizens, disgusted with the state of politics, disgruntled with the better-known parties, and distrustful of the slated mainstream candidates, announced they voted for themselves. By the time polls closed on the West Coast, the ties were broken and a new story in history had been written.

The news alerts and breaking news told the immediate tale. Voters across the U.S. had gone to the polls and elected a man with no party affiliation. Augustus became president-elect because the citizens, finally, were fed up with the shenanigans in the Capitol—and the capital. The people had forcefully decided they were tired of:

- a "do nothing" Congress which ignored the will of the citizenry
- political chicanery that stifled legislation and created gridlock
- professional politicians, who, in order to be re-elected, repeatedly misrepresented the truth and promised the world to anyone and everyone who may cast a vote
- lobbyists, special interest groups, and financial contributors that cut deals and received special legislative considerations
- legislators who voted for their party's interests rather than doing what was right for the nation as a whole.

Americans came out in droves and gave Augustus 53% of the popular vote. The Democrat received 18%, followed by 17% for the Republican, and 5% Libertarian, 2% Independent, 1% Communist, and 1% for the Green Party candidate. The remaining 3% of ballots cast accounted for nearly six million who voted for themselves. Augustus gave a heart-warming and thankful acceptance speech at two o'clock in the morning on the Wednesday immediately following Election Day. However, he was not president just yet. The Electoral College had to have its say.

Unlike their opponents, who had long-standing organizations in place to register Electors, Augustus and Forrestor had to find, identify, and register their own. They and their spouses knew hundreds of people and solicited business associates, college alumni, family, former military colleagues, friends, neighbors, relatives, and others across the country. All were told of Augustus and Forrestor's aspirations and asked if they would become a presidential Elector from their state. Of the 538 needed to occupy every position in every state and the District of Columbia, 501 were successfully recruited and enrolled.

Article II, Section 1, of the Constitution outlines the Electoral College process beginning with "Each State shall appoint, in such Manner as the Legislature thereof may direct, a Number of Electors, equal to the whole Number of Senators and Representatives to which the State may be entitled in Congress." Augustus and Forrestor had researched each state's requirements, including deadlines, necessary affidavits, and notification procedures. At least twenty states required the write-in candidates to provide the names of their Electors at the same time they submitted affidavits, registered, or petitioned to have ballot access. Other states had different statutes that governed when and how names were to be provided. Regardless, the Secretary of State for each state needed to have the names of Electors who pledged their vote before they could submit the required Certificates of Ascertainment.

Each state was also allowed to create its own rules regarding an Elector's vote. In some states, Electors were listed on the ballot along with their candidates. Electors in 29 states and D.C. were required to cast their vote for the candidate they were registered to support. In many states, Electors were allowed to identify themselves as "unpledged" and were therefore free to vote for whomever they decided. Another category of failing to cast a ballot as pledged was called a "Faithless Elector." For a handful of states, failure to vote as pledged meant potential fines or criminal misdemeanor charges up to felony prose-cution. In other states, the electoral vote could be cancelled and the Elector replaced. Other states followed different procedures.

On that historic November night, Augustus won a majority of states. As expected, the Democrat won the West Coast states, plus Hawaii, New York, and Washington, D.C., for 116 Electoral College votes. The Republican took many Eastern and some Midwest winner-take-all states to garner 100 of the needed 270 votes. Nebraska and Maine results were split. In Nebraska, Re-publicans got two, Democrats one; in Maine, Republicans and Democrats each got one; and the phenomenon candidate received two from each of those states based on overall popular wins. The final tally, according to the media and based solely on a map listing the Electors assigned to each state, was Republican 103, Democrat 118, and Augustus 317. As anticipated, neither Democratic nor Republican opponent admitted defeat nor gave a concession speech. Lawyers for both sides began filing their legal briefs. It seemed the country was destined for another election fiasco similar to the one in the year 2000.

By law, Electors met and cast their ballots on the Monday after the second Wednesday in December in their respective states a month after the popular vote election ended. Several of those meetings were animated, even hostile, as some pledged, unpledged, and non-bound Electors intimated they might change their vote. A 53% popular win was not an overwhelm-ing majority, some argued. Others retorted that given the election had the largest turnout since 1964 and the next closest candidate received only 18% of the popular vote, the people clearly had spoken. A few added to the mix the argument that the six million citizens who voted for themselves was an indication the populace wanted something new in their president and government.

Throughout the months preceding the election and in the weeks immediately afterward, average citizens learned more about the Constitution, the voting process, and the how's and whys of the Electoral College. The post-election legal wrangling revealed to the public power hungry career politicians and the "control freak" nature of political parties. Voters outraged at what they deemed an attempted coup d'état took to the streets. Impromptu demonstrations were held outside local congress-ional offices and on the steps of the Capitol. Party offices were broken into, trashed, and even burned. Firms representing the political parties in lawsuits were identified and their attorneys threatened. The two mainstream losers called for restraint, peace, and for allowing legal proceedings to take their course.

The Communist, Green, Independent, Libertarian, and other party losers, prompted by cajoling from Augustus, uttered, "We lost fair and square and have no issues with the president-elect. Our constituents have accepted the results, and it is time the Democrats and Republicans do the same."

Demands by the press were made on the future president to speak out against the violence allegedly perpetrated by his supporters. Augustus responded,

> I call upon the Democratic and Republican candidates for president who lost this election, their political machines, their respective parties, their Political Action Committees, their attorneys, their supporters, and their law firms, to accept uncondition-ally, the will of the people, the will of the citizens, and the will of the voters. Cease all

attempts to overturn the results of this election. Your continued efforts will only create a constitutional crisis, which may result in more destruction, violence, and possible loss of life.

More importantly, your selfish actions are an assault on democracy and visibly demonstrate to our citizenry, to our allies, and to our enemies that America does not truly believe in her own democratic ideals. Your legal maneuvers clearly show that votes and the voting process are as irrelevant as they are in dictatorships around the globe.

Fellow citizens, our Founding Fathers created this constitutional republic on the principle that we can change our government through a peaceful system called voting. I ask you to redirect your frustrations toward the civil methodology of e-mailing, writing, telephoning, texting, and using social media to contact the political elite. Vent your disbelief of, and disgust in, the lawsuits currently being filed by the Democratic and Republican losers of this, your, presidential election.

After all was said and done and the electoral ballots were tabulated, the election was one for the history books. At a joint session on January 6, three days after the new Congress was convened, the still serving vice president opened the Electoral College results, which were then passed to tellers who announced each state's tally. The final certified vote count was Republican 98, Democrat 109, and Augustus 331.

Some in the legislative body were still not satisfied. Since 1887, under Title 3, United States Code, Chapter 1, §15, legislators can object to individual Elector ballots or a state's total electoral vote count. Luckily, for Augustus, many members were just as gridlocked as before the November election. They could not decide upon which Electoral College ballots to contest. Furthermore, because of the public's demonstrated outrage with Congress, several did not want to accept the risk of continuing to challenge the election. In addition, little support came from newly elected members, who decided to spend their political capital on future issues more relevant to their constituents.

The soon-to-be out of office vice president declared Augustus Lincoln Treatise to be the next President of the United States. That pronouncement and the flood of demands by Americans ended the standoff between Augustus and the major parties, at which point the Democrats and Republicans finally acknowledged their loss, relinquished their objections, and terminated their lawsuits. However, as a further sign of resistance, no concession speeches were made.

Ultimately, the calendar closed the door on any challenges. January 20 was upon them. The currently serving president and vice president, by the Twenty-second Amendment, were not allowed to remain in office. Neither the Speaker of the House nor the President pro tempore of the Senate wanted to give up their powerful positions. Serving Cabinet secretaries of the outgoing administration, also in the line of succession, did not want the job. Moreover, as had been their modus operandi for decades, Congress could not agree on a viable replacement.

The outsider had won.

President You

38

Chapter 4

Executive Order

Presidential Executive Orders (EO). Executive Orders are official documents, numbered consecutively, through which the President of the United States manages the operations of the Federal Government.

(Federal Register, Presidential Documents)

Since the beginning of the New Year, Augustus and Angelica had resided at Blair House. Located just across the street from the White House, Blair House had been established as America's official temporary residence for visiting heads of state and other dignitaries. Now that they had moved into the Residence, the Oval Office was still in disarray. New woven carpet depicting the Presidential Seal, his desk, sofas, chairs, coffee and end tables, lamps, bookcases, pictures, accouterments, knick-knacks, mementoes, and such things had yet to be installed.

His first official act was an Executive Order restricting lobbying efforts. The document was signed, not in the Oval Office, but in the hallway just outside. The unceremonious event occurred precisely at nine o'clock in the morning on Augustus' first full day in office. A handful of new and many long-time serving White House staff observed the formalities. A wall functioned as table.

The first lady stood by his side. Their younger children had departed earlier that morning for home, back to their routine lives. Cooper remained and acted as official photographer.

When first told of his father's ambitions at Christmas two years ago he had blurted, "Awesome. I can be a White House staffer. No. Wait. Private advisor to the president."

Augustus immediately put the kibosh on that idea. "I love you, son. But no way, no how, not on my watch, will you work in the White House. If I get that far."

Cooper, their eldest child, never married, had yet to find his path in life. He had spent most of his adulthood in and out of several colleges and universities. Nicknamed "Professor," he seemed to enjoy life as a professional student, earning two undergraduate degrees, three Master's degrees, and one doctorate. He relished learning and had yet to find that one thing to capture his interest or lifelong passion.

One might think Cooper was student loaning himself into bankruptcy or debtor's prison, or sticking his parents with a lifetime pile of invoices. That was hardly the case. Between his forays in education, he worked at odd jobs, saved money, and paid his bills. More importantly, he spent time on the Internet or in a library researching and writing. There were more than one-and-a-half million agencies, businesses, charities, civic leagues, clubs, community chests, corporations, fraternal organizations, individuals, private and public foundations that had programs and grants available to those who sought a better life through education. Cooper researched and applied to hundreds, and they responded by paying for books, tuition, room and board, school events, fraternity fees, computers or tablets, mobile phones and devices, and even incidental expenses. In addition, businesses and corporations looked for people to test products and he participated in many, often paid for his efforts or allowed to keep and resell some of the evaluated items.

Cooper was fascinated with the dichotomous nature of the White House. More than two hundred highly effective professionals and their attention to details kept the Executive Mansion running like clockwork. Juxtaposed against this efficiency was the adept political staff of the West Wing buzzing like a swarm of bees whose Oval Office hive was disrupted daily. He likened it to controlled chaos. However, within a couple weeks Cooper became bored, as Augustus knew he would, and returned to his second doctoral dissertation.

On that single sheet of White House embossed paper, President Treatise penned his signature to the first of many campaign promises. Under Article II, Section 3, of the Constitution ("he shall take Care that the Laws be faithfully executed"), Augustus banned lobbyists, emissaries for special interest groups, and agents of foreign governments from hawking their wares in all Washington, D.C. federal public facilities. Included were the White House and its grounds, executive office buildings, the Supreme Court, the Capitol, all Senate office buildings, and all similarly located Representative offices provided those sites were owned, operated, managed, leased, and/or otherwise financed by the government or any of its agencies, departments, or agents on its behalf. He did not and could not prevent legitimate delegates from conducting lobbying efforts with members of Congress on private property.

One of the reasons for his election to the highest office in the land was that an overwhelming majority of Americans believed their elected officials were too influenced by self-serving lobbyists who did not have the best interests of the country at heart. As one egregious example, in an effort to garner tax breaks, one lobbyist proudly boasted, "I represent the interests of citizens from every state in the union." A superficial investigation revealed the organization had a membership of fifty—

one person for each state.

Augustus reasoned he represented all citizens. The justices of the Supreme Court were legal guardians of the Constitution and therefore, by extension, represented the citizenry. Senators and representatives were elected agents of all the people in their states and districts. Overall, the 535 members of Congress, 9 Supreme Court justices, and the president represented all Americans; not the select few who "bought" access and obtained special dispensation.

Behind the Executive Order was the philosophy that, within reason, every citizen should have access to their member of Congress without having to compete against "hired guns." His idea derived from two early life incidents. When he was a young boy, vacationing in Washington, D.C. with his family, Augustus' parents decided to stop by and say hello to the representative from their congressional district. They knew the congresswoman, as they had worked on her re-election campaign. Upon arrival and after an exchange of pleasantries with the gatekeeper, they sat and sat and sat in the outer office as twelve or so lobbyists entered and exited the elected official's private chamber. True, his parents did not have an appointment, but the congresswoman's refusal to spare five minutes for a well-known campaign volunteer seemed downright rude. Disappointed, after more than a two-hour wait, they left immediately when a young man delivering lunch was given direct and unimpeded access.

On a later trip to the nation's capital—well before the cumbersome bureaucracy of advanced tickets and necessary security measures today—Augustus, along with his wife and children, were standing in line on the Ellipse to take a tour of the White House. Like many other people, they patiently waited their turn in the first-come, first-served line. As they moved toward the front with the next group to be allowed entry, all were stopped. Cutting in line ahead of them was a busload of tourists from a Communist regime. By the time those "VIPs" were screened, passes checked, names verified, and proceeded through security, visiting hours had ended. As a result, several Americans were denied their White House visit. That, Augustus felt, was unacceptable.

President Treatise believed that if an entity wanted some special deed or dispensation from Congress, then its leader, agent, or lobbyist should visit all 535 elected officials' offices in their home states and districts. Or, and much preferred as far as Augustus was concerned, open a branch office in each representative's and senator's district and meet the legislators when they were at home during one of the multiple recesses. That gave lobbyists about 240 days out of 365 each year to gain direct access to their targeted official on that person's home turf. After all, if special interest groups, in fact and as they often claimed, represented citizens all across America, then it should be reasonable to establish local offices throughout the country.

The added benefit of roughly 2,000 special interest groups opening 535 offices for lobbying across the nation meant the potential creation of 100,000 more jobs, purchase or lease of hometown buildings and office space, expenditure of funds to support local businesses, and additional income for hundreds of employees throughout the affected communities; not to mention increased revenues for local jurisdictions from expanded tax bases. Another consequence of the transfer of lobbyist support staff out of Washington might be a slight easing of traffic congestion in the D.C. metro area.

Naturally, members of Congress were outraged when they heard about the Executive Order. However, they had to be careful in their public remarks so as not to appear too much in favor of lobbyists at the expense of voters back home. They couched their comments in politic-speak, lamenting how the president was denying freedom of speech and the people's right to petition Congress for redress of grievances. Augustus countered by joking that he did not prohibit any free speech as evidenced by the multitudes of feckless disgruntled voices of some legislators. "They seem to have a lot to say now."

President Treatise stated he simply wanted congress-lobbyist meetings out in the open and in full public view where reporters could accost Congress members and lobbyists before and after they went into and came out of private residences, businesses, office buildings, and the like—locations where the people could see who the legislators were meeting, and perhaps overhear portions of their conversations in places frequented by citizens.

"How can citizens petition Congress if they are denied knowing what grievance exists because of deals and decisions made in closed-to-the-public congressional offices?" Augustus asked. "True, deals and decisions may now be hidden from public viewing in private venues. However, the local and national press can now publicly identify the private citizens, businesses, or foreign governments who own, lease, and occupy those facilities and openly question their involvement with members of Congress. Exposure some may not want. Besides, the Executive Order only applies within the jurisdictional boundary of Washington, D.C. Legislators are still free to meet lobbyists in federal locations within their districts.

"Moreover, in today's high-tech, social media, cyber-space environment, petitioners and lobbyists can meet officials face-to-face, digitally. Under federal law, those electronic means of communications are public property, have to be preserved, and are open to scrutiny via Freedom of Information Act requests.

Digital and video records of meetings between citizens, lobbyists, and members of Congress have to be retained."

In another effort to stifle influence peddling, Augustus unsuccessfully attempted to ban legislators from becoming lobbyists. In years past, Congress had demonstrated its two-faced ire by banning Armed Forces personnel, mostly admirals and generals, from becoming contractors for defense industry businesses—especially when those high-ranking officers retired from a weapons program they were overseeing and then went to work for the defense company selling that weapon to the Pentagon. Congress members reasoned those senior officers were too involved with the program and would exert too much influence on lower ranking military officials.

How convenient it was for representatives and senators to forget all about "being too enmeshed" when they themselves became employed as lobbyists and implored their former peers to provide tax breaks or special legislation on behalf of their new employer.

President You

Chapter 5

State of the Union

He shall from time to time give to the Congress Information of the State of the Union, and recommend to their Consideration such measures as he shall judge necessary and expedient...

(Article II, Section 3, United States Constitution)

The Constitution requires the chief executive to provide information to Congress but does not specify how. George Washington and John Adams read their "Annual Message" to joint sessions of Congress. Thomas Jefferson began the practice of providing legislators a hand-delivered written Annual Message to be read aloud by a clerk at the joint session. That practice remained in force until 1913. Beginning with Woodrow Wilson, presidents appeared before joint sessions of Congress and read the document aloud. During Franklin D. Roosevelt's tenure, the Annual Message began to be informally called the "State of the Union." In 1947, it formally became known as the State of the Union Address (SOTU). Augustus' speech was neither delivered for reading nor orated before a joint session. Through the White House communications office, President Treatise broadcast his SOTU to Congress, the Supreme Court, Cabinet secretaries, Joint Chiefs of Staff, Americans, and the world's people wherever they may have decided to watch and listen.

Breaking once again with more than 110 years of tradition, within a few days after his election, Mr. Treatise gave his first State of the Union Address from McLean House, in the village of Appomattox Court House, Commonwealth of Virginia. As with his inauguration, Augustus selected this particular site for its historical value as background for his speech on American division and his call for national unity. He also selected the music with care. The opening tunes were *The Battle Hymn of the Republic* and *Dixie*.

> Two and a half centuries ago, colonial Americans were a divided people over the issue of taxation without representation. Eventually, they fought our first revolution and created our new nation with unalienable rights of life, liberty, and the pursuit of happiness for all persons.
>
> More than one hundred sixty years ago, Americans were again a people divided as the institution of slavery fueled the War Between the States. That, our second revolution, pitted brother against brother, family against family, citizen against citizen, and state against state. When it was over, these United States retained the concept that our nation conceived in liberty was dedicated to the proposition that all people are created equal.
>
> Unfortunately, we Americans are divided once more. We are separated by views about immigration, politics, political parties, social justice, race, religion, *Roe v. Wade*, sex, sexual

orientation, wealth, and many other we-they examples too numerous to mention.

The root cause of such rupture is well known. Partial truths are divisive; comments out of context, destructive. Carefully chosen words that obfuscate facts are lying. The selective elimination of pertinent details a willful misrepresentation. These are sins of omission. All too often, the easier wrong is chosen instead of the harder right.

Founding Father George Washington is legend to have said, "I cannot tell a lie." Savior of our nation Abraham Lincoln was called "Honest Abe." Discourse must be truthful. As is stated in courtroom dramas, we must be willing to tell the truth, the whole truth, and nothing but the truth, warts and all. Failure to do so only feeds the continual distrustful narrative.

At this historic location General Ulysses S. Grant, representing Abraham Lincoln, President of the United States, offered General Robert E. Lee, representing Jefferson Davis, President of the Confederate States of America, what became regarded as the most generous terms of surrender ever conceived to end any war — the overriding principle that our divided nation must heal. Siblings were asked to set aside blue and grey rivalries. Families were asked to welcome returning kinfolk with open arms. Northerners and Southerners were asked to forgive fellow brethren.

Our third revolution has just begun—not with weapons of destruction, but with voices of reason. Now is the time and this is the place to begin a new dialogue of national unity. We must, as individuals from all walks in life, with unique experiences, and differing perspectives, as Americans devoted to the survival of one nation, our United States, accept the ideas of others with civility, self-awareness, and loving hearts. We must listen and eliminate our predisposition to judge. We must converse, not argue. We must respect, not hate. We must learn the positive attributes of others and acknowledge they contribute to our country's greatness.

I ask all Americans to join in this national effort. Only with open minds can we break the irksome barriers to understanding and, as freedom-loving people, unite once again. Should we not do these things, then we will continue to be a house divided that will surely perish from the earth.

After his presentation, the closing song was *This Land Is Your Land.*

President Treatise's emotional call for unity across the nation was based in part on his parents' teachings as well as his early childhood and teenage experiences. Both his parents were raised during the 1930s Depression Era. To survive, families and neighbors worked together as President Roosevelt's radio broadcast "Fireside Chats" offered comfort and instilled hope.

A decade later, people were asked to accept rationing of tires, sugar, gasoline, processed foods, and many other items, and to do without while supporting the war effort by recycling glass, paper, tin, aluminum, rubber, and establishing "Victory" gardens. Communities and the country endured these activities and helped sustain United States' attacks on tyranny across the globe in defense of freedom and liberty. Men departed to fight America's enemies overseas. Women assumed male dominated jobs, earning the nickname "Rosie the Riveters." In World War II, Augustus' dad fought and his mom riveted.

His father, Myles, was a skilled professional, strong telephone union man, and volunteer firefighter. A self-described patriot, Myles was Chairman of the town's Americanism Week during the anti-Communism era of the 1950s—the third decade in a row when citizens were asked to unite, this time against a Communist political and economic philosophy. His mother, Nora, was a stay-at-home mom who often took young Augustus with her to church for various activities. Mostly the church-women constructed handmade craft items to sell at fundraising bazaars or prepared meals, deserts, and homemade ice cream for upcoming socials.

By all accounts, Augustus had what was often considered a normal childhood. Nora described his early years. "He was a mischievous child. As a two- and three-year-old, each spring Augustus would pick the bright yellow flowers that grew daily in our yard and give them to me—dandelions. When he was a bit older, he graduated to harvesting the neighbor ladies' flowerbeds."

Squirrels fascinated the young boy. Myles said, "Augustus tried to feed a squirrel with an open and empty hand. He got the critter to come to him, only to have the creature take a bite out of his finger. The boy didn't cry. He was too fascinated by the blood and missing piece of skin."

Like many children, Augustus liked cookies and milk. His older brother James wrote this anecdote. "Augustus had a sweet tooth. To our mother's consternation, he would often disappear only to be found next door, sitting at a table in front of a plate of freshly baked cookies and glass of ice-cold milk, chatting away with the elderly woman of the house. Luckily, she was our parents' landlady."

Unity of family, unity of neighbors, unity of church, unity of community, unity of citizens, and unity of nation were lessons of Augustus' youth. Those teachings were tested as a teenager. Like many boys, he played and loved sports, was awkward around girls, struggled with academics, experienced exclusionary cliques, and was bullied. "Why can't we all just get along?" he would ask his folks. During summer breaks, he held various jobs: newspaper carrier, gravedigger, farm hand, jewelry store worker, grocery bagger, and steel worker.

As high school graduation approached, Myles told Augustus he expected him to attend college immediately after graduation. This was the path to a dream Myles had chosen for his son to achieve greatness. Augustus, with other ideas, went through the motions and applied to many institutions. Several college and university letters later, it became clear higher education was not in his immediate future. Rejection letter after rejection letter brought out repressed emotions in Myles. His secret plans were disrupted and belief in his son's future was shattered. Those hidden feelings exploded into a barrage of disappointed verbal assaults. "I guess you don't want to go to college." "You better find another place, but quick." "I'm not going to pay for it." "If you ain't goin', you'd better get a job." "Get prepared to move out." "Go back and speak to a counselor and find a school." Nora's protestations for Myles to calm down were ignored.

Filled with his own pent-up secrets, Augustus finally interrupted his father's diatribe and shouted out defiantly, "Shut your damn mouth!" Myles was stunned silent. That was the first time Augustus had ever back-talked. James sat awed. Nora, who always knew more than she let on, took her son's outburst calmly and in stride. This was the seminal event when Augustus broke the bonds of parental control and entered into manhood. It seemed, however, at the cost of family unity. Augustus described those last few months in high school before leaving home to enlist in the Army as "tenuous." These sensitive, open, and unreconciled wounds helped formulate the basis for his first State of the Union Address.

President You

Chapter 6

The Press

Congress shall make no law respecting an establishment of religion, or prohibiting the free exercise thereof; or abridging the freedom of speech, or of the press, or the right of the people peaceably to assemble, and to petition the Government for a redress of grievances.

(Amendment I, United States Constitution)

Well before thirteen individual colonies joined to create a unified United States, the relationship between the citizens' government and the people's press has always been somewhat tenuous, if not contentious. Early colonial writings often disputed, and even chastised at great risk, the United Kingdom's King George III and England's Parliament.

During the Civil War, Major General William Tecumseh Sherman expressed his frustration with leaks to the press: "The Northern Press either make public opinion or reflect it...All bow to it...officers instead of keeping the Executive Branch advised...communicate with the public direct through the Press so that the Government authorities are operated on by public opinion formed too often on false or interested information. This has weakened the Executive and has created jealousies, mistrust, and actual sedition."

In the last few years, differences between administration messages and media reports had resulted in open verbal warfare, giving rise to the term "fake news." To many, Hodding Carter III's decades-ago observation, as written in Don Kowet's book *A Matter of Honor: General William C. Westmorland versus CBS News*, "without fairness and balance journalism may become indistinguishable from vigilantism," had come to fruition.

Within a handful of days after his inauguration, Augustus held his first meeting with the White House Press Corps (WHPC). By then the traditional 100-day president-press grace period had disintegrated. The rancor had been fueled by earlier administration staffers, who had added an additional "C" to create the WHPCC (White House Politically Correct Correspondents). President Treatise and his staff did not continue that disdain. Their goal was to heal open wounds while creating a more congenial press relationship and better media-administration environment. It was a delicate balancing act with potentially disastrous consequences.

As a first remedy and different from other Oval Office occupants, the president and first lady entered the White House briefing room via the press corps offices. Augustus and Angelica introduced themselves by their first names and greeted every reporter with personal questions about career and family. It took more than an hour for them to reach the dais. President Treatise began by telling the journalists he would hold one press conference per month. In addition, the first lady would participate in some as well as conduct her own.

At that gathering, he laid down some ground rules. Punctuality was a sign of respect. Question and answer sessions were to be professional and civil. Clamoring to be first to ask a question and yelling over the voices of peers was discourteous and would not be tolerated. Interrupting and arguing was disrespectful. Such antics were grounds for being ignored.

Continued outbursts would result in removal from that session. Each reporter, in sequence, would be called upon to ask his or her primary question. Once every journalist had asked and received an answer to that single question, follow-up queries might be addressed—again in reporter sequence. "My intent," said Augustus, "is to give every member of the press an equal chance and equal time to ask questions and receive answers pertinent to his or her readership, subscribers, and audience."

Taking a cue from Abraham Lincoln, in an effort to lighten the atmosphere, Augustus told the story of one encounter with the press. "I was hired as a crisis manager and disaster specialist for a community. Shortly after I had assumed that role, the local newspaper asked for an interview, but gave me some time to get oriented. A month later the reporter asked how I was doing. Thinking it an interview icebreaker, my glib response was, 'We have had no disasters, so I must be doing something right.' That night a tornado passed through. The headline the next day was 'Tornado Strikes Area.' Immediately below was my photo with the article title, 'Doing Fine, No Disasters.'"

Those present chuckled. With a smile and a laugh at himself, he said, "How could the paper not use that?" Heads nodded in agreement. "The point, ladies and gentlemen, is that my remark was not self-aggrandizement and their article title wasn't written maliciously. I sincerely hope, in the serious business that is America, should I make some passing conversational remark between you and me, it does not make news. If it should, then let it be reported as intended and in context."

The chief executive ended the briefing by commenting he hoped they understood that he and the first lady had some pressing duties. Neither of them took any questions. The WHPC would be notified of their next gathering.

Less than a fortnight later, Augustus completed a promise—

his first full press conference. It was billed as a "Private Meeting" held on Friday afternoon before the Super Bowl. Attendees were told to come empty-handed and were asked to arrive an hour earlier than normal. That heightened media curiosity. Invitees were introduced to stricter screening designed to ensure no recording or video devices accompanied the journalists. Each member of the White House Press Corps entered the East Room with, basically, the clothes on their backs. This event was to be more of a presentation than a conversation or question and answer session.

Precisely at 3 p.m., President Treatise entered the room, and the Secret Service sealed the area. Three members of the press who did not arrive on time were denied entry, had their credentials confiscated, and were escorted off the premises. They had been advised about punctuality.

At this meeting, the chief executive outlined his philosophy about working with the press. He began with an old army story about a soldier, rank of private, who was told by a non-commissioned officer to report to headquarters. Dutifully the young man immediately marched over to the headquarters, halted on the sidewalk outside, faced the front of the building, saluted, and pronounced in a loud, professional military voice, "Private Joe reporting to headquarters, as ordered, sir!" Augustus was making the point that the White House was an inanimate object.

He lectured the attendees: "The White House does not speak or make statements. Personification is not to be used. There will be no 'anonymous' or 'unnamed sources close to the White House.' In your days at school, did you justify a doctoral dissertation, a master's thesis, or cite references on term papers, and present facts in debates, by using anonymous, unnamed, undocumented sources? I would bet not. I, the first lady, White

House staffers, members of the Cabinet, and any member of the Executive Branch who say anything to the press, are to be named and quoted as a source."

Augustus tempered those remarks by stating he knew he could not prevent reporters from keeping their sources' identities secret. He could not stop journalists from using that as a reporting technique. Nevertheless, he had already informed officials in his administration that nothing they said was off the record; whatever they said could be quoted, and their names used.

President Treatise also told the attendees neither they nor anyone else would receive advance copies of any of his speeches. That was his policy and he did not, and would not, explain. Augustus did not like that anyone with an opinion, regardless of venue or title, often commented and put their spin on what he might say before the American people heard it "from the horse's mouth." Augustus preferred that citizens had the chance to hear what he said before pundits postulated their own interpretations. Why should he provide material earlier than need be to "talkies and writ-ies," as he called them? Once he had said what he had to say, there would be plenty of analyzing, complaining, critiquing, espousing, fretting, interpreting, prognosticating, speculating, and whining.

Regarding comments concerning local or specific current events, the commander in chief told the story about a conference of senior military officers. "A few junior generals in charge of strategic missions were lamenting to a senior general that too much of their time was spent responding to day-to-day issues. After an earful, the senior general responded, 'Generals, you are paid to insure, if the time comes, our missiles launch, our aircraft drop bombs, our submarines sink ships, and our armies defeat enemies. You are not paid to unclog toilets. You have subordinates for those tasks. Now, if you want to unclog toilets, I will demote you and give your job to someone who understands the role of a general.'" Augustus' point was this: Other administrations had gotten into the habit of injecting their views on local incidents, even before the facts were known, the situation stabilized, and professional or elected officials had the opportunity to address their own community.

"The people of the United States require and pay me to focus on America's place in the world and to function on the international stage. Citizens elect, and expect, local officials to respond to the challenges within their communities. Therefore, I do not intend to comment on local events."

The second half of the meeting dealt with workspaces. The White House was where he and his family lived, slept, ate, relaxed, and worked. It was part residence, part museum, part war room, and part executive chambers. It was his temporary home, and he was the most important caretaker of the "People's House." In addition, it was originally the President's House and was not really designed as an office building. The magnitude of America's role in the world and the growth of government eventually necessitated expansion of the building to accommodate some executive offices.

With all that as a lead-in, he said, "Future media access will be restricted. The White House, its grounds, and the Press Room are no longer available on a daily or routine basis. All space occupied by any reporter will be cleaned and vacated by the end of tomorrow. Your passes are revoked and are no longer valid. New access badges will be issued Monday at the Eisenhower Executive Office Building directly across the street. That site will also be the location of your new offices. That concludes this meeting."

His words and abrupt ending took everyone aback and

angered those present. Members of the WHPC were furious. They complained bitterly about what he said, the manner in which it was done, and the timing. Upon conclusion of the meeting, several journalists reported to their bosses and refused to cover President Treatise in the future. The weekend news, competing with the Super Bowl, was filled with acrimonious commentary regarding the blatant violation of the First Amendment and the people's right to know.

The chief executive, commander in chief, and head of state was not ignorant. He fully recognized the purpose of a free press, sometimes called the Fourth Estate or Fourth Branch of government. He was cognizant of the importance of Thomas Paine's writings and the commentaries of Silas Dogood to the American Revolution. He knew an abiding press aided success during World War II and an opposing media negatively influenced the Vietnam War. He was aware that throughout history, reporters informed the citizenry of the good, the bad, and the ugly of government's actions—or inactions.

A properly informed public is an important part of America's greatness. "The survival of a democracy, "wrote Aldous Huxley in *Brave New World Revisited,* "depends on the ability of large numbers of people to make realistic choices in the light of adequate information." The operative words, "a properly informed public" and "adequate information" were, according to Augustus, the heart of the problem.

Who decides what constitutes a properly informed public? Who decides what adequate information is? All governments and media outlets have their spin, angle, and perspective. As a soldier in Germany during the Cold War, Augustus had listened to Soviet Union news broadcasts. Their reporting on events in the United States was decidedly different from that of the *Stars and Stripes* newspaper and the Armed Forces Network.

Before Augustus' election, one news advertisement touted they reported what they knew to be the truth. That prompted the question, "Are the other networks reporting what they know to be a different truth?" Another program advertised theirs was the "real" news. Did that make other news illusory?

Augustus was reminded of an old adage that said there are three sides to every story—yours, mine, and the truth lies somewhere in between. He wondered, "Why does the press report their version of truth? Of reality? Is today's media so infatuated and enmeshed in their myopic, parochial, and dogmatic world they are incapable trusting the citizenry? If people have a right to know, cannot news report the facts and let people reason the truth?"

These and other questions reminded him of a story he once heard during the Nixon administration's overtures to China. Apparently, at one of President Nixon's speeches, an American reporter and a Chinese journalist were sitting side by side. After the president had finished, the American asked his foreign counterpart if he needed assistance clarifying what Nixon said. The response was, "No, I understood perfectly."

Then the U.S. reporter asked if the journalist had any questions. The Chinese correspondent wanted to know if Americans were ignorant. The puzzled reporter asked why the journalist had asked such a question. "Because," he said, "before your president spoke, you told your people what he was going to say. After your president spoke, you told your people what he said."

"Here we are," mused Augustus, "more than half a century later, and the media are still translating what a president says. Has our education system deteriorated that much? Have we lost the ability to think and reason on our own? Do we really require interpretation by so-called experts telling us what they thought somebody said, or meant to say, or should have said?"

The White House Press Corps, however, was not just any group of correspondents. They were seasoned media veterans, experienced in Washington reporting, and very knowledgeable. Augustus knew he needed these journalists if he was to succeed, which made his actions even more puzzling. Over time, many came to realize their anger was purely emotional— bruised egos, the WHPC mystique deflated, and loss of status— when all that had really happened was relocation. Access to the president, first lady, Cabinet, White House staffers, and administration officials continued. The Press Pool still existed, and travel on Air Force One occurred, as did trips to Camp David. Especially helpful in healing the rifts were the president and first lady's subsequent amiability toward reporters and their bosses.

A White House dinner was held for media moguls. Augustus solicited their help in fighting terrorism, reducing the nation's mass murder epidemic, healing racial tensions, restoring citizens' respect for law and order, and uniting the country. His request was simple.

"Stop the incessant, weighty, 24-hour-a-day, for several days, nationwide reporting of local events. Do not send your evening news anchors, for days on end, to the scene of terrorist bombings, mass shootings, riots, or anti-police rallies. Report on the event, sure, then move on to other news occurring in the country or happening across the globe. Allow local news outlets to cover their local incidents. Stop making social media postings national news."

Augustus' request was based on his experiences in Europe where anarch groups were bombing American military installations, local and national government facilities, and international airports. The constant reporting and association of identified groups with terrorist events only emboldened their cause and acted as free advertisement for their recruiting efforts. It led to copycat groups committing similar attacks. A de facto competition took place for public recognition between anarchists in order to create greater headlines and significantly more coverage for their separate causes.

European leaders asked heads of their media to stop nationwide news reporting of terrorist atrocities in their home countries. Classified briefings were presented regarding the nature of the insurgent threat. In return, media widely reported governments' successes in the capture or killing of insurrectionists, results of trials and subsequent imprisonment, but not the terrorists' attacks.

An immediate result was the reduction of copycat incidents. The long-term impact was threefold. Without media headlines, smaller groups eventually disbanded. Less dedicated malcontents melted back into the fabric of society. Committed organizations, frustrated at their loss of news coverage, planned bigger attacks. Thus, the more members who were involved, the less secretive their intent and the more exposed their identities became. That led to infiltration of organizations by undercover authorities or exposure by confidential informants. In less than four years, the law enforcement agencies across Europe ended a significant number of homegrown terrorist threats.

The chief executive conducted a similar bold action to eliminate the clamor for 15 minutes of fame. He presented a Homeland Security briefing on gangs, terrorist, hate, and criminal groups operating in the U.S. At that meeting, he requested that traditional media no longer provide the identity, photograph, or personal data regarding any individual mass shooter or terrorist. He asked Internet and social media CEOs voluntarily shut down posted videos of horrendous crimes and claims of responsibility. Augustus desired the focus be on victims and not on glorifying perpetrators. He solicited their support of these measures to stop the violent acts of aggression and deaths of innocent Americans—whatever the motive. His requests were met with some success from the more established and traditional press but not so much by the younger, more aggressive social media outlets.

The first couple did not stop giving press conferences or one-on-one interviews; they continued to take the White House Press Corps on trips across the country and around the world. They scheduled monthly all-day press meetings. Both remained for as long as reporters had questions to ask. In addition, President and First Lady Treatise hosted private, individual, and intimate dinners for each member of the WHPC and their family, including spouses and children, parents, grandparents, and siblings. Dress was casual, private tours were given, and conversation focused on guests and family—not policy or politics. During those evenings, the first lady let it be known that should those guests have other career opportunities or plans, to inform her so the president and she might provide a fitting farewell. These dinners, over time, smoothed any initial animus.

President You

Chapter 7

Federal Budget

No Money shall be drawn from the Treasury, but in Consequence of Appropriations made by Law; and a regular Statement and Account of the Receipts and Expenditures of all public Money shall be published from time to time.

(Article I, Section 9, United States Constitution)

The President shall transmit to Congress on the first day of each regular session, the Budget, which shall set forth in summary and in detail...

(The General Accounting Act of 1921, a.k.a. the Budget and Accounting Act; Pub.L. 67-13, 42 Stat. 20 - Public Law 67-13, Chapter 18, Title II-The Budget, Section 201)

On or after the first Monday in January but not later than the first Monday in February of each year, the President shall submit a budget of the United States Government for the following fiscal year.

(United States Code, Title 31, Subtitle II, Chapter 11, § 1105)

It took one hundred years, a Great Depression, two World Wars, a Police Action, several smaller wars and regional conflicts, multiple recessions, suffrage and civil rights movements, and desegregation, before a Democratic president and a Republican Congress balanced the nation's budget, slowed government spending, and kept the country's debt around $3 trillion. One generation later, two administrations—one Republican president with his Republican Congress, who financed a war, and one Democratic president with his Democratic Congress, who funded social change—ceased balancing the budget, dramatically increased the borrowing limit, and incurred a seven-fold national debt to pay for massive spending.

In the first years of the twenty-first century, the executive and legislative branches were so divisive and entrenched in their political ideologies that government shutdowns and continuing resolutions were the norm. One continuing resolution financed the government for two years. That way senators and representatives would not have to deal with budget questions during their re-election campaigns. Members seemingly violated federal statutes regarding their fiduciary respon-sibilities. None were prosecuted or even charged with a criminal offense except in meaningless speeches on the floors of the Capitol and from the Oval Office.

Normally, the chief executive submitted an annual budget to Congress in which were outlined the dollars deemed necessary to finance existing programs (some increased, others decreased) and pay for campaign promises and political agenda items. The Legislative Branch reviewed that budget to which each of the 535 members added spending to cover their own campaign promises or cut funds for programs—most often military spending. Every one of them, along with their staffers, would "wheel and deal" and haggle to sort out what "pork" they could get for their constituents. At the same time, A-listers, agencies, corporations, foreigners, industries, lobbyists, organizations, powerful persons, special interest groups, small businesses, unions, wealthy individuals, and anybody and everybody who wanted something inundated members of Congress with their requests. Nothing had changed since the thirteen separate original colonies decided to become a unified country.

President Treatise's daunting task was to put a stop to it. Before presenting his budget, Augustus went directly to the people with a nationwide broadcast from the Oval Office.

> The country's current $34 trillion debt and its more than $145 trillion in unfunded liabilities are not only a threat to United States security, but also a direct threat to each American's way of life. The debt is a domestic enemy to the future of our children, grandchildren, and great-grandchildren.

> Citizens who struggle with too much borrowing, individual debt, or bankruptcy fully understand how their own lives and dreams have been disrupted or destroyed; and how their children's lives have been negatively impacted. It is my job and the job of every member of Congress to ensure America is not disrupted, negatively affected, or even destroyed because of fiscal irresponsibility.

> On the world's stage, since going off the gold standard, the United States dollar has been the legal tender on which nearly all other currencies have been based, secured, and guaranteed. Now nations across the globe are demanding a different standard by which global financing should be measured.

> These are expressions of anxiety and fear that America's economic stability is at risk. Even drug cartels and dictators are diversifying their portfolios, hedging their bets by stockpiling other countries' cash instead of one-hundred-dollar bills freshly printed from U.S. Mints and distributed by the Federal Reserve.

Augustus recalled how, when visiting the Eastern Bloc before the Berlin Wall and Iron Curtain came down, restaurateurs and businesspersons clamored for the almighty dollar. When Angelica and he vacationed in western democracies, the dollar was in high demand. However, since America incurred its massive debt and unfathomable financial liabilities, many nations preferred their own currency. On a few occasions, dollars were not accepted at all. Augustus recognized that America's debt had a far greater impact across the globe than in just the treasuries and banking systems of other lands. He would use that knowledge in the formulation of his budget proposal.

President Treatise reminded fellow citizens that America had its war on drugs, war on poverty, war on homelessness, war on hunger, war on AIDS, war on cancer, war on racism, and even a war on women. He asserted, "Now is the time to declare war on debt!"

It meant sacrifice and cutbacks probably not seen since World War II. "In my Inaugural Address, I discussed the triad instruments of national power. Economic stability is one of those strengths. One goal of my budget will be to cut government spending. With your help we can eliminate our national debt."

In this unprecedented broadcast, he remarked, "Follow me on a trip to the next battlefield," at which time the scene faded from the Oval Office and opened with the chief executive standing inside the United States Mint next to a machine printing thousands of sheets of brand new one-hundred-dollar bills. "They say money does not grow on trees, but it sure takes a lot of trees to print money. My budget is the first step in slowing, if not stopping, the continuous running of these printing presses."

The scene faded out a second time, and Augustus reappeared in front of the Treasury building at 1500 Pennsylvania Avenue. "Here at the U.S. Treasury are hardworking public servants. They are responsible for paying all the bills your government incurs."

Walking into a room filled with cubicles, he stopped at one desk, pointed to several piles of paper, picked up a handful of forms, and commented, "These invoices include your income tax refunds, Social Security benefits, Medicare expenses, interest on government loans, funds for research grants, sustainment of our Armed Forces, benefits for federal employees, numerous entitlement programs, costs to maintain the nation's infrastructure, disaster relief and assistance, congressional pork projects, even my salary, and yes, fraudulent claims. As a country, America must pay her bills, balance her budget, and become debt free; just like every one of you at home. With your help we can win America's war on debt, put our financial house in order, and recover national economic security."

Next, his budget tour appeared on Capitol Hill. With the Capitol as his backdrop, he said, "This, ladies and gentlemen, is the greatest battlefield of all. As citizens, we must convince all—not some, not everyone else's—but our own representatives and senators in Congress to change. Have them cease and desist wasteful spending. Get them to cease and desist funding pet projects. I need your help in making them fiscally responsible for their actions. And I need you to vote them out of office should they not!"

Back in the Oval Office, the president continued his presentation and addressed the "ten years" budget reduction fallacy.

> Nearly every politician speaks in terms of how their particular spending program will save millions of taxpayer dollars "over the next decade." There are many facets wrong with that oxymoronic thinking.
>
> Spending programs are based on several assumptions—inflation will be this, unemployment will be that, Gross Domestic Product will have "X" growth, trade deficits will reduce by so much, and "Y" will remain steady. In reality, it is basic algebra, when the value of any assumption in the formula changes, the result of the entire calculation then changes, and thus the value of costs or savings to the program changes. In other words, neither I nor any president, nor the White House Office of Management and Budget, nor members of Congress, nor the Congressional Budget Office, nor any agency, department, economist, or person can guarantee the assumptions upon which programs are based will remain constant, even predictable, over ten years.
>
> Politicians rely on the concept of "once

passed, always forgotten." They know the immediacy of public furor today will have been long forgotten and ignored in ten years' time. When, if ever, has the federal government conducted an audit of any program and subsequent to that audit required a bean counter, Cabinet secretary, senator, representative, or president to speak loudly, openly, honestly, and publicly, to announce, "Remember that program a decade ago which Representative X and Senator Y introduced, that Congress passed, and President Z signed, and how it was guaranteed to save billions of dollars? Well, after ten years this is the final tally." Never!

The problem with legislation enacted for a ten-year period is that it is always tweaked. The law simply may have been bad. Instead of, heaven forbid, eliminating the statute, and beginning anew, the Legislative Branch typically makes marginal alterations and adjustments because lobbyists meddle on behalf of special interests, and congressional membership changes. Program revision occurs when the occupant of the White House is replaced—at least once and sometimes twice during a given program's decade-long funding cycle. Every modification costs additional dollars not originally programmed, planned, or forecast.

In practical terms, the issues with constant changes were

many. Individuals, the self-employed, small businesses, corporations, and organizations could not keep up with the ever-changing laws. That inability to keep pace was compounded by the rules, regulations, policies, and procedures promulgated by various government departments and agencies which changed with every elected official and political appointee. Every time an adjustment was made, an additional, unanticipated expense arose. The ultimate and final cost was always more and savings were always less than originally stated. Augustus continued,

A challenge in the budget process is word games played by members of Congress when it comes to allegedly cutting programs. Democrats desire a ten percent increase in funding. Republicans want only a five percent increase in spending. Consequently, Dems blame the GOP for cutting programs. In actuality, a seven or eight percent increase is enacted and no real reductions occur. This "game" is continually played by both parties at the expense of the taxpayer.

Lastly, in determining the budget, what is the difference between debt and deficit? Politicians are experts at interchanging both words and concepts as if they mean the same thing. Democrats pronounce their budget proposal will reduce the debt, only to be denounced by Republicans for increasing the deficit and vice versa. The result is all too often an increase in both the national debt and deficit spending to the detriment of all Americans and the destabilization of United

States economic security.

Augustus recalled two personal experiences. When he worked for different international charities, every employee and volunteer was inculcated with the concept of "being a good steward of the donated dollar." Reputable Non-Governmental Organizations took very seriously their fiduciary responsibility to ensure every contributed dollar went to the recipients and programs espoused in their charter or mission. That was required for two very good reasons. First, revenue was limited, so expenses were tightly monitored. Second, any perceived abuse or diversion of funds in the public eye could cause the charity to fail—donors might stop contributing.

"It is time for members of the Legislative Branch and all government employees," the president demanded, "to become good stewards of the taxpayer dollar! To see, find, and 'employ more efficient and economical ways to getting tasks accomplished,' as written in the government Code of Ethics enacted by Congress."

With that background, Augustus presented his proposed budget. There were two primary tenets. First, instead of an annual budget filled with programs extended for ten years, his budget covered only the four years of his first term in office. Both he and members of Congress would be held responsible. No new program legislation would exceed four-year funding, and all prior funded ten-year programs expired at the end of this budget's fourth year. Second, once enacted, no changes were permitted to any of the laws tied to the four-year budget. That allowed every individual, organization, business, corporation, and jurisdiction to rely upon the legislation and provided a reasonable amount of time to determine the actual effects before adjusting statutes. His four-year budget proposal provided the chief executive de facto line item veto power yet allowed him room for approving emergency funds such as in disaster declarations.

He used as his starting point the last $5 trillion budget passed by Congress and signed by his predecessor. Augustus' key budget aspects set actual reductions in funding, across the board, for the Cabinet, and all executive departments and agencies except the Defense Department, Homeland Security, Justice Department, and Veterans Administration; 1% the first year, 2% the second year, 3% the third year, and 4% the final year. Cost reductions were accomplished in many other ways, as well.

Inside his budget proposal was the elimination of discretionary funding for all religious groups at the rate of 25% per year until zero outlays was achieved. Years ago, family took care of family. When that failed, neighbors and churches picked up the mantle of support. Government was the agent of last resort. Despite all its legislative and financial efforts, it has never provided people with family values, moral compasses, or local community standards. Government was too big, wasted too much money, was not responsible to its citizens, and attempted, in many areas, to replace families, churches, and communities at exorbitant cost. This part of budget reduction returned control of people's lives to themselves and got government out of their places of worship.

That same reduced funding concept also applied to nonprofit organizations that received taxpayer dollars. Donors to causes, charities, and non-government organizations expect their contributions to be used effectively and responsibly. People donate to activities with which they have a relationship or affinity; they do not contribute to organizations that are contrary to their beliefs. More importantly, they expect their donation to be directly utilized as intended and not siphoned off for use elsewhere. Government funding of nonprofit organizations, in essence, was using citizens' money for programs not supported by every taxpayer. The president's charity employment taught him if a not-for-profit's cause was worthy, then it succeeded through private donor—not government—assistance.

Based on Augustus' local jurisdiction experience, taxpayers influenced local programs run by local politicians to a greater extent than they influenced federal programs enacted by Congress. His proposed reduced spending combined with tax code revisions would return more dollars to the wallets and purses of Americans—as well as control of those assets.

Throughout America's history, the military took the brunt of political whims. Expansion and reduction of personnel strengths and funding occurred before, during, and after every conflict. The commander in chief reminded Americans of the second pillar of national power—the Armed Forces. He said, "It is time to stabilize military personnel end strength at one percent of the population based upon the latest official census. When I was elected, the population of the U.S. was roughly 335 million people. That means, for the purposes of my four-year budget, the peacetime strength of our Armed Forces will be 3.35 million personnel.

"Also, for more than two hundred years the Coast Guard has been known as the saviors of mariners in trouble on the high seas. Nearly everyone is familiar with their heroic efforts to save the lives of endangered anglers, merchant marines, sailors, watercraft enthusiasts, and yachtsmen along coasts, shorelines, harbors, and seaports. What is less well known is that the same mission applies to lakes, rivers, and waterways. In addition, the Coast Guard has the responsibility of protecting the country from seaborne terrorists, assisting with migrant interdiction, and conducting environmental protection. My budget triples the strength of the Coast Guard, at the rate of 20,000 coast-guardsmen per budget year, to a final 120,000 men and women. It doubles the number of aircraft and watercraft for air-sea rescue, ice breaking, drug interdiction, and coastal, port, and waterway security, as well as marine safety and navigation aids.

"In response to demands from the people to 'fix' the justice system, my budget authorizes and funds additional judges, United States attorneys, and legal staff for both criminal and civil cases. That is designed to allow courts to open for evening and weekend trials and to adjudicate the backlog of defendants' cases awaiting their day in court. Additional attorneys can prosecute hate crimes and law enforcement abuses. More public defenders with accompanying resources will enable them to match the assets available to prosecutors. Government payments to defendants' private civilian attorneys and law firms are eliminated."

His budget included doubling the number of federal agents at a rate of 100 street agents per every one supervisor hired. Those additional agents were deemed necessary to conduct counter-terrorism operations, strengthen efforts to fight drug and human trafficking, reduce the illegal purchase of weapons, prevent mass murders, catch identity and industrial technology thieves, stop the counterfeiting of currency, track down fraudulent Medicare and Medicaid abusers, obstruct robo-calls and cyber-crime, and deter a plethora of other illegal activity.

Finally, Augustus requested $10 billion the first year, $20 billion the second year, $30 billion the third year, and $40 billion the fourth budget year in grants to allow communities, towns, cities, counties, and states to double the number of full-time police officers, deputy sheriffs, and state troopers. The goal was two law enforcement officers per vehicle per shift. The resources were designated to hire street cops, not supervisors, or administrative staff, or to buy military-style equipment.

These were some of the major tenets and objectives in President Treatise's budget proposal covering the first four years of his presidency.

While his budget proposal worked its way through Congress, Augustus began immediate taxpayer savings. Remembering his second group of personal experiences in government, private sector, and nonprofit employment, he implemented several Executive Branch policies.

At his former state job, receipt of personal mail at the office was not allowed. That eliminated delivery and opening of boxes of mail order items and Internet ordered products on government time. In private business, the company's Information Technology department blocked all employees' private e-mail addresses, websites, and internet service providers. Only company-designated portals were authorized for access on company computers and mobile devices. At a nonprofit organization, every landline and cell phone call was tracked, and monthly records were sent to each supervisor. Personal calls and text messages were identified, and the employee reimbursed the charity for those non-work related costs. At another business, use of the Internet was tracked. The time conducting personal business during work hours was deducted from the employee's paycheck. Applying these simple policies in the Executive Branch saved thousands of hours of labor and millions of dollars. Because of these directives, employees performed their jobs, significant work was accomplished, and backlogs were cleared.

The advent of multiple means of social media communication eliminated the need for government employees and supervisors to schedule, host, attend, and spend taxpayer money on expensive conferences at luxurious resorts in exotic locations. Teleconferences and webinars became the norm. Presentations were loaded onto agency websites for employees to access. Records of individual attendance at web-based training were recorded and reported to the appropriate supervisor. These innovations had been standard practice during Augustus' work in the private sector, in professional organizations, and as an anti-terrorism contractor. Applied to the federal government, the reduced travel expenses saved tens of millions of dollars.

Bonuses for federal employees were curtailed. Managers and supervisors, especially Senior Executive Service personnel—at the top of the Government Service employee pay scale—did not receive bonuses; monetary incentives were for workers only. In addition, any employee, regardless of position or pay grade, who was in arrears to the Internal Revenue Service received no bonus, no step or time in service pay increase, no promotion or transfer to a higher pay grade, until back taxes were paid. Retiring federal employees had portions of their pensions and annuities garnished until owed income taxes were paid in full.

Congress did not like or accept Augustus' entire four-year budget proposal. Referring to the Constitution and the "power of the purse," members preferred the annual business-as-usual budget, which gave them more control. However, some aspects were enacted. Congress supported military end strength, increasing the Coast Guard, funding to fix the justice system, granting dollars to local law enforcement, and reducing taxpayer resources supporting religious organizations. Citing prior entitlement legislation, proposed reductions in funding of many portions of the Executive Branch were rejected. Increases in federal law enforcement and reductions aimed at many nonprofits were not approved. The president was presented with an annual budget that included ten-year programs and associated funding. Augustus vetoed the legislation, and Congress overrode his veto.

At the beginning of his second year in office, President Treatise submitted to the Legislative Branch a three-year budget proposal. It reduced the prior year's budget by more than $270 billion by eliminating several Executive Branch agencies and departments. Legislators had been stonewalling, filibustering, delaying, and otherwise stopping the confirmation of several political appointees. Augustus put the onus on the various congressional committees: "Since committee members have apparently decided that political appointees are not necessary for managing selected Executive Branch agencies and depart-ments, I can only conclude that Congress feels those same entities are not essential for operating the government. In which case, elimination is the most logical course of action." For the second year in a row, Congress forwarded to the president annual budget legislation, which Augustus vetoed, and Congress overrode.

The third year Congress was presented a two-year budget with predictable results. That year Augustus spoke directly to the people and told them the names, political party, pork project, and dollars he felt were wasted by legislators; followed by claims the pork was payoff to campaign contributors and that those identified senators and representatives did not care about current and future citizens. He included the names of campaign and party donors who benefited from the pork.

Unfortunately, that approach was not too successful either. Congress continued adding pork, borrowing more money, enlarging the debt, funding special interests, increasing the deficit, and raising the debt limit. Augustus felt his failed war to significantly reduce the country's debt, curtail government spending, and strengthen America's economic instrument of national power was "a major disappointment of my presidency."

Chapter 8

Political Appointees

> The President...shall nominate, and by and with
> the Advice and Consent of the Senate, shall
> appoint Ambassadors, other public Ministers and
> Consuls, Judges of the Supreme Court, and all
> other Officers of the United States...
>
> (Article II, Section 2, United States Constitution)

President Treatise sought out and nominated for appointment to positions in government doers, not talkers — men and women with compelling records of personal achievement and professional accomplishment. Like their sponsor, each one had experience in all three of these categories:

- served at one time in city, county, state, tribal, or federal jurisdiction or political subdivision;
- worked in corporations or small businesses or were self-employed;
- hired by a non-governmental organization, commonly referred to as charities or not-for-profit organizations. Serving as a board member, volunteer, or managing his or her own family foundation did not qualify.

Their fourfold mission designed to accomplish Augustus' ultimate goal of returning to the people faith, trust, and confidence in their government included:

- eliminate inappropriate regulations, rules, policies, directives, procedures, guidelines, memorandums, etc.
- stop the fraud, waste, and abuse in their agencies and departments
- create a more efficient government by streamlining operations, and
- dismantle the bureaucracy through combining functions.

Managers coordinate things. Supervisors direct workers. Leaders, on the other hand, efficiently manage resources, effectively supervise people, and possess the communications skills and personality traits that enhance cooperation, buy-in, and support from employees at all pay grades. Leaders make the time to look at a situation and listen to what they are told — then assess the information before decisions are made. Leaders are not afraid to get their hands dirty and perform menial tasks when necessary. Leaders foster a positive work environment and encourage individuals to better themselves. These were some of the attributes and qualities possessed by the men and women the chief executive brought into his administration.

All too often political appointees became enamored with the pomp and circumstance of the White House and Washington. To counter that attitude, Augustus directed that individuals appointed to high office conduct their swearing-in ceremony in his or her hometown. The events took place not in a federal building, not in the state capital, not at the county courthouse, not at city hall, not in any government facility, but in the most open and public place—outside in the city park, town square, county fairgrounds, or similar open-air venue. The activity was completely open to the public; costs and invited dignitaries were kept to a minimum.

Additional instructions from the president included:

- Personal expenses for the event were to be paid by the appointee and would not be reimbursed by taxpayers.
- The appointee was to make it clear to local officials and invited guests that expenses were to be kept to a bare minimum—the less cost to the taxpayers, the better.
- Any expenses incurred were to be paid with private funds, and use of volunteers was encouraged.
- Balloons, bands, banners, chairs, drinks, food, placards, platforms, parades, reviewing stands, signs, tables, and all those things normally associated with similar events were to be discouraged.
- Complex, expensive staging and sound systems were to be avoided. All one really needed was a soapbox for slight elevation above the crowd and a handheld speakerphone to carry the sound of voices far enough to reach the people who stood in the back.

Special guests were limited to the appointee's family and the official administering the oath of office. As a professional and protocol courtesy, invitations were extended to the governor of the state, commonwealth, territory or head of the Indian nation; county board chairperson, judge executive, parish leader or borough president; city or town mayor or tribal government leader; corresponding state-level office holder; and their spouses. Only two speeches were made at each event: one lasting less than one minute to introduce the appointee to the public and the second, limited to five minutes, by the appointee.

The new officials were to spend a minimum of one week, preferably two, in their hometown with family, friends, and everyday people before coming to Washington. They entered establishments or visited work sites, introduced themselves, mentioned their new job, took an interest in those they met, asked questions, and most importantly—listened, mostly in one-on-one conversations with individuals in the workplace. They sat in on classes at the local public and private K-12 schools as well as colleges, universities, and trade schools. They avoided speaking engagements to organized groups that represented the interests of individuals, clubs, organizations, unions, businesses, and the like to preclude the impression of favoritism.

During their time at home, appointees freely granted interviews to local newspaper and television reporters and appeared on radio, cable, and television programs with local talk show personalities. Interviews with national news networks, affiliates, and their reporters were discouraged—the focus was local. Another purpose of this mandated time in their home region was to visit the offices for which they provided governance and oversight. Their task was to find out from local agency employees' perspectives what did or did not work. As a courtesy, they met with managers and supervisors, but the focus was on the worker, preferably without the boss in attendance or earshot.

The purpose of executing and accomplishing such guidance was to achieve Augustus' ultimate objective to bring government closer in touch with its owners—the people. In addition, to demonstrate the adage that actions speak louder than words.

Cabinet Secretaries

Cabinet meetings were held on the second Saturday of every month. They began promptly at 9 a.m. Sometimes they would end by noon. More often than not, they would last through the night and well into early Sunday morning. Gatherings were rarely held at the White House. Each Cabinet office and separate agency or department hosted these work sessions in his or her respective buildings. In that way, Cabinet secretaries and senior officials were able to see their counterparts' environment—a technique used to break down barriers and reduce fiefdom attitudes. In addition, it sent a visual message to all federal employees regarding cooperation and teamwork between agencies. It also provided Augustus the opportunity to meet and tell what he was trying to accomplish and why to employees working on the weekend.

Those sessions were mandatory— no exceptions. The Cabinet secretary, agency, department, service, and administration head attended along with that organization's chief counsel. On very rare occasions, a subject matter expert was utilized, but only for the necessary portion of the discussion. Each primary official defended or supported his or her position on the issues addressed.

At these meetings, Augustus, Forrestor, and the attendees reviewed Signing Statements—those words of support or disagreement written by presidents as an attached memo or directly on the cover page of legislation passed by Congress. If some executive action had been taken and was deemed to have exceeded the intent of the statute, Augustus directed that all procedures associated with that Signing Statement be voided, modified, restricted, or not permitted. If the wording was merely an accolade or an admonishment of the legislation and no executive action had been taken, then no further proceedings were necessary.

Along with the Signing Statements, Executive Orders, Memorandums, Presidential Decision Directives, and other written chief executive documents were reviewed, cussed, and discussed. For the particular enactment being reviewed, each official presented the impact, positive and negative on the government, but more importantly, on the people. If the decree benefited the nation and her citizens as a whole, it remained in force. On the other hand, if the procedure was determined not to be in accordance with the intent of the law passed by Congress, was unlawful, exceeded the constitutional authority of the president, or had an overall negative impact on the country and its citizens, then the document and all subsequent regulations, rules, policies, directives, and guidelines were overturned. During Augustus' time in office, nearly one thousand prior executive documents either were modified or were revoked in their entirety.

Big government often created programs that, once established, never went away—even after they had outlived their usefulness or purpose; moreover, and much worse, they continued to be funded. Cabinet secretaries, executive agency and department heads, along with their inspectors general, were directed to conduct a thorough review of all programs and associated funding. By adding these to the review process, more than 6,500 defunct programs since the time of George Washington and the first Congress were found to be still on the books. An example was the Office of Intra-Agency Officials Collecting Revolutionary War Debts.

Nearly one hundred Advisory Councils, Boards, Commissions, Committees, Panels, and Research Projects were abolished or disbanded. The job descriptions of eighty-three Senior Executive Service members included aspects of many programs that no longer existed. Some of those non-programs comprised a significant part of the basis that supported their six-figure incomes. Removal of the non-existent programs from SES job descriptions eliminated the justification for high salaries. Seventeen political appointee positions were discovered that granted a title, paid a salary, required neither an office nor any responsibilities, and for which the employee spent all his or her time at home. Those, too, were eliminated.

The review also revealed a vast number of identified defunct programs were still funded. There were no offices, no staff directly managing, supervising, or working those programs, no files, no records to maintain, and no actions being taken whatsoever. Low level employees had been given responsibility for a dead program under the "other duties as assigned" portion of their job's KSA (Knowledge, Skills, Ability) in order that the agency or department justify funding that was ultimately diverted for use elsewhere. Overall, the bottom-to-top investigation and research determined $27 billion in taxpayer money had been wasted annually on extinct government programs. These dollars were reprogrammed.

By far the most challenging aspect of Augustus' mission for the leaders of the various entities was effecting attitude changes within the federal bureaucracy. The primary problem was career employees were tired and abused. Every time a different party took control of the government, its henchpersons, in the form of political appointees, who may or may not know anything about government—let alone the department or agency over which they were placed in charge—ordered adjustments be made that suited the agenda of the new administration. Those appointments often led to abuses of authority that changed the original intent of statutes those same appointees were supposed to uphold. Repeatedly, federal employees were directed to alter regulations, policies, and procedures—with the result of reinterpreting the original document with a different understanding of what was meant. That "reinventing of the wheel" wasted workers' time and tax dollars. Worst of all, it demoralized employees and disenfranchised millions of citizens who had to react to the constant, often back-and-forth changes in a politics-driven bureaucracy.

The commander in chief had seen and experienced the same waste of resources in the Army. One commanding officer was showy in his approach to running the outfit. Consequently, it was important that round rocks appeared as landscape and lawn edging next to every sidewalk in front of every barracks and unit building—and the rocks must be painted white. Another commanding officer thought white too stark a color and had the rocks painted red and yellow to match the unit's official colors. A third commander had all the rocks removed altogether, only for them to be replaced when a fourth officer took command.

Changing federal employee attitudes and fostering buy-in to stabilize bureaucracy operations took time and effort. The new appointees' tasks were to create an environment such that workers would uphold existing laws. They would be encouraged to resist efforts by future political appointees who wanted to make changes based on "Look what I did for you, Mr. President," or to make a name for themselves, add to their résumé, enhance their speaking fees, or negotiate book deals.

Ambassadors

The head of state required each ambassador to possess what was known as a five-by-five-by-five rating in the language of the nation to which he or she was assigned. In other words, they read, wrote, spoke, and comprehended the foreign vernacular as if they were a native. Each ambassador had to have taken college courses specific to that country; most had obtained a Bachelor or Master's degree in studies of that land. The appointee must have at least visited that country in some capacity as a tourist or dealt with foreign nationals on a business trip. Ideally, they had lived in that nation as a direct result of their parents' employment or their own employment, military service, or exchange student status.

Ambassadors had to demonstrate their knowledge of a country's history, culture, and societal norms and possess the ability to represent the United States as the world's leader and partner with the land of their assignment. They had to appreciate that nation and its people and not act like the proverbial bull in a china shop. Too often Augustus, while vacationing in other parts of the world, had seen and heard American tourists yell at local sales clerks because they did not speak English. He thought his fellow citizens rude, ugly, and conceited, and recalling his own interactions with residents of other countries, required ambassadors to be courteous and consummate representatives of all that was good about the U.S.

If no individual met his requirements, then the position of Acting Ambassador fell on the shoulders of the highest-ranking career diplomat in the Foreign Service familiar with the country to which he or she was assigned. No one was appointed, let alone recommended, solely because of friendships, business relationships, monetary donations, political payback, or because somebody knew somebody who knew somebody.

Judges

Historically, the appointment of judges was based mostly on judicial acumen. In the previous and current century, skill had been all too obviously replaced by advocacy. Politicians preferred judges with attitudes parallel to their own. This was deemed appropriate to ensure a political agenda was successful and would not fall to challenges in court. Even though the

Judicial Branch was designed to be an equal partner with the Legislative and Executive Branches as part of the checks and balances established by the Founders of the United States, judges openly and actively predisposed to the ruling party's beliefs were nominated by the White House and approved by a spiteful Senate. That political nomination and approval system often denied qualified judges because they did not possess the appropriate perspective.

Those and other instances of partisanship, which placed the interests of political parties above those of the United States and her people, in Augustus' view, compromised the integrity of the judicial system and prostituted the separation of powers concept established under the Constitution.

President Treatise nominated judges who were inclined to have a stricter interpretation of the Constitution. Especially considered were judges who believed the judicial system was an independent branch of government and not subordinate to any political party. After a review of their legal history and adjudication record when determining suitability for appointment, the chief executive asked only two questions: "Do you believe in the Constitution of the United States?" and "Would your role be to interpret law or make law?" Unfortunately, many benches remained vacant while the socialist left and alt-right members of Congress argued incessantly.

Other Political Appointees

Unlike his predecessors who filled political appointee positions based on family, business relationships, party recommendations, or high-dollar campaign contributions, Augustus opened all opportunities to the people. He wanted everyday citizens who, like himself, believed in less bureaucracy and greater organizational effectiveness. Even though nearly 45,000 applications and résumés were submitted, it was hard finding the more than 3,000 replacements needed who met all the chief executive's requirements for appointment. This was exacerbated by a disbelieving Congress that routinely disapproved close to 87% of all nominations. Consequently, nearly 800 positions remained unfilled. Augustus was fine with that, as vacant positions meant expense reductions and ultimately led to the elimination of many positions unnecessary to government operations.

On the other hand, many career federal employees had the talents to perform in positions of higher authority. Augustus sought out those individuals, interviewed them, and many, though they did not always agree with his mission, accepted the offered leadership role. They retained their Government Service rating, maintained their status for retirement purposes, and received additional compensation for the increased respon-sibility.

As with judges, ambassadors, and Cabinet secretaries, those appointees, too, had to return to what they considered their hometown for their appointment ceremony and all that the president's entire mission encompassed.

President You

Chapter 9

Name

name *n.* **1** That by which a person or thing is called.

Beginning with his pronouncement, throughout the campaign, Election Day, continuing to his inauguration and beyond, most newshounds assigned to discover all they could about Augustus too often regurgitated unconfirmed second- and third-hand stories as if they were facts. A few journalists conducted due diligence. Who was the interloper who refused to conform to the decades old societal norms established by the political class and powerbrokers of Washington?

It started on a plateau a few miles and several minutes' drive by modern conveyances from where a single five-hundred-foot high monolith of rock stood like a chimney, its base a pile of rubble forming a circular pyramid. That Nebraska landmark called Chimney Rock, visible from as far away as thirty miles, was used long ago by adventurous souls who left behind the old world of the east and ventured toward an unknown life in the new west. Their Conestoga wagons, towed by teams of oxen, were laden with precious possessions, crates of dried meat, bags of salt, barrels of flour, and casks of water. They traveled into the foreboding future alone, in clusters of three or four families, or caravans more than a mile long, across a landscape where the population of rattlesnakes far exceeded the number of pioneers making the journey.

Those settlers, whose stiff wide-brimmed hats became weather-beaten floppy vestiges of what they had once been, mostly trod the ten-mile-a-day trek for the entire four-month-long trip. The women folks' once brightly colored bonnets were bleached dull from bright sunlight, and the bottoms of their gingham dresses were permanently stained brown from dirt and mud and were laced with thistles from miles of stepping beside the wagons. All except the youngest of children walked, their sun-reddened skin covered with a fine makeup of beige dust. So many made this precarious move that more than one hundred fifty years later, the earth still showed where wagons' wheels carved ruts into bedrock on the California, Oregon, and Mormon Trails.

Life for President Treatise began nearly a century after the Transcontinental Railroad was completed, on his mother's bed, in the second floor apartment rented by his parents. Opossum Flats was a rural community located in the far reaches of the Nebraska Sandhills. A veterinarian attended his birth, a man who was more accustomed to the physiology of farm animals than of humans—the basic principles of Homo sapiens birthing being similar to those of bovines, canines, equines, and felines—at a cost of fifty dollars.

The bed on which the newborn arrived was made of black forged steel. Its head and footboards were vertical rods capped by upper and lower cross members that gave it the appearance of jail cell doors. Attached to its frame were interwoven metal strands and springs that squeaked anytime someone sat or lay on it. Two full size mattresses, each about three inches thick, rested on its metal skeleton; there was no box spring. Three goose-down feather pillows adorned the bed. Over the plain white sheets was a hand sewn, patchwork quilt assembled from scraps of used cloth his mother's mother had stitched long ago.

Bedroom walls were painted a pale yellow that looked brighter than they really were against the backdrop of a dark brown-stained hardwood floor. There were no rugs. Most of the room's light came from a single double-hung window on the south wall. Other than the bed, the only pieces of furniture were a dresser for underclothes and a small lamp that rested on a nightstand. With no closet, most outerwear hung from inch-thick, half-foot long wooden pegs inserted into or affixed to the walls.

The warped wood floor extended through a doorway that led to another room. In it were positioned a couch covered in pink peony and green leafed tapestry, a predominately red and navy paisley patterned over-stuffed chair, a solid kelly-green vinyl hassock, a brass floor lamp, a neutral-stained pine wood coffee and end table set, and a small black plastic portable radio. This room's walls were the same pale yellow color. Ambient light entered from windows on the south and east walls. As there was no second bedroom and the living space was too small for either a twin bed or a crib, seven-year-old brother James' bed was the couch. Augustus was relegated to the chair, which was protected by a plastic cover.

The front door of their apartment led to a mirror-image apartment across the hall that was rented by another couple and their daughter going through her "terrible twos." At the end of that hallway, in what was once a storage closet was a shared bathroom that consisted of a toilet, sink, and cast iron, claw-foot bathtub resting on asbestos manufactured flooring. The toilet tank mounted high upon the wall above the commode was activated by yanking down on the rusty metal pull chain. All the fixtures were white except where iron-laden water had created a brown stain on the porcelain. Brass faucets attached to lead pipes controlled the flow of sulfur-odor well water. There was neither a shower nor medicine cabinet. The room's walls were coated with several layers of light blue, lead-contaminated, oil-based paint. A single 60-watt exposed light bulb, attached to a knob-and-tube wire, hung down from the cobwebbed ceiling. One ten-penny nail for hanging towels or clothes protruded from the plain solid wood door. As there was no window for ventilation or airing, the room often displayed mold and should the light bulb burn out, the room became dark as a cave.

An interior staircase led down to the ground floor, where the proprietor and his wife lived. Their private bath was in the back of the house positioned just below the upstairs bathroom. The kitchen with its wood-burning stove, on which all meals were prepared, was to the left of the bathroom. A used refrigerator had replaced a leaky icebox. Four other rooms filled the main floor. One was the proprietors' bedroom, and the second was their separate living area. The third space had been converted into a dining room where all tenants met for meals three times daily—except twice on Sunday. Original to the building, the parlor took up the front of the first floor, in which the families could gather to read, play cards, visit, or discuss the happenings of the day. There was no television; even the most rudimentary TV was considered an unaffordable luxury.

The root cellar below the house had been altered to accommodate an oil-burning furnace. Every so often, a truck would arrive and the black liquid was dispensed into the holding tank in the basement. The only rooms that received the benefit of direct heat were on the ground floor; none upstairs had any sort of ductwork for warmth in the winter. In the summer, open windows and a floor fan provided air con-ditioning. The front porch on the east side of the building had been converted into a glass-enclosed greenhouse in which vegetables were grown year-round. Milk, butter, cream, and cheese were delivered weekly, the local newspaper every Thursday, and mail, if any, occasionally.

The two-story structure itself had been constructed before World War I and was aligned in a neat row with several others of similar design. Streets were nothing more than dirt alleys and not named. With a town population of less than two hundred, none of the homes had numbers; they were known by their original occupants' names. The future president's parents lived in the Emery House, as it was called, because a Mister Emery built the place and was its original occupant. Delivery of goods and services was never an issue, as everyone in town knew where each other lived. Keeping one's own personal business secret from gossiping busybodies and small town talk was always a challenge.

All village businesses were clustered around a one-block-long main street. On one side were the filling station, run by the local Farmers Cooperative, a grocery mart, and a privately owned bank used by farmers, ranchers, and residents. On the other side was the general store, which also served as the post office and telephone exchange, and a café that served breakfast, lunch, and opened its bar during evening meals. The one-room schoolhouse, with its sole teacher who provided education for children kindergarten through sixth grade, was utilized as the town hall on weekends. There was no pre-school. Older students either rode farm equipment driven by their siblings or were bused the twenty miles to the county's combined middle and high school. Two nearby churches fulfilled the religious needs of most everyone in the community; a cemetery on the north edge of town met the needs of both.

Between the cobblestone town street to the smooth pavement

of the two-lane, asphalt state highway lay three miles of gravel road that featured dust in the summer, mud in the spring and fall, and ice in the winter. Once each summer the county roads department graded the road, spread new gravel, and coated everything with a concoction of stone chips, oil, and tar. It was designed to smooth the road as well as keep down the dust. All it really accomplished was to splatter automobiles with sticky, black sludge. In this environment lived and worked the Treatise family.

The baby's mother was of Dutch-English ancestry—a blond haired, green-eyed beauty. Nora was raised in Deadwood, South Dakota, during times of gambling parlors, saloons, houses of ill repute, and gunfights. She had gotten pregnant the night of her senior high school prom and married her sailor lover six months after graduation. That union yielded a boy named James whose father was reported to have fallen overboard, lost at sea during a hurricane, and ultimately was declared dead by the Navy.

To make ends meet, Nora worked as a bookkeeper in a department store while her parents watched the child. Some years after her first husband's death, she met and married a much older man, a World War II combat veteran turned semi-professional musician. Myles was of Welsh-German ancestry complete with brown hair, blue eyes, and an explosive temper. He, too, was raised and educated in Deadwood, delivered newspapers to those same dens of iniquity, and drove a taxi before being drafted and sent to war.

As a musician with a meager income and family to support, he discovered the demand for traveling bands had waned, and weekend-only work did not provide enough money to raise a family. Myles eventually obtained employment with the telephone company as a lineman and installer. After a brief period of initial training, he transferred and took his wife and her son from the fir trees and mountainous terrain of the Black Hills to their residence in the desert-like, rural grassland outback of the American Plains.

Well-read and with a gift for languages, Myles had easily learned French in New Caledonia and Cebuano from his time on Cebu Island, The Philippines after the Leyte Gulf campaign. He had a fervent belief his biological son was destined for greatness, and the new father decided the boy, who was to grow up and become a renowned person, needed a suitable name; a name, that when spoken, identified that man with inherent eminence. Augustus, from one of the Caesars, and Lincoln, the 16th president, seemed worthy.

Such was the small world the eight-pound, 10-ounce, 19-inch-long, sandy-haired and blue-eyed Augustus Lincoln Treatise entered.

President You

Chapter 10

Political Correctness

Article the third. Congress shall make no law...
abridging the freedom of speech...

("The Bill of Rights," The 1789 Joint Resolution of
Congress Proposing 12 Amendments to the U.S.
Constitution, September 25, 1789)

political *adj.* Pertaining to government. **-'ically**
adv.

correct *adj.* Right, lacking fault or error; exact,
accurate; proper, as *correct* behavior. *Correct*
means without fault according to a standard, as
correct speech **-'ness** *n.*

"**A**mericans, as a people," Augustus often said, "abhor
Political Correctness."

If the Pilgrims had been politically correct,
there would be no Plymouth Rock. Had
British subjects been politically correct, James
Oglethorpe would have had no one to
colonize Georgia. Were Thomas Jefferson
politically correct, he would not have written
the Declaration of Independence. Should
Abraham Lincoln have remained politically
correct, the Emancipation Proclamation

would not exist. Suffragettes remaining politically correct would have meant no voting rights for women. Had President Truman fostered political correctness, our Armed Forces would have remained segregated. If our youth remained politically correct in the 1960s, the "Sex, Drugs, Rock 'n Roll" revolution would not have taken place. Were the rock group *The Doors* politically correct, they would have sung different words on *The Ed Sullivan Show*. The Civil Rights movement remaining politically correct would mean separate whites and coloreds' only lines still today. The LBGTQ community would still be in the closet had they abided political correctness.

Continuing their offensive, the Politically Correct (PC) rabble had turned its focus onto Broadway, movie and film, music, television, and video game industries. Ultimatums were uttered and retribution demanded if scenes were not retouched, voiced over, or edited out altogether; words in scripts and music had to be replaced and all acts of violence removed. Television programs and movies stereotyping Native-Americans as ruthless savages, African-Americans as lawless criminals, Mexican-Americans as drug dealers, Asian-Americans as sex traffickers, and Muslim-Americans as terrorists were declared bigoted. Demands were made that those productions be destroyed. White actors and actresses who portrayed Indians, Africans, Hispanics, Asians, or Arabs were labeled racist. So, too, were the producers, writers, stunt persons, camera operators, editors, and casting directors—anyone in any way associated with "incorrect" entertainment was vilified for misappropriating cultures. Everyone named on the list of credits in films and programs was identified, addresses determined, and politically correct (hate) mail sent. Television, cable, satellite, Internet movie networks, and their sponsors were boycotted. Live performances were picketed. Books were banned or burned.

Micro-aggressionists demanded software companies and graphic artists stop creating offensive geometric figures, symbols, clip art, and emoji. The crowd's argument was any person who used any colored mathematical geometric figure or any symbol in any capacity that offended anyone else was a bigot. As illogical and irrational as that seemed, other interpretations by some in the PC gaggle posited that "incorrect" individuals were actually against the symbol they used or displayed. The country was still moving that direction when Augustus became president.

The end—the proverbial straw that broke the PC camel's back, came rather quietly—in the form of games. The overly thin-skinned and all too sensitive politically correct minority asserted that card games were repugnant. The common deck of cards was emblematic. *Spades* connoted· racist sentiments and were renamed shovels. *Diamonds* indicated the top 1% wealthiest and had to be called parallelograms. *Clubs* were deemed weapons of violence. Initially they were retitled *Shamrocks*, but that was Irish cultural appropriation and showed favoritism to one nationality, which was not allowed, so the more generic *Clover* was selected. *Hearts* remained—they exhibited love, peace, and kindness.

Poker was declared offensive because the name itself indicated violence toward women—when pronounced it sounded too much like "poke her." *Seven Card Stud* was overtly sexually explicit. *Old Maid* was challenged—too mean to elderly ladies. *Black Jack* was considered blatantly racist. *Three-Hand Bridge* called attention to physical deformities, and *Idiot's Delight* offended those with learning disabilities. *Go Fish* and *Frog* brought on the ire of environmentalists. Advocates wanted to ban *Pig*, but anarchists convinced the minority to leave the disparaging remark about police. Anti-gun proponents protested against *Shotgun* as too violent. Those against alcohol suppressed any game with the word *Gin, Rum, Six Pack,* or *Rummy*. Games that mentioned nationalities such as *American Pinochle, Chilean Canasta*, and *Russian Bank* were targeted. *Spit in the Ocean* was an obvious elimination.

Even board games could not escape PC wrath. Those that acquired property, built wealth, or generated money, such as *Monopoly*, were petitioned to include a rules change which required players to equally distribute all assets to the other players. On the other hand, games in which a player apologized for his or her actions, *Sorry* for example, were left unscathed.

Political correctness, in Augustus' view, had gone too far and had become tiresome and boorish. The chief executive decided enough was enough. Americans needed independence from thought and speech police. He provided the push, the spark, and the catalyst to a nationwide and overt rejection of PC.

On July 1, his sixth month in office, President Treatise selected Thomas Paine's Cottage in New Rochelle, New York from which to broadcast his message. He stood in front of the white two-story, wood-framed house. A small roof over the porch, held up by two square posts, protected the single-door entrance. Augustus was attired in America's national colors: oxblood shoes, red socks, tapered navy trousers, and a white, open-collared golf shirt.

In his 1706 work *Thoughts on Various*

Subjects, Jonathan Swift wrote, "Some Men, under the Notions of weeding out Prejudices; eradicate Religion, Virtue, and common Honesty." That is what Political Correctness accomplishes. In its attempts to weed out every kind of prejudice and offense, it has begun to eradicate all forms of religion, replace virtue with violence, and make honesty in plain speaking impotent.

I stand before you today in front of the historical residence of Thomas Paine, Founding Father who coined the phrase "United States of America" and authored *Common Sense*. It is just plain common sense that Political Correctness is wrong.

It is unconscionable the United States of America—the only country in the world that stands for freedom; the only land to which generations of people came to flee oppression and the suppression of their thoughts, words, and faiths; the only nation which represents liberty on earth—is now divided into fiefdoms that ban art, bags, books, cats, dogs, drinks, flags, foods, games, icons, movies, murals, music, people's names, pictures, plays, prayer, religious symbols, sports, statues, straws, words—anything and every-thing that piques some person's fastidious feelings.

It is today's self-appointed, self-righteous, politically correct thought police who claim freedom of speech, yet are themselves police-state oppressors, dictatorial suppressors, and purveyors of hate. Our ancestors faced and rejected such ideologues, and today's immigrants shunned those attitudes by coming to a free speech America.

I ask, "How long are we, as the freedom loving citizens of a constitutional republic, going to allow an insignificant number of PC whiners to destroy the first and foremost amendment to our Constitution and abuse the first tenet of our Bill of Rights—the right to free speech?" I answer, "Not anymore!"

This week, as we celebrate our nearly two and a half centuries of independence from the tyrannical rule of a monarchy, let us declare our independence from restricted speech and controlled thought by modern day PC tyrants.

I declare the Political Correctness way of living, breathing, and thinking ended. As far as I am concerned, it stops now. If you do not like what you hear, see, or read from this president—tough!

The people, tired of being bullied silent from expressing their thoughts for fear of offending someone, reveled in the freshness of the man who led the new "freedom from fear of free speech" movement. The heretofore-silent majority, once again became the voice of America.

National Language

language *n.* **1** Human speech. **2** The speech of one people as distinguished from that of others.

The president was against establishing English as the national language. "In America, one does not converse, listen, scribe, or peruse the way one does when one is born, reared, educated, and lives in England, does one. In the United States we talk, hear, write, and read American, don't we. American is our national language."

Four decades after the ratification of the Constitution, efforts were made to change how words were spelled and pronounced. Using our Constitution, for example: defence (English) was scribed, not defense (American); Yeas and Nays were written as opposed to Yes and No; and chuse was penned instead of choose. Noah Webster's 1828 dictionary, in part motivated by nationalist fervor, introduced many spelling reforms. Emphasis on syllables was altered in many words; similarly, sentence structure changed.

A cursory look inside any dictionary reveals the philology and/or etymology of words, including colloquial expressions. U.S. citizens' everyday grammatical use of words comes from nearly all nations on the globe. As the melting pot of all races, creeds, colors, ethnicity, cultures, and vernaculars, America has adopted and incorporated many foreign words and associated definitions into its lexical—hence, American is not the same as English.

Augustus solidified his "American is the national language" belief while he worked in state government. He discovered the state spent hundreds of thousands of taxpayer dollars to convert and produce forms and brochures into Spanish, Vietnamese, and other languages. "Why?" he would ask. The common answer was the state had a significant population of Hispanics, or had just accepted a large influx of Vietnamese refugees or other immigrant groups.

"What is 'significant' and 'large'?" he would ask. "Were they based on a percentage of population or was there a numerical threshold that, when reached, triggered the need to create foreign language forms?" He got no direct answer. Prevailing comments highlighted the decision to help immigrants become citizens, and the best way to make them feel welcome was to create forms they could complete in their native tongues. Since there were no quantitative measurements and there appeared to be only emotional reasons, Augustus' next logical questions were, "Are we going to reproduce forms in Japanese, Swahili, Hmong, Gaelic, or Farsi? After all, one state employee's parents are from Saudi Arabia. How about Hebrew? We certainly have an extensive Jewish population."

Creating universally understood Hispanic forms was, in and of itself, challenging. Chilean, El Salvadoran, Guatemalan, Honduran, Mexican, Panamanian, Venezuelan, and many other Central and South American vernacular contained some form of dialect and idiom of Spanish, each with their own unique and subtle differences. It took months of time, labor, and expense, rewrite after rewrite, and review after review by state employees, university language professors, and immigrants to arrive at an "acceptable" all-encompassing document.

"Is the state prepared to conduct the same process for the reported three hundred dialects of Chinese or two hundred dialects of Philippine?" Augustus would ask.

Responses ranged from, "We have to accommodate these people" to "We must do this for them to receive benefits; to make it easier for them; to demonstrate we are a welcoming state."

"Then shouldn't we similarly integrate all foreigners moving into our state?" he inquired.

"We will, when enough of them arrive. And don't ask for the definition of enough!"

"Then isn't the state fostering government-sponsored discrimination when it accommodates some immigrants and selected refugees while not bestowing the same assistance on other foreign nationals?"

To which Augustus received only a guttural sound of exasperation.

As he continued his education into the ways of state government, Augustus noted the only department that was obliging was Social and Human Services—the agency that provided most taxpayer funded "free" things. None of the other agencies and departments was taking the trouble to generate foreign language forms. Delving deeper into the mechanisms of bureaucracy, he concluded the accommodating effort boiled down to money and power.

Augustus described it as a very simple, self-perpetuating concept. As he saw it, offering more programs required additional employees; that meant greater expenses, which necessitated increased budgets, and in turn created a larger bureaucracy—empire building, it was called. The added benefit to any official was an enhanced résumé based on the quantity, not quality, of programs overseen, the number of employees supervised, and dollar amounts managed. Small wonder Augustus' proposal to invest a one-time capital expenditure of $50,000 in computer technology designed to save the department and taxpayers $3 million in operating costs were ignored.

Based on that and other experiences, President Treatise proposed American, not English, as the country's national language—a small, but in Augustus' mind, significant distinction. While legislation snail-paced itself through the halls of the Capitol, he issued an Executive Order that enjoined all federal entities cease offering the choice between English or Spanish and any other language except TDD on telephones, websites, e-mails, the Internet in general, and social media sites more specifically. Federal forms, pamphlets, brochures, and documents were included in his directive.

The Executive Order instructed the Department of Education to withhold funds from those schools where classes K-12 were taught in a foreign tongue. He was not referring to English as a Second Language programs and did not target classes that taught children a foreign language. He specifically targeted public school districts where algebra, chemistry, history, literature, math, physics, physical education, science, and other subjects were taught in any foreign language. Americans, and immigrants who desired to become citizens, educated in U.S. schools, must be instructed using the American language. This was the president's goal.

Another aspect of the Executive Order directed federal departments to review the status of all entities—public or private sector—which had contractual, fiduciary, monetary, proprietary, statutory, or other relationships with the government and utilized foreign languages. They were to be scrutinized. Continued use of other than American vernacular for general contact by the public could result in the reduction, withholding, or cancellation of government resources.

An additional basis for the chief executive's language agenda arose when Angelica and a fellow federal agent were on assignment in a Southern state. Her law enforcement partner became violently ill, and he was taken to a local hospital. Everyone in that health care facility spoke Spanish—emergency room staff, doctors, nurses, and those who cleaned his room—and no one spoke American. The agent was there three days before a doctor communicated with enough skill to discuss the agent's medical condition. No melting pot had taken place in that locale.

Finally, in almost every other country in the world, immigrants learned to read, write, and speak the language and understand the history, culture, government, laws, business, ways of life, forms, documents, and everyday aspects of living. The process was difficult and required a commitment to citizenship and a demonstrated willingness to become a knowledgeable and productive resident. President Treatise believed Americans were an exceptional people and becoming a United States citizen should be hard as well: "When you work for and earn something, you cherish it more than when it is given to you." Learning the American language was part of that effort.

Augustus was not anti-foreign language or anti-persons of another culture. He and Angelica had traveled to many countries around the world as private citizens. They appreciated the ability of local inhabitants to communicate in American, especially when they vacationed, rented cars, used public transportation, stayed at hotels, ate in restaurants, purchased products, sought directions, watched the news, needed medical care, or required emergency assistance. President Treatise and the first lady knew from experience that people in other lands were very much delighted in their efforts to speak the local vernacular. Moreover, from his own inter-actions with foreigners who vacationed in the U.S., those visitors valued Americans even more when they found he, or anyone, could communicate in their native tongue.

As an international tourist, Augustus had experienced countries that made significant efforts to assist visitors. Many established "hot lines," such as the 112 system in South Korea, through which tourists seeking assistance could contact a person who understood their particular language. This was not designed to facilitate becoming that country's citizen, but was a tool for foreigners who sought aid in a variety of situations. A similar system was contained in the proposed language legislation. It would create jobs, especially for new immigrants.

He also incorporated a technique used by a nationally renowned charity. That organization offered its services without the expense of developing individual language forms or creating a cumbersome bureaucracy. Simply, a chart of the flags of all the countries of the world or an up-to-date atlas was kept available at each office. When anyone came in for assistance who could not understand American, the charity's employee showed the flag chart or world map and the client would point to their native country. Then the charity contacted their network of volunteers for assistance as translators. That network con-sisted of university and high school professors and teachers; religious leaders from local churches, synagogues, mosques, and temples; college and high school students seeking extracurricular activity credit for schoolwork; immigrant advocacy groups; new green card holders; or citizens who knew the requisite language.

The program was so successful that law enforcement used the charity's resources to assist foreign tourists. Prosecutors, public defenders, legal aid groups, and attorneys employed some of those same volunteers to aid during criminal, civil, or administrative cases. Emergency management, hospital, ambulance, and fire department personnel, who often interacted with immigrants, used the same resources as well.

As a soldier assigned to Germany, Augustus had attended a Department of Defense program designed to immerse soldiers in the German culture, laws, and language. The chief executive proposed legislation to provide grants for the Department of Education and the Small Business Administration to enact something similar in the U.S. Those funds were designated for schoolteachers, college professors, and new immigrants to open additional language immersion camps for children during the summer break from school. The added benefit was another job creation venue.

Augustus was proficient in German and could get by in Italian and Japanese. Angelica was a better Spanish and French linguist. Both were strong advocates of citizens learning at least one and preferably two other languages. That accomplishment would pay positive dividends to any American's future anywhere on the globe. Incorporated into the proposed legislation was additional education funding to hire teachers for schools that offered foreign language classes beginning in Kindergarten and extending through high school graduation. In order to prepare America's children for their role on the international stage, enhanced language education and foreign exchange opportunities would be provided.

The president's objective in making American the national language was six-fold. First, re-instill the idea that Americans have their own vernacular, adopted from all cultures, and their own methods of writing, reading, and speaking. Second, continue assimilation and integration of immigrants from across the globe into the country's norms and create within them a new national identity as Americans. Third, reduce government spending by utilizing existing public-private-nonprofit partnerships that already provided language interpretation services to new citizens and visitors. Fourth, expand volunteer linguistic services by using immigrants and guest foreigners as interpreters. Fifth, create jobs in education and tourist assistance services. Sixth, expand language education for the nation's youth.

The legislation became law. American was adopted as the official language of the United States; funding was allocated to hire more teachers in public schools; a nationwide tourist help line was established; and resources were made available for organizations to identify, recruit, and utilize foreign language volunteers as well as establish language immersion camps. Withholding of funding for public schools that taught classes in other tongues was not included, and businesses were not "punished" for offering foreign language choices. The president's original Executive Order was revised and applied only to the Executive Branch; both the legislative and judicial branches continued to offer language options. Despite the portions of the proposal that had been eliminated, Augustus considered it a substantial victory.

International Relations

international *adj.* Relating to or affecting two or more nations at once.

relation *n.* **6** The position in which one thing or concept stands with regard to another.

At state dinners held in the White House for leaders of other nations or while conducting America's business with foreign governments on their home soil, Augustus and Angelica would regale their international visitors, hosts, and hostesses with anecdotes of earlier visits as private citizens to their countries. Those stories went a long way toward endearing the president and first lady to many leaders of the world and tended to ameliorate some of his more controversial foreign policy decisions.

The head of state's first overseas trip occurred a few months after he took office. His trip to the Middle East began to repair the chasm created by previous administrations and congresses. He stopped first in Israel, where he met with its prime minister and president and addressed the Knesset. "People of Israel, know this—as long as I am President of the United States, America will stand with you."

President Treatise reminisced about the time he and the first lady toured Israel several years earlier. "We crossed the Sinai Peninsula from Egypt and observed the rusted, burnt steel hulk remnants of the Yom Kippur War in 1973. As there was no toilet on the bus, the eight-hour trip from Cairo to Tel Aviv was broken by a stop halfway to allow passengers to answer nature's call. Since there were no public toilets in the remote village, Angelica and I conducted our necessary business behind a two-meter-high wall made of straw and mud-baked bricks, sharing the space with several camels." That story received a generous laugh from Knesset members.

Augustus described how the tan colored, barren and seemingly endless desert sands became a plush, green oasis upon reaching Israel's border at Kerem Shalom—a testament to persistence, ingenuity, and irrigation. He talked about several members of the tour group who purchased camel saddles—the "thing to buy" in Egypt. Unfortunately, the saddles were stuffed with straw that was infested with insects dangerous to Israel's agriculture, so the saddles were confiscated and burned. This tale reminded Augustus of his parents' story about their honeymoon to San Francisco in 1948. At the border between Nevada and California, agriculture agents confiscated his mother's wedding corsage, as they feared it carried some insect or blight dangerous to California's agriculture.

The head of state recalled how he and the first lady's first real introduction to Israeli culture began the day they arrived at their Tel Aviv hotel just in time to experience Yom HaShoah—Holocaust Remembrance Day. That was the beginning of an eleven-day countrywide tour which included Jerusalem, a city destroyed, besieged, attacked, or captured more than forty times over three millennium; and Temple Mount, the location of King David's Temple. Masada, the former palace of King Herod where 900 Jewish Sicarii held at bay a Roman Legion for several months and where new Israeli Defense Forces recruits take their oath of service was visited. There was also an overnight stay at a kibbutz near the northern border that was shelled by Lebanese artillery while they tried to sleep in a shelter.

The commander in chief acknowledged Israel's survival concerns, stating, "From a strategic national defense and tactical military perspective, it is easy to see why retention of the West Bank is so important." He recounted how he and First Lady Treatise, those many years ago, actually waded across the Jordan River. Augustus continued with the most striking aspect of their vacation, which occurred at an elementary school located in the Golan Heights. Three colorfully painted Soviet anti-tank destroyers—fire engine red, bright sunshine yellow and deep royal blue—served as playground equipment. "Americans could not fathom their own children using such weapons of war as a jungle gym in school yards."

His speeches, meetings, and overall visit were a resounding success.

In Jordan, America's head of state parleyed with leaders from several Mideast countries and Persian Gulf states and labored to renew United States' tattered relationships. Some limited agreements with individual nations were reached, but due to prior administrations' vacillations and perceived unreliability, any unified consensus on fighting terror, regional trade, arms sales, and joint patrolling of the Persian Gulf to deter piracy remained unresolved. Russia, he was told, was seen as the greater stabilizing force in the region. Still, President Treatise's negotiations were viewed as a positive first step towards American re-engagement in the region.

Syria, even with Russian military aid and political support, was still embroiled in its civil war. As a combat fighting force, ISIS no longer occupied any significant portions of land in Syria and Iraq. Their Caliphate had been essentially destroyed. However, they continued to control small pockets within larger cities, much like street gangs in American communities ruled some neighborhoods. Moreover, ISIS, or some form of it, still existed as ideological cells in countries around the globe. In addition, as a sovereign nation, Iraq had ceased to exist except as a puppet colony of Iran.

His follow-on flight took him to a highly publicized visit to the U.S. Air Force Base at Incirlik, in Adana, Turkey. There he openly met with military personnel and their families. Behind the public scenes at a secret meeting with Turkish, Syrian, Iraqi, Iranian, and Kurdish leaders, Augustus built on the Kurdish people's vote years earlier to create a separate country. He opened the door a little wider towards the formal reestablishment of a separate Kurdish state.

These discussions revolved around Turkey, Syria, Iraq, and Iran designating a portion of their territory—historical lands claimed, pre-World War I owned, and currently occupied by the Kurds—for creating a new Kurdistan, provided the Kurds cease all attacks inside those countries. All Kurds living in Turkey, Syria, Iraq, and Iran who did not reside in the designated areas would abandon their homes and businesses and move to their new country. Kurdish prisoners would be released into the new Kurdistan.

In return, United Nations peacekeepers would patrol Kurdistan borders to prevent incursions into Turkey, Syria, Iraq, and Iran for twenty-five years, with a possibility of remaining for a second generation. It was hoped that at the end of that time, many family and historical feuds would have been forgotten. In addition, Turkey would receive military aid and Syria and Iraq would receive economic assistance from the United States. Some sanctions against Iran would be lifted. However, the Iranian nuclear deal, signed and later cancelled by previous administrations, remained a significant barrier to

Iran's support of a separate Kurdish homeland. Negotiations between all parties and in the UN continued throughout Augustus' presidency without definitive resolution.

In a side deal with Turkey, Augustus broached the subject and secured the reopening of Mount Ararat to exploration for Noah's Ark. The United States would finance the entire expedition. If the Ark were discovered, Turkey would get the lion's share of the credit, if they wanted it. The U.S. would pay for the construction of any museum and research facility to protect and analyze the ancient wooden vessel. The site would surely become an instant location for Christian pilgrimage. For Turkey, the tourist industry alone would certainly be an economic windfall.

Throughout his entire Mid-East trip, Augustus attempted to secure a lasting peace in the Middle East. At every locale, in each nation, with their individual leaders, America supported efforts to make the City of Jerusalem a separate City-State along the lines of the Vatican. Each of the major religions would control all the religious sites, as they currently operated, and a joint governing body would manage city affairs. If the effort were successful, the U.S. embassy would be relocated outside the boundaries of the newly established City-State of Jerusalem. Unfortunately, because of the continued religion-based tensions throughout the region, nothing fruitful resulted from those discussions.

Back in the U.S., in an effort to destabilize hard line regimes that supported terrorism, denounced the West, and called for "Death to America," the president initiated a new approach to warfare. Limited and selected use of bombs and drones on hand-picked targets by former White House occupants were to a degree successful, but risked war—not that America was not already engaged in combat operations in many regions.

Moreover, sanctions were only as strong as the number of nations that supported those efforts. The chief executive's goal was to demonstrate America was not the "Great Satan."

Augustus wanted to reach the young, modern, future economic and moderate political and social reform leaders of targeted countries. He desired to show what life could be once the oppressive shackles of denying women's human rights were removed. His objective was to fight the ideological war with an economic strategy—gifts.

President Treatise's plan involved the purchase of female clothing from the best design and fashion houses across the world. Coordinated outfits of all sizes were assembled into individual packages, flown by drones, and parachuted into selected countries. Inside was a note that offered this gift from the people of the United States. In addition, propaganda leaflets explained getting an education, driving a car, voting for leaders, and freedom of choice were all part of women's rights. Notes also clearly explained that wearing burqas or other religious attire, or not, was their right. This form of warfare executed on a limited basis throughout his presidency had some, but not immediately determinable, long-term degree of success. Feedback from U.S. and foreign intelligence services indicated positive short-term results despite angry statements from the political and religious leaders of some affected nations.

Secure in the knowledge that European allies, the North Atlantic Treaty Organization and European Union were stable (despite BREXIT—England's departure from the European Union), the head of state's second overseas trip focused on Far East Asia. In Japan, South Korea, The Philippines, Communist China and Nationalist China (Taiwan), Augustus reassured allies and advised foes that while he was commander in chief, the United States would uphold defense treaties with America's friends and resist efforts made by expansionist and saber-rattling regimes.

In Japan, using his best Japanese, President Treatise told the prime minister of his trips to the country while fighting the Global War on Terror decades before. On one occasion, Augustus had gotten lost in downtown Tokyo and he was thankful to several Japanese for helping him negotiate that city's transportation network. The president also reminisced about his temporary duty assignments as a soldier to Kadena AFB, Okinawa, and shopping for pearls, pink coral, kimonos, and obis in Naha. To ease tensions with Japan in general and Okinawa in particular, the commander in chief agreed to remove the vast majority of Army, Navy and Marine Corps forces from the island, and turn most U.S. facilities over to the Okinawan government. USAF airmen and assets, however, would remain at Kadena Air Force Base. Army soldiers were to be relocated to South Korea. Navy sailors and Marines would be temporarily stationed in The Philippines or on Guam. His decision was well received.

In The Philippines, he entered into a new phase of treaty discussions for a more permanent U.S. military presence. Negotiations centered on a location that would support an airfield, provide a harbor, minimally disrupt the local inhabitants, and infuse capital into their national economy. Only the initial framework was discussed. The secretaries of state and defense would have to work on and determine the details amenable to both nations.

President Treatise met with South Korean leaders and pledged continued support for a unified Korea. He was provided an update regarding North and South Koreans freely crossing the Demilitarized Zone for family visitations and recently successful cross-border trade. Despite being called a "warmonger" by North Korea for proposing to move Army assets from Okinawa to South Korea, Augustus thanked the South Koreans for offering facilities for the temporary relocation of U.S. military forces.

Even though the United States, North Korea, South Korea, Japan, China—and to an extent Russia—had successfully denuclearized the Korean peninsula, brokered an end to the Korean War, lifted sanctions placed on North Korea, and opened that dictatorship to economic development, the "Hermit Kingdom" had not stopped its nuclear ambitions. The Democratic People's Republic of Korea (DPRK) still benefited from its Supreme Leader-U.S. President meetings propaganda coup a few years before.

Reportedly, "North Korea's nuclear weapons brought South Korea's president to Panmunjom. DPRK's Inter-Continental Ballistic Missiles arcing over the 'Land of the Rising Sun' forced Japan to the negotiating table. Nuclear-tipped ICBM threats to destroy Guam, Alaska, Hawaii, and the west coast of the United States compelled America's president to meet in Singapore and Vietnam. DPRK's strength pressured the President of the United States to visit Panmunjom and enter North Korea. It was DPRK's strategic doctrine that ended the Korean War and began North Korea's new era of prosperity."

Propagandists continued, "We no longer need to actually possess nuclear-tipped missiles. We know the science, engineering, and technology, retain the research and documents, and employ the trained scientists, engineers, and technicians to reestablish our nuclear missile program at any time."

For North Korea, it was an easy trade to access financial wealth—world banking systems and currencies, International Monetary Funds, foreign investments, and open markets—riches that could be used to buy a nuclear arsenal. Secretly, the

DPRK had moved its scientists to Iran, where development of nuclear weapons and ICBMs continued. North Korea could claim the Korean peninsula was nuclear free. Iran could claim they were not in violation of any "Nuke Deal" or U.N. sanctions.

In China, Augustus met with its leaders and recounted his enjoyment at the Beijing Olympics, his tour of the Great Wall, Imperial City, and a visit to the Terracotta Army near Xi'an in Shaanxi province. Down to brass tacks, he denounced North Korea's secret nuclear weapons and long-range missile programs as threats to the stability of the region as well as world peace. Even though the denuclearization treaty secured the Supreme Leader's life-long rule over North Korea, continued violation of the spirit of a nuclear free peninsula necessitated regime "reorientation." Augustus solicited China's support and pushed for a unified peninsula under South Korean leadership. In return, when successful, the commander in chief would withdraw all of America's military presence from South Korea. China, however, used North Korea as their point man in ruffling the feathers of the world. It was their thermometer, their trial balloon for testing the reaction of Western nations. Nothing was resolved.

In addition, China refused to curtail its own military expansion in the region. Consequently, Augustus ordered the cessation of earlier planned U.S. troop withdrawals from South Korea and in a move of brinksmanship, flew to Taiwan, where he negotiated a return of American Armed Forces and renounced the "One China" policy.

After this trip, Augustus focused on foreign aid cost-cutting measures. There was an old saying that went something like, "As long as you have money, you will have friends; run out of money, and you no will longer have friends." That had been the

United States' foreign policy approach for decades. For far too long, many friends and foes alike banked America's cash payments in private, offshore, or in Swiss accounts for themselves and their cronies instead of using the dollars for the benefit and improvement of the lives of their own citizens. Even dictators who were paid to remain "friendly" to the U.S., which America eventually overthrew and replaced with other dictators, were paid by the government as long as they professed allegiance to the West. In many other cases, the United States was simply blackmailed for more money by a simple threat by a despot to realign with an enemy or government hostile to America. Those pay-for-loyalty efforts mostly stopped under Augustus' presidency.

When it came to foreign aid, America as a cash cow was closed. The budget for foreign aid was reduced or curtailed altogether as treaties were renegotiated. Based on State Department recommendations and CIA analysis, future cash or direct dollar assistance for many "friends" was converted into products and services. Partnerships and joint ventures between governments and private businesses were formed in which both parties cooperated in the construction of infrastructure, planting and harvesting of crops, development of energy, purification of water and air, and treatment of sewage and waste. U.S. Reserve units continued to provide medical and dental assistance and treat the poorest of the poor as well as construct roads and bridges. Volunteer agencies, as they had been performing since the Kennedy administration, maintained their missions of education and agriculture and other assistance.

Many long-standing international relationships were retained, maintained, and sustained. However, for the leaders of some countries, if the president's actions meant America's quasi-friends turned to America's enemies for aid, so be it. Augustus declared, "Let our enemies go bankrupt, borrow themselves into massive debt, print money, risk future massive inflation, and devalue their currency." Meanwhile, the United States used other means to deal with rogue nations such as banning tourists from traveling to those countries, U.S.-flagged cruise liners from entering their ports of call, and American air carriers from landing at their airports. In addition, those countries were removed from Most Favored Nation status and the Preferential Trade Program.

America's apparent withdrawal from the world stage engendered by these and previous policies only strengthened her enemies and emboldened questionable friends. To counter possible threats, the commander in chief reinforced the security, protection, and defenses of overseas military installations, consulates, and embassies. The vast majority of U.S. Armed Forces presence in other countries resulted from Status of Forces Agreements or other longstanding treaties. Those arrangements were periodically reviewed and renegotiated, and most military installations were upgraded as part of normal operations. Nearly every permanent or temporary military presence on foreign soil was exactly that—foreign soil. Often, the U.S. leased the land.

Embassies and consulates were another situation altogether. By international law, treaty, or custom, the ground upon which a foreign country's embassy or consulate was located is considered the sovereign territory of that nation. In other words, American embassies and consulates located in other countries are on terra firma as if that facility or compound was located in any city, county, or state in the U.S. As such, any unauthorized entry onto an embassy compound or into a consulate facility might be construed as an attack on the United States, just as any illegal entry into a person's home might be viewed as an attack on that family. Foreign governments are responsible for using their local or national police or military forces to protect every embassy and consulate of each country located in their homeland. However, once an invader crosses the boundary, fence, wall, or threshold onto a visiting country's terrain, the protection responsibility reverts to the guest nation's security forces.

Under Augustus's watch, security, protection, and defense of American military and diplomatic facilities focused on several areas. Additional external lighting, loudspeakers, and security cameras were installed—enough to illuminate, broadcast toward, and observe the exterior walls of the compound and buildings, each with overlapping coverage and connected to electrical circuits independent of local utilities. A combination of fixed and drone-equipped cameras utilized zoom, night vision, and thermal imagery, and were linked and networked in order to broadcast live images directly to the Pentagon's National Military Command Center, the State Department's Emergency Operations Center, and the White House Presidential Emergency Operations Center. The entirety of each location became self-sufficient for up to seventy-two hours— infrastructure, communications, generators, fuel, utilities, food, and water. All systems were enhanced and tested once per year for a minimum of six hours during peak activity; used materials were replenished, and broken items were repaired or replaced and tested.

Every ambassador, Foreign Service officer, State Department, Government Service employee, civilian contractor, and U.S. citizen assigned to the embassy or consulate spent a week at the Federal Bureau of Investigation's training facility in Quantico, Virginia, and took firearms, explosives, security, and anti-terrorism training. Those who refused or failed training either were not assigned overseas or were removed from their foreign duties. Standard government service practice required federal employees to sign a mobility agreement that allowed their reassignment to other locations, including other countries. Failure to comply meant no lucrative assignments, potential reassignment to a position outside the State Department, retirement, or processing for discharge. Those serving overseas assignments took annual refresher training with the Marine Corps contingent responsible for the defense of each embassy and consulate.

Not disclosed to the public was that secured in every room, at every embassy and consulate, were an M-16 semi-automatic rifle and a 9 mm semi-automatic pistol, both with one full magazine of ammunition, and with a single, high explosive, fragmentation hand grenade.

Historically, in response to selected crises or security threats, facilities were temporarily closed and staffs were advised to remain at home. It was common to ban travel to a particular country or region. Severe steps included the voluntary or involuntary evacuation of U.S. citizens from the troubled area. When necessary, evacuation plans were accelerated from months and weeks to days or hours. Other measures directed embassy or consulate employees to return to America up to and even including complete closure of the facilities.

Augustus had other ideas. In a decisive classified policy decision, he directed, since embassies and consulates were considered American soil, U.S. facilities were never to be abandoned in a crisis. In the best tradition of the Navy, where the captain went down with his ship, the ambassador and the Marines were to remain at all costs. The United States of America would not cede sovereign territory as happened in Benghazi, Libya, in 2012 and Tehran, Iran, in 1979. A Top Secret plan was developed to defend embassies and consulates to the last person.

According to the plan, at the beginning of any trouble, host nation officials were to be contacted, apprised of the situation, and asked for additional security forces. Phase One began with requiring foreign nationals visiting the embassy or consulate, who were conducting business or seeking immigration to America, to be escorted off the property. As the situation evolved, employed local nationals were to be directed to leave the premises and their credentials confiscated as they departed. The Marines were required to be on full alert with weapons and ammunition distributed. The requisite authorities in Washington were to be made aware of the situation. Coordination between embassies' staffs and their host nation counterparts would begin in earnest. The Department of Defense was to place relevant resources on alert and launch drones to overfly the area.

Phase Two was to be implemented should host nation police, security, or military forces prove incapable of dispersing or suppressing the local threat. All U.S. personnel were to take defensive responses against intruders who invaded compound grounds, scaled walls, crashed through gates, climbed fences, or occupied the designated protection zones located immediately outside embassy and consulate boundaries.

Initially from building rooftops, the Marines were to defend with riot gas, flash-bang grenades, and other nonlethal weapons. Facilities were to be placed on lockdown; all external structures, interior offices, room doors, and windows were to be sealed and locked as if inside a submarine underneath the surface of the sea. The weapons assigned to each room were to be removed from their secure containers. Messages were to be broadcast over the loudspeaker systems directing the invaders to leave. Cameras were to be activated and live feeds sent to the appropriate command centers.

Special lines of communication were to be opened. The ambassador was to call his counterpart first; if not available, then that country's leader; if also not available, then that land's military head. The President of the United States would be contacted next. The second senior executive on site was to contact the U.S. Secretary of State. The commander of the Marine contingent was to contact the Secretary of Defense directly. The National Security Council was to convene as soon as possible while the president engaged that host nation's leader. In accordance with the plan, the Department of Defense was to launch armed drones, order Air Force bombers into the air, direct Navy ships to code and arm cruise missiles, and move other military assets towards the region.

Phase Three was to occur when the embassy or consulate building was breached. Intruders then became enemy combatants, and deadly force was automatically authorized. No decisions from on high were required. No stand down or wait and see orders would be issued. Marines could fire into the intruders at entrances, through windows, and down hallways and staircases. Embassy and consulate staff were to prepare to defend themselves by "locking and loading" their room's M-16 and pistol. Any persons forcing entry into their room were to be shot. Once the ammunition was expended, the grenade was to be used against the attackers. If the intruders were successfully repelled, a defensive posture was to be established along with reinforcement of weak points. Armed defensive resistance ended and the on-ground battle was deemed over when local security or military forces stabilized and controlled the external situation. If not, and the intrusion continued with hostages taken or unarmed staff killed, and overall control of the embassy or consulate was jeopardized, Phase Four could be implemented.

Phase Four was a "Black World," Top Secret, Sensitive Compartmented Information, Special Access Program known only by three officials on location: the ambassador, the Central Intelligence Agency station chief, and the commander of the Marine contingent. Of those three, the senior official present during this phase of the crisis, could make the decision to implement "Socrates." It executed the total destruction of the embassy or consulate and would certainly kill all remaining U.S. personnel, destroy all classified materials and equipment, and deny access to the site by any adversary.

Fortunately, the entire plan was never implemented; portions, however, were. During one Phase Two incident, Augustus told the foreign leader, "Your people are violating America's sovereignty and their actions are tantamount to an attack on the United States. As commander in chief, I have personally ordered the ambassador, the Marines, and all embassy staff to take up arms in defense of American soil. And, unlike previous commanders in chief who acted either injudiciously or cautiously during similar events, I and the American people are going to react as we did after Pearl Harbor."

The head of state's boisterous pronouncement did not convince that regime's leader—but Phase Three did. In addition to the fighting on the ground, armed drones and Navy fighter-bombers pounded intruders and terrain around the embassy buildings with laser-guided bombs and continued until the host nation met its obligation to safeguard Americans. Air Force B-1, B-2, and B-52 bombers flew along that country's borders as an additional "show of force," ready to implement Phase Four. To aid in the defense, U.S. Special Forces arrived on scene to deter, and prevent any possible retaliation.

Although some countries condemned America's actions, and the press criticized the president for his military response, the vast majority of the populace supported Augustus' decision to defend United States territory and her citizens. The most positive result was not only open support from many previously silent allies, but less friendly countries also took heed and subdued many of their anti-American factions.

President You

United Nations

The United Nations is an international organization founded in 1945. It is currently made up of 193 Member States. The mission and work of the United Nations are guided by the purposes and principles contained in its founding Charter.

United Nations, an international organization of nations to maintain peace.

United Nations Charter.

WE THE PEOPLES OF THE UNITED NATIONS DETERMINED to save succeeding generations from the scourge of war, which twice in our lifetime has brought untold sorrow to mankind, and

to reaffirm faith in fundamental human rights, in the dignity and worth of the human person, in the equal rights of men and women and of nations large and small, and

to establish conditions under which justice and respect for the obligations arising from treaties and other sources of international law can be maintained, and

to promote social progress and better standards of life in larger freedom,

AND FOR THESE ENDS

to practice tolerance and live together in peace with one another as good neighbors, and

> to unite our strength to maintain international peace and security, and
>
> to ensure, by the acceptance of principles and the institution of methods, that armed forces shall not be used, save in the common interest, and
>
> to employ international machinery for the promotion of the economic and social advancement of all peoples...

Before becoming head of state, Augustus noted there seemed to be no logic to the manner of refugee resettlement across the globe and within the U.S. Not every nation accepted refugees, and neither did many American communities. It seemed strange that mostly wealthy and economically strong countries welcomed refugees, while many of America's rich and famous preferred refugees were resettled in other cities and towns. Now president, he decided to take action on the international stage and domestically.

As the newest leader of the United States to host the annual General Assembly meeting of the United Nations, President Treatise gave two speeches at his first session. His initial remarks, as was customary, opened the conference with a broad and generic welcoming of the world's leaders, foreign ministers, ambassadors, envoys, and delegates. He highlighted that he had lived, worked, vacationed, visited, and traveled through many of their countries.

Augustus' most important comments, which were presented just before the annual session closed, concerned refugees and the mass migration of men, women, and children.

The United Nations has accomplished a

great many tasks to the benefit of all humankind throughout its history, and continues to achieve important objectives. However, regarding the involuntary migration of people across the face of the earth because of war, famine, climate change, disease, or persecution, the United Nations has not lived up to its full potential. The world's refugee challenge is a direct result of the negative political, economic, education, religious, social, or cultural malfeasance within some of our member states. People are not only losing their lives, but their families, homes, culture, heritage, history, religion, and communities, as well.

Before the next annual General Assembly session, the United States will lead efforts within this body, as written in its founding charter, to effect change to "fundamental human rights, the dignity and worth of the human person, equal rights of men and women, promote social progress and better standards of life in larger freedom, employ international machinery for the promotion of the economic and social advancement of all peoples."

President Treatise emphasized that not every country accepted refugees.

While the United Nations often works towards influencing the internal affairs of selected member states, in accord with its Charter, the world's countries continue to have an obligation to assist all people of the earth. Therefore, the United States proposes all member nations accept a proportion of the globe's displaced population.

Events in which that process may occur are national, regional, or global crises that result in the mass migration of people from their homelands; necessitate the establishment of United Nations operated refugee camps; and require housing, feeding, clothing, healing, and educating displaced persons. At those times, the United Nations will call upon *all* member states to accept refugees.

Key to Augustus' proposal was that ALL member states were to accept refugees.

Under the president's plan, the number of refugees accepted by every country was based upon a member nation's population as a percentage of the world's overall population. For example: if the earth's population was 7.4 billion and the population of the United States was 325 million, computations calculated the U.S. had 4.38% of the world's people. Therefore, if the refugee population were 1,000,000, America would accept 43,800 of them. Using the same formula, and as examples, the following countries would be required to accept refugees in these numbers: Andorra–1; Australia–3,239; Bolivia–1,448; Botswana–3,054; Central African Republic–662; China–185,900; Costa Rica–650; Laos–919; Nepal–3,853; Switzerland–1,122; Trinidad and Tobago–182; and Tajikistan–1,146. All one million refugees would be absorbed into the fabric of every member nation.

The percentage formula was designed so that no single country took the significant cultural brunt and economic responsibility of refugees, as had been the case in the past.

> By accepting an identified percentage of the displaced population, individual nations will be able to retain their own heritage and language and not be overwhelmed by a disproportionate influx of people who want to retain their own cultural identities in their new country.
>
> From another perspective, if the United Nations believes in the concept of globalization, then the proposed refugee acceptance program and calculations should be met with open arms and without resistance. Many in this body have repeatedly posited the influx of people from foreign lands into another nation add to a country's economy rather than drain its resources. The best way to accomplish economic, social, and cultural globalization is require *every* member state to accept refugees from other lands.

Augustus closed his remarks with a warning. Should the United Nations take no meaningful action toward effecting internal change in member nations that treat their own citizens poorly, the United States would make adjustments unilaterally. In addition, the U.S. would do the same should a universal agreement on accepting refugees not be adopted by the time of the next annual General Assembly.

There were several obvious arguments against the proposal. Nations that were current or historical adversaries did not want to accept citizens of their foes. Other countries feared the extermination of their citizens who were forced to relocate to the lands of their devout enemy. Homelands that had their own economic challenges did not want the financial burden of accepting refugees. Some leaders would be placed in the prickly situation of providing resources and opportunities to foreigners that they had repeatedly denied to their own citizens. The argument was made that refugees may not want to go to their assigned host nation.

For each challenge, President Treatise had a response. As a historical starting point, the 1864 Geneva Convention outlined the treatment of sick and wounded on the battlefield. Subsequent conventions added additional protections including those due to civilian persons in time of war. The United Nations adopted its Universal Declaration of Human Rights in 1948 that established "fundamental human rights to be universally protected." The UN Refugee Convention of 1951 outlined the rights of displaced persons and the legal obligation of States to protect them. Its subsequent 1967 Protocol expected States to cooperate in ensuring that refugee rights are respected and protected. The International Bill of Human Rights in 1976 defined the rights and protections due to all the world's citizens. If need be, those rights would be protected and international laws enforced in established refugee camps operated by the UN and secured and defended by UN Peacekeeping Forces.

The United Nations already financed the vast majority of the cost of taking care of forced migrants until their acceptance into a host country. The UN would still incur those expenses, and unnecessary economic burdens would not befall the poorest host countries. Refugees, generally, do not seek to immigrate to and become citizens of the country that generously agrees to accept them on a temporary basis. Refugees hope to be able to return to their native lands and abandoned homes once the threat to their lives and freedom are diminished. In the president's mind, the citizens of a host country need not worry about any loss of opportunity to those temporarily housed, and their leaders should not fear any political backlash. Against every naysayer, Augustus reasoned accepting refugees accomplished the stated mission of the United Nations and, by extension, forced leaders to address the challenges within their own borders, which often were the cause of international crises.

Unfortunately, the original Refugee Convention allowed several countries to exempt themselves from accepting refugees. Many would not change that option. After a year of intense negotiations, the United Nations failed to reach an agreement on the president's proposal and did not take any significant worthwhile actions in the internal operations of select lands. Consequently, President Treatise withheld a set dollar amount of America's financial contributions to the UN for every refugee accepted into the United States. In addition, and in concert with his immigration policy, an equal dollar amount was withheld for each citizen of a foreign country found to have entered or remained in the U.S. illegally and who was eventually deported. Once that total dollar amount equaled America's normal dues payment to the United Nations, at the same calculation, America's foreign aid to the applicable countries was withheld. Secondly, Augustus significantly reduced the number of refugees accepted into the United States, and, in some cases, refused displaced persons altogether until countries that had never accepted any evacuees took in refugees.

Domestically, Augustus found some government operations downright confounding. For example, rice farmers from hot, humid, wet Southeast Asia were resettled in America's coldest northern states. Those with agricultural backgrounds were placed in metropolitan cites. Refugees who operated and managed small family-owned businesses were established in rural communities whose own local businesses struggled to make ends meet.

Conspiracy theorists often postulated Democrats were so lax and open to refugee resettlement because they saw foreigners as potential voters, and that immigrants were resettled in Republican communities to sway elections. In reality, refugees were often resettled in predominantly liberal, accepting regions typically oriented more towards Democrats than Republicans. A petulant President Treatise directed, over time, the resettlement of displaced persons into locales where rich, famous, and wealthy advocates resided—regardless of political persuasion.

What became blatantly obvious was many who yelled the loudest and longest about America's compassionate need to accept refugees were not personally willing to provide finances or resources. They were, however, vociferous proponents of spending billions of taxpayer funds for foreigner resettlement—as long as the downtrodden were settled in someone else's community.

Pro-refugee resettlement supporters who became refugee resettlement objectors took to the airways and cast blame on the president, alleging falling home prices, reducing property values, increasing crime, the resurgence of pandering on the streets and in city parks, and changing the culture of their community. Sensing he was losing in the court of public opinion, Augustus issued a direct challenge to the top one percent wealthiest citizens—sponsor refugees. By sponsorship, instead of paying higher taxes to a bureaucratic, cold, and faceless government, the president insisted the rich and famous demonstrate their human caring and warmth by using personal wealth to house, clothe, and feed these newcomers.

He identified the wealthy and their properties all across the U.S. "Certainly your many bedroom and several bathroom mansions on lush estates and your multi-floor palaces in the tallest skyscrapers could accommodate three, five, even ten refugee families. Hire them as au pairs and nannies, butlers and maids, caretakers and gardeners, chauffeurs and vehicle mechanics, chefs and cooks, house sitters and security guards. Use your own riches to pay them a decent, living wage of $15 per hour. Contract tutors to teach a skill, trade, and English as a Second Language. Use your network of contacts to establish those refugees with experience in private business or to finance entrepreneurs. Help them become Americans. There are enough multi-millionaires and billionaires in the U.S. that a goal of sponsoring 250,000 refugee families could easily be attained.

"It is easy to be magnanimous with other people's money. If you are so principled in your refugee welcoming beliefs, then open your mansions, ski chalets, lakefront cabins, high-rise condominiums, beach houses, ranches, and villas. Become a modern version of the Statue of Liberty and, as Emma Lazarus wrote in her 1883 sonnet *The New Colossus*, move these 'tired, poor, huddled masses yearning to breathe free, the wretched refuse, the homeless, tempest-tost' into your vacant, hardly ever used second, third, and fourth homes. Be your own 'lamp beside the golden door'!"

The head of state got no takers, decried the elitists' hypocrisy, and continued with refugee relocation.

President You

Sanctuary Jurisdictions

sanctuary *n.* The most secluded and sacred part of a temple; a place of certain shelter; a refuge.

jurisdiction *n.* Legal power or authority; extent of authority and power.

While President Treatise pondered his application of America's economic instruments of national power to cajole foreign governments into making political, economic, social, religious, education and moral changes within their own borders, he decided to test his tactics inside the U.S. His targets were sanctuary cities, counties, and states.

America fought a Civil War from 1861 to 1865 that was a violent rehash of the original Constitutional Convention. Slavery was the determinant of that armed and nationwide conflict that pitted states' rights and the three-fifths rule against federal power and all men being created equal under the law. The result of the War Between the States reestablished a nation united and validated the federal government's overall legal authority under the Constitution. Augustus reasoned America faced another battle between state and local jurisdiction rights and federal power—and this time the issue was foreigners in the United States illegally. As was decided more than a century and a half ago, the federal government retained national authority. Augustus applied that substantive and distinct conclusion to sanctuary jurisdictions—cities, counties, and states that enacted their own laws in violation of federal immigration statutes.

The first salvo fired was wording included in his budget proposal.

> All jurisdictions subordinate to the federal government and all public and private entities whose people fall under the jurisdiction of the Constitution of the United States of America shall not be eligible for federal public funds where those subordinate jurisdictions and public and private entities enacted or may enact legislation in conflict to federal immigration statutes.

That attempt failed in negotiations with Congress.

His second, short-term effort was more successful. As the country's chief executive, Augustus directed all executive offices to withhold, deny, or divert outlays of discretionary funds from sanctuary jurisdictions as well as from public and private entities within those jurisdictional boundaries. Many previously promised multi-year outlays were delayed for "review." Those broad fund categories included agriculture, commerce and housing credit, community and regional development, employment and social services, energy, general science, income security, international affairs, justice reform, natural resources and environment, space and technology, and training. Some specific examples included grants for education, fire, infrastructure, land use and erosion control, libraries, police, research, and transportation. Money for block grants, charter schools, and enterprise zones were also realigned.

Discretionary funds were prioritized to those communities, counties, and states that did not offer or provide sanctuary to persons in the U.S. illegally. Sanctuary cities in massive debt had requested federal support in preventing bankruptcy. Augustus rejected those requests.

As part of his second effort, which had a longer lasting effect, the president directed all executive departments and agencies begin moving out of sanctuary cities and counties into communities more amenable to complying with federal statutes. On a larger scale, Executive Branch officials were to begin planning to move all federal resources out of sanctuary states. Several non-sanctuary locations had General Services Administration facilities lying idle that were reopened and reoccupied. In addition, selected official government travel to and through sanctuary areas—such as conferences or conventions—was banned. Other venues for administrative procedures or judicial matters were changed to non-sanctuary cities and counties. It was hoped, at the very least, the loss of jobs and revenue and the closure of facilities would bring local, pro-sanctuary politicians to their senses. At best, citizens would vote the sanctuary leaders out of office and replace them with more law abiding and rational individuals—who would then revoke local sanctuary laws. In his calculation, Augustus recognized some communities would dig in their heels and never change.

On his third front, the chief executive attacked sanctuary cities from a legal perspective by stricter enforcement of current law. Harboring or aiding and abetting a fugitive from justice were criminal offenses. Where federal law enforcement agencies had indisputable proof that undocumented individuals wanted by authorities for criminal offenses resided in a sanctuary community, and when a federal judge was convinced, warrants for the arrest of the perpetrator and accomplices were issued.

Accomplices included former and current elected officials, as part of a larger criminal conspiracy, who enacted and voted for local sanctuary legislation. In other cases, those officials were detained and held as material witnesses. Once a legal precedent had been established for local officials, the chief executive could focus on governors and state legislators. As expected, Augustus was vilified and burned in effigy as a dictator.

Augustus' fourth point of pressure denied discretionary benefits to persons who resided in sanctuary jurisdictions. Much of the funding for local and state social programs came from the federal government—the taxpayer. The vast majority of citizens did not want their tax dollars to pay benefits to foreigners who were here illegally. Denying "free" benefits cut off one of the primary reasons for remaining in the country without proper documentation; those here illegally would leave as many had before during periods of economic downturn or recession. Affected communities and their leaders would have to make up the difference by cutting other programs or raising local taxes and fees. For some officials, a political tightrope they did not want to walk.

As his last direct impact approach, the president resettled refugees into sanctuary cities. After all, he reasoned, if those communities were willing and able to support aliens in the U.S. illegally, then they certainly were just as willing to accept foreigners brought into the country legally by the federal government on humanitarian grounds. He started first with the less populous sanctuary communities, often resettling the number of refugees equal to ten percent of that town's current population. The economic and social impacts were immediately obvious. In other cases, the chief executive relocated refugees into the hometowns of congressional representatives, senators, and governors who openly supported sanctuary cities, thus creating potential ramifications for those politicians. Finally, refugees were sent to cities where many of the pro-illegal alien rich and famous resided within their gated communities, on private estates, in guarded mansions.

Whenever possible, throughout all the efforts against sanctuary jurisdictions, President Treatise used his bully pulpit to reveal the dangerous nature of sanctuary policies. He quoted crime statistics not only in the sanctuary cities but also in nearby communities which were affected by "safe-haven" policies. Augustus blamed the sanctuary city for the rise in crime in the neighboring towns. He used federal law enforcement agencies, state troopers, county sheriffs, and local police departments to identify and publish the names and faces of terrorists, murderers, rapists, child molesters, robbers, and other wanted violent offenders who resided in sanctuary cities. Local politicians and community leaders could no longer ignore the once nameless and faceless criminal elements in their midst.

Augustus recalled his conversation with the owner of a German brewery who had attended an international brewers' convention in an American city. This was during a time when immigrant unrest and terrorist attacks were taking place across Europe in general and Germany in particular. Upon his arrival at the convention, a local reporter asked the brewery owner, "Given all the killings in your country, why should Americans vacation in Germany?" Herr Jocheim's response was, "The population of your city is about one million. Germany's population is over 86 million. Last month more people were killed in your city than in all of Germany last year. Perhaps this convention should not be held here and Germans should not vacation in your city." Using that conversation as his foundation, Augustus strongly discouraged domestic and international tourists from visiting, organizations from conducting conventions, and businesses from developing and investing in sanctuary locales.

His multi-pronged approach was generally successful. The citizens of roughly two hundred fifty sanctuary communities exercised their own political will and economic instruments of local power and elected less liberally minded officials to city and county leadership positions. Sanctuary laws in many were repealed. About half of the remaining cities were in the midst of heated debates. As the president predicted, nearly twenty of the larger communities and three states with greater wealth and significant public support continued to ignore federal law. For them, the chief executive proposed a more radical offensive.

Declassified White House meeting notes revealed Augustus considered applying even greater political pressure. He intended to close the terrorist detention center at Guantanamo, Cuba. Then, escorted by U.S. Marshalls, the remaining terrorists would be delivered to the governors, county board chairpersons, and mayors of the more obstinate sanctuary jurisdictions. Accompanying them would be a note stating, "This terrorist is seeking sanctuary from persecution by the federal government."

"Let's see how those state and local politicians who provide safe havens to criminal aliens react to that!" Augustus offered. The notes indicated the White House General Counsel and the Attorney General vehemently argued against such action. They pointed out delivery of the terrorists would be viewed as a validation and acknowledgement of a sanctuary jurisdiction's legal position. In addition, Cabinet secretaries recalled the public outcry when a prior administration proposed to house terrorists in the maximum-security prison, United States Penitentiary, Leavenworth, Kansas. Eventually, their arguments convinced Augustus to avoid that highly emotional Executive Order.

Pundits were his continual nemesis as the president employed his sanctions methodology, and his Justice Department fought the plethora of lawsuits filed by states, counties, cities, individuals, and immigrant rights groups. Lower courts rejected some of his methods as unlawful, but ultimately the United States Supreme Court in *Treatise v. Sanctuary* upheld the federal government's ultimate authority over immigration. However, SCOTUS severely rebuked Augustus' administration for its inconsistent policy positions regarding sanctuary jurisdictions.

President You

Repeal the Seventeenth Amendment

The Senate of the United States shall be composed of two Senators from each State, chosen by the Legislature thereof, for six Years; and if Vacancies happen by Resignation, or otherwise, during the Recess of the Legislature of any State, the Executive thereof may make temporary Appointments until the next Meeting of the Legislature, which shall then fill such Vacancies.

(Article I, Section 3, United States Constitution)

The Senate of the United States shall be composed of two Senators from each State, elected by the people thereof, for six years; When vacancies happen in the representation of any State in the Senate, the executive authority of such State shall issue writs of election to fill such vacancies:

Provided, That the legislature of any State may empower the executive thereof to make temporary appointments until the people fill the vacancies by election as the legislature may direct.

(Amendment XVII, United States Constitution)

After winning freedom from England, colonists in general and the Continental Congress in particular had to decide not only what type of government to establish but also how that government would function. They had roughly 3,000 years of history from which to draw and decided on creating a representative democracy and republican form of government based on a constitution. Three independent branches were created as a "check and balance" to ensure one function did not garner too much power over the other two and lead, as often happened throughout history, to the dissolution of opposing government bodies.

One significant issue revolved around colony (state) rights versus a central (federal) body. Some Constitutional Convention delegates argued a strong centralized government was essential to accomplish tasks each state could not, such as defense and treaties. Other delegates wanted decentralized control left to the states to ensure against a too powerful national government. A compromise was reached and written into the legislative articles of the Constitution regarding how the Congress would operate based upon the election of representatives and senators. Peoples' interests in each state would be represented by the popular vote and direct election of U.S. Representatives. This allowed for citizens' "passions and prejudices," "fads," "flavors of the month," or current issues of the day to be presented in the central government. States' interests would be represented by the indirect election of U.S. Senators via the state's legislature. States would have input into the central government with the added benefits of not being subject to the whims of the people and as a state legislature check against federal government overreach.

Within a few decades, challenges against state legislatures electing U.S. Senators were begun. Allegations were made that seats were "bought and paid for" by powerful interests. Stories of intimidation and bribery were published. One senator's election was challenged in court based on a plurality of votes, not a majority. Divided state legislatures resulted in Senate vacancies in Congress. These and other issues led many states to elect their U.S. Senators by a popular vote of the people, not by the legislature. The Populist movement across the country noticed, took advantage of, and built upon those local changes to push for a national referendum, the result of which is the Seventeenth Amendment to the Constitution, ratified in 1913.

More than 100 years later, many of those same assertions were levied against senators in Congress. One was tried for corruption. Allegations of sexual misconduct and use of public funds as payoffs for silencing accusers were made. Lawsuits were filed claiming voter fraud, lost ballots, improper counts, or violations of campaign election laws. "In essence, the Seventeenth Amendment only shifted the problems at state legislature level to federal level," Augustus opined. This guided the president's efforts to repeal that amendment to the Constitution and his encouragement of state legislatures to follow Utah's 2016 lead and pass a Joint Resolution in that regard.

An unintended consequence of the amendment was degradation of states' rights and a lessening of their ability to rein in the passions of the federal government. Legislation was now enacted or quashed based on senators appealing to the whims of their base. Far left or alt right constituents drove Senate votes. The will of the majority of citizens in favor of legislation was being obstructed, and legislation that the majority of citizens were against was being approved by a Senate that was under the influence of a minority of vocal activists from each state, regardless the side of the aisle. This is what our Founding Fathers, as presented in the Federalist Papers, wanted to avoid when they wrote in the original Constitution that senators "shall" be chosen by the state legislature and not by popular vote.

Senate gridlock, infighting, doing nothing, and party line voting, were real consequences of the Seventeenth Amendment. The majority party was able to impede the minority party's agenda or ram through, against the will of the majority of people, any serving president's agenda. Also, during four congressional sessions, when Republicans controlled the House of Representatives and Democrats controlled the Senate, senators were able to stifle nearly every piece of legislation for the greater portion of eight years. The reverse was also true with a Democratic House and a Republican Senate. That wielding of centralized power by the federal government was a fear expressed by some Founding Fathers who supported states' rights. The Seventeenth Amendment took away states' rights to restrain the central government and to hold the Senate accountable.

Augustus believed the constituent-based, party-first decisions of the Senate were a direct result of the amendment — senators were in the Legislative Branch too long. Referring to the original Constitution in which the legislature of each state elected its U.S. Senators to serve in Congress, the chief executive offered, "When the political makeup of a state legislature changed from one party in control to another, that state's United States Senators changed." He used this example:

> Suppose a state elects its legislature every four years. The Democratic majority in that legislature elects two Democrats to serve a six-year term in the United States Senate. If four years into a six-year senatorial term in office the people of the state vote in a Republican majority to their legislature, that legislature could then elect two Republican

U.S. Senators. The state legislature's election would result in the ouster of current serving Democrats in favor of the Republicans. In the U.S. Senate, where one vote means a great deal, the political balance of power shifts.

Multiply that scenario by fifty. Before the Seventeenth Amendment, based on a state's election cycle of its legislature, the Senate was in a consequence of flux and party-in-power realignment. The constant change or potential for change in political party representation forced senators to work with everyone, negotiate, cut deals, trade votes, and otherwise get things done. There was no guarantee the next senators sent to Congress from a newly elected state legislature would go along with existing, hard fought, negotiated deals—let alone be of the same party. In addition, those ever-changing political party realignments required the president to build coalitions with current serving senate members because at any time that chief executive's party could move from majority to minority status. Gridlock was lessened.

Augustus argued,

> The greatest negative under the Seventeenth Amendment is United States Senators are no longer elected by a state's legislature, but elected by popular vote by the citizens of each state for a term of six years. Regardless of the makeup of the local legislature, the elected U.S. Senators remain in office until the next federal election cycle, making any state legislature irrelevant to the national scene. The amendment seemed like a good

idea at the time; however, after more than 110 years, it has proven blatantly and obviously detrimental to the country and interests of the people.

With research, a calculator, rounding some numbers and averaging others, Augustus was able to provide the following data. Beginning with the first Congress in 1789 until the 63rd in 1913, more than 1,100 citizens were senators. Since the 64th Congress in 1914, when the Seventeenth Amendment took effect, to the 115th in 2017, just over 850 citizens were elected as senators; nearly 250 fewer—despite the increase in the number of states admitted to the union. In the first 125 years, the longest one senator served was 35 years; only five served more than 30 years. In the second 105 years, the number of senators who served, or were serving still, came to three more than 50 years, nine between 40 and 49 years, and twenty-four between 31 and 39 years. Moreover, those continuous years of service as senator did not include time as a member of the U.S. House of Representatives. Talk about Washington insiders!

Additionally, nearly 90% of senators from America's pre-Seventeenth Amendment history left after two terms (twelve years) or less in office. They followed George Washington's lead, encapsulating his farewell address: "If our government is going to work the way we envisioned it, then other citizens need to take up the mantle of representing the people." Since the amendment's ratification in 1913, however, rather than leaving office after two terms, 70% of senators remained in office for more than two terms.

"Just who did those senators benefit all those years?" Augustus asked rhetorically. "Do citizens really want to retain in office careerist politicians who provide Americans with a do-nothing, divided, and gridlocked Congress?"

Prior to the Seventeenth Amendment, legislation was processed through the power brokers in charge of the various committees. If a proposed law was only applicable within the realm of any particular committee, it was resolved within that committee. When a proposed statute affected other committees, coordination, compromise, "horse trading," and "tit-for-tat" agreements were reached. Powerful committee leadership and membership often changed when the state legislature voted in a new U.S. Senator, especially from a different party.

According to Augustus,

> Mark Twain is credited with stating, "Politicians are like diapers, they need to be changed often and for the same reason." After enactment of the Seventeenth Amendment, and over time, too long a retention of fuddy-duddies, although experienced, has led to entrenchment of thought, word, and deed. Senate majority and minority leaders have too much influence over their respective party members, which often leads to block voting along strict party lines. Those "titles" did not exist before the Seventeenth Amendment. Moreover, those obstinate leaders would most likely have been returned to civilian life had state legislatures retained authority to elect a U.S. Senator, especially from a different party.

President Treatise thought there had to be a physiological or psychological term to describe a person who felt no one else could perform the job or task better than he or she. "We have all heard of the professional sports athlete who participated yet ignored his or her reduced performance level; known of an over-worked co-worker or boss who denied his or her failings and did everything themselves; seen aged parents who continued to drive well beyond their physical capability. All firmly convinced no one could do the job better than they; hanging on at all—and whatever—cost."

Augustus believed America's Founding Fathers were a group of very smart and wise individuals who would be dumb-founded at senators' obstinacy today. A vigorous America depended on new application of its founding principles by younger and forward thinking citizens. The chief executive felt if people did not change the status quo, voters had only themselves to blame for retaining a Senate where, as Jonathan Swift wrote in *Gulliver's Travels*, "Ignorance, Idleness, and Vice are the proper Ingredients for qualifying a Legislator. That Laws are best explained, interpreted, and applied by those whose Interest and Abilities lie in perverting, confounding, and eluding them." Or a government, as Henry David Thoreau observed in *Civil Disobedience*, "equally liable to be abused and perverted before the people can act through it."

Party leaders and senators who vehemently believed that Congress in general and the Senate in particular could only function properly while they remained indefinitely in office thwarted the proposed amendment. Senators adopted the same thoughts as members of the first Congress who wanted George Washington to serve as president-for-life because they too believed no one else could possibly perform the job as well as he. Those Founding Fathers were proved wrong by Adams, Jefferson, Madison, Monroe, and succeeding presidents, just as senators' unwavering beliefs eventually proved them wrong, as well. Nevertheless, the public and state legislatures were unable or unwilling to cure a politicized and self-serving Senate by repealing the Seventeenth Amendment.

President You

Clean Water

The Clean Water Act (CWA) establishes the basic structure for regulating discharges of pollutants into the waters of the United States and regulating quality standards for surface waters.

(United States Environmental Protection Agency, 33 U.S.C., 1251 et seq., 1972)

The Federal Water Pollution Control Act. The objective of this Act is to restore and maintain the chemical, physical, and biological integrity of the Nation's waters.

(Title 33 United States Code, 1251 et seq., Section 101, As Amended Through Public Law 107-303, November 27, 2002)

In the land of Sacajawea, near the confluence of the Gallatin, Madison, and Jefferson Rivers, at the headwaters of the Missouri River, President Treatise made his case. This site had been discovered and mapped by the Lewis and Clark Expedition (1804–1806) as authorized by President Thomas Jefferson. At the Missouri Headwaters State Park in Montana, the modern day successor delivered his televised oration.

Augustus had authorized his own expedition. With the Environmental Protection Agency in the lead and support from the National Science Foundation, Centers for Disease Control, National Institutes of Health, Public Health Service, United

States Geological Survey, Army Corps of Engineers, Coast Guard, Interior, Agriculture, and Energy Departments, interns and volunteers, multiple task forces had been dispersed across the country. The purpose of that armada was to collect water samples from the nation's longest 100 rivers, streams, and waterways.

Beginning at the head of each source of water, and every mile downstream thereafter until it intersected another river or reached the ocean, each flotilla team gathered one quart of river water to be analyzed. The Global Positioning System was used to record the locations where samples were taken. When finished several months later, the government had the most current, best possible, and fullest analysis of the chemical and biological content along the entire length of the targeted hydrological systems. It was that compiled data that formed the basis for his speech.

On that overcast January day, a brisk cold wind flowed from the north and lowered the temperature to nine degrees above zero while snowflakes dotted the air. The president's 6'2", 220-pound body was protected from the weather by layers of cotton long underwear, white long-sleeved dress shirt with a paisley tie, dark blue pinstriped suit, and navy cashmere overcoat with matching leather gloves. Although his feet were covered by wool socks and inserted into heavy boots with one-inch-thick soles, Augustus shivered. Standing on the sandy and pebbled strip of ground where patches of dormant grass and shrubs peeked through a thin blanket of snow, he told the people where he was, gave a brief history of the area, and then offered,

Today, I announce my proposed legislation for Congress to revise the existing
Federal Water Pollution Control Act, better

known as the Clean Water Act, which will allow the creation of new regulations that shall provide all Americans with cleaner water for drinking, cooking, bathing, and other basic human needs.

For the past year, in the tradition of Lewis and Clark, teams of fellow citizens, comprised mostly of volunteers and interns, floated down waterways and gathered samples for analysis. The results of their magnificent efforts are well documented. From those examinations, we know the chemical and biological composition of water along the entire length of America's major rivers, streams, canals, lakes, and reservoirs.

Based on those findings, I request the Congress immediately enact my Pollution Control legislation outlined as follows:

First, all *existing* entities that create man-made pollutants and materials currently dispensed into nature's and the nation's natural water resources shall ensure the content of any pollutants and materials shall have no more than the same chemical and biological composition contained in the waters ten miles upstream from where those pollutants and materials enter the water systems.

Second, all *new* entities that create man-made pollutants and materials to be dispensed in the future into nature's and the nation's natural water resources shall ensure content of any pollutants and materials shall have no more than the same chemical and biological composition contained in the waters twenty-five miles upstream from where those pollutants and materials enter the water systems.

Third, should the headwaters of any waterway fall within the ten mile and/or twenty-five mile limits established above, then the composition of said pollutants and materials shall be no greater than the baseline sample taken at mile marker zero by the expedition for that particular water system.

The samples currently on record as a direct result of the past year's expeditions shall be used as the chemical and biological baseline standard.

These new statutes shall be effective the date I sign them into law.

Some detractors will say these are challenges too difficult to achieve. I say this legislation will create opportunity. Opportunity for America's bright young minds to use their God-given talents in biology, chemistry, medicine, physics, and other sciences to achieve cleaner and less hazardous pollutants or waste materials and ultimately purer water. Opportunity for America's entrepreneurs to create new technologies, develop new manufacturing processes, and establish new industries. Most of all, opportunity for America's citizens to enjoy nature's greatest necessity for human survival — clean water.

For a nation who put men on the moon in less than a decade, certainly Americans can solve this challenge not only for us, but also for all the inhabitants of the world.

His proposed legislation, supported by many environmental groups, worked its way through Congress and eventually became the law of the land.

President You

Health Care

health care. the prevention, diagnosis, and treatment of disease, illness, injury, and other physical and mental impairments in human beings.

Universal *adj.* All-pervading; relating to the whole world, general, common to all.

socialized medicine. A system under which medical service would be provided by govt. for everyone, without direct charge to the recipient.

single-payer. *adj.* of, relating to, or being a system in which health-care providers are paid for their services by the government rather than by private insurers.

Single-payer healthcare is a healthcare system financed by taxes that covers the costs of essential healthcare for all residents, with costs covered by a single public system.

multi-payer healthcare system is one in which private, qualified individuals or their employers pay for health insurance with various limits on healthcare coverage via multiple private or public sources.

It may seem obvious, but it is important to note that "access" is not the same as "insurance" and insurance is not the same as "health care." Too often, in health care debates, those words are used interchangeably. So too are the words "universal," "socialized," "single-payer," and "Medicare-for-all." The incorrect use and political application of those words has led to many an ill-informed and confused citizen.

In reality, every American and foreign visitor to the United States has access to health care. Health care can be defined as efforts made to maintain or restore physical, mental, or emotional well-being of people. Under the Emergency Medical Treatment and Active Labor Act established in 1986, hospitals within the U.S. are required to provide medical care of an emergency nature. That statute applies to 75 million annual visitors, 12 to 20 million people who reside illegally, foreign government officials, foreigners who attend college or university on student visas, employees of foreign businesses with work permits, migrants using guest worker cards, and the citizens of the United States. By federal law, everybody has access to America's healthcare system. They just need to go to any emergency room or urgent care facility.

However, not every aspect of treatment in an emergency room is paid in full by the medical provider or state or federal government. Based on lawsuits, court interpretations, and subsequent statutory amendments, various definitions of Emergency Medical Condition, Medical Screening, Stabilizing Treatment, and Transfers have arisen. That means a patient may not receive treatment for every ailment, injury, or malady—the focus is on emergencies and saving lives. Individuals may have to bear some financial liability and personal responsibility to pay for treatment received not directly related to the emergency. Some form of medical insurance (individual, employer, organization, or government) provides options for expanded medical care beyond emergency and lifesaving treatment as well as establishes conditions under which received health care may be paid.

Varieties of systems are currently in use throughout America. The Department of Defense (DoD) Military Health System–Defense Health Agency appears more in line with universal treatment since active service members, their spouses, and children, as well as military retirees and spouses, are covered. The Department of Veterans Affairs (VA)—Veterans Health Administration seems closest to socialized medicine, since government employees provide treatment. Medicare and Medicaid resemble a version of single-payer because health-care providers are reimbursed at defined amounts by the federal and state governments. There are private insurance companies that pay providers for a variety of treatments and other medical expenses, depending on the type of plan in which the patient is enrolled. The Patient Protection and Affordable Care Act (Obamacare) offers health insurance plans through either the federal government or individual states via various health exchanges and their participating private insurers.

The DoD and VA healthcare systems are virtually free—mostly at no cost to the service member or veteran. They are free in the sense that a large portion of military personnel enrolled in these systems pay little to no medical bills, as nearly all treatments are paid in full with taxpayer funds. With Medicare, those bills are primarily paid by taxpayers from the payroll-deducted Medicare tax and Parts B, C, and D premiums. Private health insurers pay for medical treatment from the premiums charged to individuals, families, organizations, and employers.

Unfortunately, for the people, during Affordable Care Act legislation discussions, politicians and special interests tended to conflate access, insurance, and health care, or lack thereof, into one blended definition or broad categories that too often obfuscated what they really meant. So too were later proposals of Medicare-for-all, single-payer, socialized, and universal health care for all Americans. The challenge for the chief executive and citizens were too many competing—and often conflicting—interests. Associations that offered health programs for members, criminals who committed fraud and perpetrated scams, health-care professionals, medical insurance providers, Medicare and Medicaid funding recipients, nonprofit organizations, private businesses and public corporations, private and public hospitals, state and local governments, the self-employed, unions, and members of Congress had their own agendas, demands, wants, and information campaigns which often confused the masses. In addition, there were thousands of perplexing, possibly contradictory, federal, state, and local statutes, laws, regulations, codes, policies, procedures, and forms.

Augustus believed each political party or self-interested entity that offered only talking points that supported their agenda and ignored the pitfalls, misinformed the public. What was required was a knowledgeable citizenry. The people needed a common sense, layman's explanation of the pros and cons associated with any Medicare-for-all, single-payer, socialized, or universal health-care system—especially the costs. The chief executive used a combination of his bully pulpit, op-eds in major publications, the White House website, social media, and public service announcements to inform the voters. He provided a balanced and objective argument, with examples and facts—devoid of lawyer-speak political hyperbole, or accountant number juggling. He believed citizens armed with knowledge never before heard from other politicians or special interest groups could make better decisions regarding the future of America's—and their own—medical care.

President Treatise cautioned citizens regarding four oft-used terms. "When a politician mentions Medicare-for-all, single-payer, socialized, or universal health care, be sure you ask, 'What exactly does that mean?' As the old saying goes, 'The devil is in the details.' You must ask your elected officials, 'What government program has ever been more cost effective and less expensive than its private enterprise counterpart?'"

He advised, "The ultimate cost of total conception-to-death health care is too exorbitant and its expense cannot justify the benefit, without a massive increase in taxes. By massive increase, I mean no deductions for anything and every person paying the government a significant portion of his or her gross income. Yes, I said gross income."

Before Augustus took office, some politicians, as a "proof is in the pudding" example of a successful single-payer medical program, posited Americans would be better off if Medicare were made available to all citizens. Medicare and its associated programs were not free. Both employees and employers paid a 1.45% Medicare tax based on income. That equated to about $725 per year per worker given an estimated $50,000 annual income. However, if a Medicare-eligible person had not worked or did not meet the forty "quarters" of employment under Social Security rules, Medicare Part A (Hospital Insurance) premiums were as high as $5,200 per year. Part B (Medical Insurance) cost a minimum of $1,600 per year, but could be as much as $5,500 per year. The costs to Medicare recipients enrolled in Part C (Medicare Advantage Plan) and Part D (Prescription Drug Coverage) were based on numerous individual factors.

"Would those same politicians expand Medicare-for-all to offer a Part E (Dental Insurance) costing $129.1 billion? Or a Part F (Long Term Care) adding a projected $440 billion to the annual budget? Perhaps the $18.2 billion Children's Health Insurance Program would become Part G. Maybe Medicaid's $581.9 billion expense would be incorporated into Medicare. Currently, neither Medicare nor Medicaid covers Americans living or traveling abroad. Will Medicare-for-all under a Part H cover the estimated nine million U.S. citizens overseas, adding possibly $108.8 billion? Would there be an additional fee to cover the medical care expenses for the 75 million foreigners who visit America every year?" Augustus asked. "After all, some politicians tout Medicare-for-all as a human right.

"What might be eliminated under a Medicare-for-all, universal, single-payer, or socialized healthcare system? Since 1965, when Medicaid was enacted, states have been permitted to recover costs of treatment from the estates of deceased Medicaid recipients or impose liens on their property. Would that provision of the law be repealed?

"Congress included a provision in the Omnibus Budget Reconciliation Act of 1993 that required states to implement a Medicaid estate recovery program. OBRA 93 requires states to recover, at a minimum, all property and assets that pass from a deceased person to his or her heirs under state probate law, which governs both property conveyed by will and property of persons who die intestate. At a minimum, states must recover amounts spent by Medicaid for long-term care and related drug and hospital benefits, including Medicaid payments for Medicare cost sharing related to these services. However, they have the option of recovering the costs of all Medicaid services paid on the recipient's behalf."

Early enthusiasm for Medicaid Estate Recovery was based on the state of Oregon's early successes in the 1940s. Extraordinary savings to the state-run Medicaid programs, as much as five-fold, were projected. That is typical of the way past presidents and many in Congress explained how the costs of health care plans would be funded. However, a study revealed out of Medicaid's year 2003 multi-billion dollar expenditures, only 0.13% was recovered. What had not been made been clear was the cost of operating the Estate Recovery Program.

Computing health care costs is not rocket science; it is simple math. The total government medical program funding in dollars (A) divided by the total beneficiaries served or enrolled (B) yields a cost per individual (C). Multiply "C" times the total population of the United States (D) based on the latest census data, and the result is the projected annual expense for that health care program if it is available to every person from conception to death.

The Center for Medicare and Medicaid Services website in the spring of 2019 presented a fact sheet on the National Health Expenditures for 2017. That year Medicare spent $705.9 billion on 58.4 million enrollees for an average annual cost of about $12,087 per person. Multiply that by the 328.7 million people in the U.S. per the April 2019 census estimate, and the cost for Medicare coverage for all Americans approached $3.973 trillion per year. In non-technical language, the $4.529 trillion United States fiscal year 2019 budget had to nearly double to $8.5 trillion in order to provide Medicare for every citizen from conception to death.

That same 2017 analysis revealed America's National Health Expenditures amounted to $3.492 trillion—17.9% of America's GDP and $10,739 per capita. Contained in that total cost are Private Health Insurance $1,183.9 billion, Medicare $705.9 billion, Medicaid $581.9 billion, Children's Health Insurance Program $18.2 billion, DoD $42.3 billion, VA $72.1 billion, and Other (including out-of-pocket) $888 billion. Using the population of 328.7 million and per capita cost of $10,739 yields a

Medicare-for-all cost of $3.529 trillion that would bring the national budget to $8 trillion.

That report also projected National Health Expenditures continually increase each year until $6 trillion is reached in ten years. If a Medicare-for-all healthcare system were to absorb all National Health Expenditures, in 2027 the U.S. budget (taking into account continued government spending) would approach $12 trillion.

These were some facts Augustus provided his fellow Americans.

"Voters, ask your elected members of Congress how that will be financed. The media reports a projected cost of $32 trillion. However, that is over ten years. Medicare-for-all, single-payer health care doubles or triples the budget forever!"

From Augustus' point of view, universal, single-payer health care was socialized medicine. The government covered all medical costs. Individuals paid nothing, except taxes to pay all expenses. From one perspective, America's Veterans Health Administration fit that concept. All health-care providers, ambulance services, clinic workers, dentists, doctors, nurses, pharmacists, physical therapists, medical personnel, hospital staff, and those who manage the system are employees of the nation-state. VA hospitals, clinics, and medical facilities are owned, operated, managed, and maintained by the federal government. Enrolled veterans receive medical treatment at no or minimal cost. Taxpayers pay the government so veterans can receive relatively free medical services.

We all heard stories how well Veterans Administration health care worked with bogus appointment lists, backlogs of patients, lack of responsive care, long wait times

seeking treatment, and deaths while government employees were paid regardless—many
received bonuses—and suffered no or limited
penalties for causing harm in the "Do No
Harm" world of medicine. For every
American to receive the same health care
provided to our aging World War II, Korea,
and Vietnam veterans who are in their 60s,
70s, 80s and 90s, when medical demands are
at their highest, more than $2.6 trillion must
be added to the national budget annually
($72.1 billion divided by 9.12 million veterans
treated times 328.7 million people). That
expense would increase America's current
budget by nearly 50%. I ask citizens to
confront their politicians on how we are
going to pay for that increase. And it ain't
only gonna' be the top one percent.

President Treatise considered the DoD Military Health System analogous to universal health care. Every military person on active duty, retiree, spouse, and child up to age 18 is eligible to receive medical treatment wherever and whenever they want for whatever the reason. As long as one parent is on active duty, nearly every conceivable medical, dental, or mental condition a human being could possibly encounter and every accident, ailment, disease, or malady that requires counseling, surgery, treatment, or prosthetics is covered. Service members can travel to any military facility anywhere in the world and obtain available health care. Military hospitals, clinics, dispensaries, aid stations are government facilities, and medical personnel and workers are government employees.

> For every American to receive the same health care as our typical 18- to 44-year-old military men, women, their spouses, their fetuses and babies through teenagers, when individuals are healthiest, nearly $1.5 trillion must be added to the national budget. Members of Congress, I ask by what method are taxpayers going to finance all that additional cost? The top one percent is not wealthy enough.

When Augustus first joined the Army, he was told one of the benefits of serving the country and attaining retirement from service was lifetime free medical care. That same benefit applied to Angelica once they were married. By the time he reached retirement, as with Medicare, Medicaid, the VA, and the enactment of the Affordable Care Act, several congresses and presidents modified military health care, as well.

Expenses were relatively low when the country had a draft under the Selective Service System and more than ninety-five percent of the Armed Forces personnel were single. Once the draft ended and the volunteer military was created, and more married persons with children joined the services, health care costs skyrocketed. The OB-GYN, prenatal, delivery, and child illness costs became a significant portion of the DoD budget. It was such an issue that the system was revised from a 100% no cost to an 80/20% structure similar to that of privatized and commercial health insurance. Health care remained free on installations with military hospitals. However, when seeking treatment off post or off base, the service member, and family were subject to paying 20% of their medical bill to the civilian health-care provider, with 80% paid by the government based on the concept of allowable expenses and if a given ailment was covered under the new treatment guidelines.

As a retiree, Augustus, along with Angelica, became eligible for free health care at most military installations on a standby, first come, first served, no appointment basis, behind five other higher priority patient categories. Sometimes, a "standby" retiree had to wait all day or return the next to receive treatment. There was an additional caveat—assuming medical services were even available. Moreover, at retirement, the 80/20% cost-sharing program for off installation health care became 75/25%.

A couple of challenges to military retirees were a direct result of Congress-mandated Pentagon force structure reductions, changes in programs, and budget cuts. During one major conflict, Armed Forces medical professionals were deployed to the combat theater. Consequently, those deployments and the earlier medical reductions caused health care at many military hospitals to be reserved for Active-duty personnel and their families only. Retirees were told to find somewhere and someone else for medical care. Later program adjustments forced military hospitals to accept only those enrolled in the annual fee based "Prime" version of the retirees' health care plan. Augustus and Angelica were enrolled in the no fee "Standard" version and subsequently were denied treatment at those installations. Armed Forces budgets were reduced, as were military medical facilities and health care availability. Full service hospitals became limited Medical Treatment Facilities. Imagine a local hospital and trauma center being reduced in staff and scope to the point it became an urgent care center or closed altogether—courtesy of funding cuts.

These were Augustus and Angelica's personal experiences, in which initial government and politicians' promises of free, fully covered, no-cost health care were later changed to cost-sharing or reduced services programs.

Some politicians touted the free or low cost and great health care provided to citizens of other nations by their homeland's medical community. President Treatise thought it curious those same proponents never mentioned the universal, socialized, single-payer, Medicare-for-all type, government run systems of China, North Korea, or Russia. He asked, "Is there something neglectful with those countries' medical care?" Also not mentioned were the healthcare systems of our predominantly socialist democracy neighbors to the south—Mexico, El Salvador, Guatemala, Honduras, or Venezuela. Augustus wanted to know, "Are there too many deficiencies in those medical systems?" African nations were totally ignored, as were Middle Eastern countries, including Israel. Even our Asian ally Japan and Western Pacific friend New Zealand failed to make public health discussions. "Why not? What are Congress, politicians, and former presidents keeping from Americans?" questioned Augustus.

The socialized medicine focus seemed to center on Canada and the European Union countries of Sweden, Holland, Germany, and England, but not Hungary. President Treatise could not personally speak to Sweden's system, but he had some knowledge of the others.

The Canadian healthcare system was not one hundred percent single-payer or universal. Canadians could purchase privately insured supplemental health care plans, as their government's system did not cover all medical conditions or treatments. In addition, undocumented (illegal) immigrants were not covered under Canada's universal system. Some members of Congress referred to Canada as one healthcare system for America to emulate, until voters saw, heard, and read news reports about Canadians leaving their country and coming to the United States for medical treatment. Funny how soon politicians became mute on promoting Canadian health care.

President Treatise told the story about one of his pre-presidency business trips. On a flight from Europe, when the Affordable Care Act was being debated, Augustus was discussing the subject of health care with a native Hollander. According to his seatmate, the Netherlands at one time had both government provided and private health care. The private system was disbanded by the socialists in power in favor of the single-payer system, which offered five choices of plans. A Dutch citizen could purchase the plan they could afford or pay for a plan aligned with their medical concerns. The government did not pay for expenses outside of the enrolled plan. If a person needed treatment for an ailment not covered under the plan they had purchased, health care was unavailable unless that individual reimbursed the government for those health related costs; or Dutch citizens had to find treatment in another country and pay for it at their own expense.

Before the Iron Curtain collapsed, West German citizens reportedly received up to six weeks paid time off each year, at full pay, for medical treatment. There were stories of a boss asking an employee to perform extra work, to which the employee replied, "That stresses me out. I'm taking next week off." The employee spent the following week, without fear of employment termination or other reprisals, at a combined health spa and casino—fully paid courtesy of universal, social-ized medicine.

To finance health care, a German worker pays 8.2% of his monthly gross income, and the employer pays 7.3% of the business's monthly gross income into the national Health Care

Fund. In America, Medicare charges only 1.45% on individual and 1.45% on business income.

After the Berlin Wall came down in 1989, it was reported that so many East Germans stressed the West German health care system that six weeks paid medical time off was reduced to four weeks. In addition, to cut costs, individual co-pays were implemented for the first time. Otherwise, the German system may have become insolvent.

Someone once quipped, "If government run health care is so good in England, why does the Royal Family have a private doctor?" In fact, England has two healthcare systems—socialized National Health Service and private health-care providers. According to Augustus' British friends, their government run medical system was terrific and free (paid for by taxes) for general routine medical things like birthing of babies, broken bones, childhood illnesses, emergency care, examinations, prescriptions, some surgery, and vaccinations. The taxes to pay for England's National Health Service (conception-to-grave) version of universal, socialized health care ranged between 9% and 11% of an individual's gross income.

A major issue with British government provided and taxpayer funded health care, however, is that medical professionals, especially nurses, often leave the socialist system to make more money in other countries. That transfer of specialty medical skills from the public to the private sector creates shortages and extends wait times—sometimes many months—for National Health Service treatment. British nationals are often better off finding a specialist in private practice. Englanders need to save money to afford specialized medical care or purchase their own expensive medical insurance. In America, we have already experienced health-care professionals who no longer accept Medicare, Medicaid, or TRICARE insured patients because of government mandated and restrictive reimbursements for treatments.

While on a trip to New York City celebrating a wedding anniversary and attending a Giants versus Jets football game, Augustus happened to sit next to and converse with the Chief Executive Officer of a Hungarian health insurance company. That man grew up under Communist, later socialist, rule and its universal socialized medical care. Every Hungarian received the same level of care—described by that CEO as "generally poor."

"Which is why," he said, "Hungary is moving towards a privatized, free enterprise, market driven system—to improve health care! I have traveled across America and met with executives of the largest health insurers to learn more about private medical care processes."

Augustus asked purveyors of Medicare-for-all, single-payer, universal, or socialized health care, "If former Communist and current socialist countries are looking at America's excellent privatized medical systems in order to improve the health of their people, why are forces in our democracy demanding health care become more like the medical systems in Communist and socialist nations—often described as poor?"

America's officials and competing special interests need to be honest and tell us the bottom line costs as I have done. Had our politicians used sixth grade math and advised us of the results, we could have made significantly better decisions in the voting booth. We could have told our elected representatives what should, or should not, be contained in any Medicare-for-all, single-payer, socialized, or universal health care coverage, the deductibles, and catastrophic coverage limits. We could have stipulated what taxes and tax rates we would or would not be willing to support. In short, a handful of blueprints for revising America's health care were and are already available without the need to create an additional new and government run system.

Just what is the ultimate and long-term goal in establishing either a Medicare-for-all, single-payer, socialized, or universal health-care system? Is it politicians or special interests' intent that the federal government, the state as in Communist and socialist countries, control and finance one hundred percent of all medical care costs for every individual? Several have so intimated.

Many have attributed the rising costs of health care to exorbitant lawsuits and the lack of tort reform. One facet of military health care relates to legal tort differences. Civilians are allowed to sue doctors for malpractice. With very few exceptions, under *Feres v. United States* (the *Feres* Doctrine), members of the Armed Forces are not allowed to sue the government—no malpractice lawsuits for medical mistakes and errors. "Ask your legislators, will their Medicare-for-all, single-payer, socialized, or universal health care plans apply the *Feres* Doctrine to all government-employed health-care professionals? Do we want all health-care professionals to be government employees who may not be sued for malpractice? Do average citizens want to lose the ability to sue doctors who make mistakes?" asked Augustus.

Military doctors are paid the same salary regardless of the location of medical services performed. In addition, military doctors do not require malpractice insurance since the U.S. government is the indemnifier. Certainly, if every medical care provider were a government employee, were paid a fixed income, and were protected from lawsuits, there would be no need for malpractice insurance, which, in theory, should reduce the costs of health care. Logically, a fully comprehensive, government-provided, taxpayer-financed, universal, Medicare-for-all, single-payer, socialized, conception-to-grave, healthcare system would eliminate the need for health insurance companies. There would be no need for employer provided coverage for employees, individual and family insurance plans, travelers insurance, Medi-gap policies, or the health insurance market place under the Affordable Care Act (Obamacare). That is true for many veterans and Active-duty military; they have little to no need for private health insurance coverage.

"I did not require private medical insurance while on active duty, as a retiree, and as a disabled veteran with a back injury incurred during a parachute jump," Augustus pronounced. "Eliminating health insurance companies would put thousands of people out of work, unless they were rehired as government employees to run the expanded government bureaucracy."

Angelica paid $6,000 per year and her employer paid $12,000 per year for privatized health insurance. Augustus asked, "Taxpayers are you prepared to pay Congress $18,000 per year, per family, for government health care? Or $36,000 to cover a less income solvent family that receives government subsidized medical care? Would the Legislative Branch implement an income means test?" He provided more facts and asked.

"Should each individual be assessed a standard annual fee based on his or her state of residence, regardless of age or sex?"

Information by the Center for Medicare and Medicaid Services recorded the annual per capita health care costs by payer, per beneficiary, per state:

- Medicare costs ranged from a high of $12,614 in New Jersey to a low of $8,238 in Montana.
- Medicaid paid a North Dakota high of $12,413 to an Illinois low of $4,959.
- Private health insurance covered Alaska's high of $5,958 to Nevada's low of $3,417.
- Personal health care spending was highest in Alaska at $11,064 to the lowest in Utah at $5,982.

"Should each individual be charged an annual premium based on age and sex, regardless of employment status or state of residence?" That same report presented per capita per person personal health care spending based on sex and age:

- $10,739 regardless of age, sex, working or unemployed, paying taxes or not, insured or not, citizen or not
- $6,788 cost for males and $8,315 cost for females (23% higher than males)
- $18,988 over age 65 (14% of the population and 34% of the cost) with cost per male $18,251 and cost per female $19,558 (7% higher than males)
- $6,632 per working adult age 19 to age 64 (61% of the population and 54% of the cost) with cost per male $5,822 and cost per female $7,430 (28% higher than males)
- $3,552 per child age 0 to18 (25% of the population and 12% of the cost) with cost per female $3,399 and cost per male $3,698 (9% higher than females)

Prescription medicines were also of interest. Drugs were free when Augustus used military pharmacies while on active duty or as a retiree. The prices of prescribed medications from the VA were means-tested based on his income and cost $40 per quarter. On the other hand, those same prescription drugs costs $6 per quarter when he used his wife's private company plan and a local pharmacy. Medicare covered no prescription costs, as he was not enrolled in Part D. The prices were different in each situation because they were different programs; DoD — universal, VA — socialized, Spouse of an Employee — privatized, Medicare — single payer. In addition, costs for medicines were different because of the various contracts negotiated between federal agencies, private industry, and competing pharmaceutical companies. He speculated whether politicians were going to combine every prescription drug system and pharmacy into a single government program.

Medical care for members of the Armed Forces was not only transportable all across the U.S., but worldwide, as well. Augustus questioned whether the politicians' health care plans included similar transportability. Could Americans travel anywhere in the world and, should they suffer some accident or illness, have health-care providers in foreign lands direct bill the United States government? Currently, Medicare and Medicaid are not available to Americans vacationing, working, or living in other countries. Would Medicare-for-all, single-payer, socialized, or universal health care change that?

There were multiple other issues for citizens to consider. Should each type of medical treatment be a fixed price across the country? Private health insurance policies varied greatly depending on many factors, such as whether the plan was for individuals or groups, and in which state the plan operated. The costs of treatment in rural America were often several thousand dollars less than the same treatment in a metropolis. Services available in the same provider network would be different depending on location. Experimental treatments and medicines were often not covered. Government could always be counted on to change its programs and fees; Social Security benefits increased 2% the same year Medicare Part B fees jumped 28%. President Treatise wondered what entitlement programs citizens would be willing to decimate. What government services could or should be cut or eliminated? Should exceptions for special interest groups be allowed to remain?

If congresses, presidents, political parties, and special interest groups were serious about giving every individual a 100% funded, "free" Medicare-for-all, single-payer, socialized, or universal healthcare system with full conception-to-grave care for every medical-related issue at a reduced and fixed cost, then the only solution was to nationalize. That meant all health related entities and industries had to be taken over by the government. Included would be: public, privately owned, insurance-based, nonprofit and religious operated hospitals, clinics, urgent care centers, nursing homes, and assisted living facilities; ambulance and aero-medevac services; dentist offices and oral surgeons; acupuncturists, chiropractors, and faith healers; dieticians, nutritionists, and health food stores; abortion providers and midwives; pharmacies and pharmaceutical companies, manufacturers, and distributors. Added would be diet, weight loss, and exercise businesses; sports clinics and physical therapy centers; health clubs; IV therapy rejuvenation clinics and spas; and mental health and addiction treatment facilities.

Additional logical questions that demanded answers were, "How could Americans afford to pay for adding all that expense to the national budget?" "Were taxpayers willing to accept a 20, 30, or 40 percent tax on gross income and eliminate every deduction?" "Were citizens willing to adopt a 20 percent national sales tax?" "How much were citizens willing to pay to provide coverage for those who can't afford the costs?"

As a basis to start discussion, Augustus put forth several preventative medicine treatments to be included in any standard Medicare-for-all, single-payer, socialized, or universal coverage package and, within the same proposal, a list of treatments to be dropped from coverage. He felt that Benjamin Franklin's "an Ounce of Prevention is worth a Pound of Cure" argument was just as applicable to reducing today's medical costs as his statement did in its application to Philadelphia fire safety in 1735.

President Treatise also believed privatized medicine was a better way to augment health care and that those who did not take care of themselves should pay more for any treatments received. He offered the idea of riders on health insurance policies. All types of automobile, homeowner, life, and business insurance policies had standard provisions and optional coverages. Augustus' listing of options for which individuals could purchase additional health care coverage included smoking, drinking, recreational marijuana or illegal drug use, contraceptives, abortions, voluntary cosmetic surgery, playing sports, and sex change operations.

While Congress, politicians, pundits, the president, and special interests continued to grapple with health care, one aspect of Augustus' agenda that received wide bipartisan support and was eventually enacted dealt with Medicare and Medicaid fraud. New restrictions, regulations, and fees were established to reduce systemic and system-wide fraud. It was very simple. Every individual, organization, self-employed person, small business, entity, company, or corporation involved with and which received Medicare and Medicaid reimbursement for services needed to comply with several requirements.

First, only American-based and owned entities could apply for and receive reimbursement.

Second, providers paid an annual fee of either $10,000 or one percent of their gross revenues, whichever was greater, to be licensed and receive a federal registration number. That license and registration number were linked to the primary address of the provider. Should the primary address of the Medicare and/or Medicaid business change, federal authorities had to be notified and a new license and registration number would be issued for the new location. In addition, a copy of the provider's annual Internal Revenue Service tax forms submission was to accompany the annual fee payment. Where the provider had multiple locations that conducted Medicare-Medicaid business, each location had its own license and registration, paid the annual fee, and submitted separate IRS tax forms.

Third, primary applicants provided a set of fingerprints, a certified birth certificate, and background checks provided by local, county, state, and federal law enforcement. Copies of two types of photo identification were also required. Every five years, background checks and copies of photo identification of primary applicants were to be resubmitted. These requirements also applied to subordinate branches and offices of the overall provider organization.

Finally, and most importantly, primary applicants were required to sign a contractual statement of pecuniary liability that acknowledged personal liability for all cases of Medicare and/or Medicaid fraud that occurred in, by, and within the provider organization, or were caused by the primary applicant, family members, or employees. By agreeing to those terms, notarized signatures acknowledged the government could implement the same asset forfeiture process it took against drug cartels, warlords, smugglers, dealers, pushers, sellers, or users involving illegal drugs and legal medicines abuse.

The statutes were restrictive because prior to this law, in 2017, approximately $60 billion in fraud (about 9% of the entire Medicare budget) took place, and the government recouped only about $3 billion—less than ½ percent of the total Medicare budget and 5% of the amount stolen—in criminal judgments. More restrictions were therefore deemed appropriate.

One of the primary reasons the chief executive wanted Medicare financial reform was the repeated shortage in the Medicare Trust Fund over the past few years, which endangered its solvency. Congress clumsily made up the differences by transferring dollars from the General Tax Fund to cover the shortfalls—"Robbing Peter to pay Paul," as the saying went. To make up the losses in the General Revenue Fund, Congress annually extended the nation's debt limit so it could borrow more money and print more dollars. One major impact of that process was America's $34 trillion debt that Augustus inherited.

Congress refused to budge on most chief executive proposals for health care reform. However, the poll-conscious politicians were able to increase Medicare's hospital insurance rates to 1.75% (up from 1.45%) for employees and employers and 3.2% (up from 2.9%) for the self-employed.

When President Treatise left office, nothing significant regarding Medicare-for-all, single-payer, socialized, or universal health care had been accomplished. National health expenditures increased to $7 trillion, private health insurance provider premiums rose, Affordable Care Act subsidies grew, catastrophic caps for enrollees were expanded, and Medicare and Medicaid coverages and allowable expenses were reduced. Congress overrode all Augustus' vetoes of cuts to Medicare benefits, treatments, prescription drugs, and services. Voters realized the exorbitant costs for a universal, socialized, single-payer, Medicare-for-all, government-owned and operated healthcare system, and kept the Legislative Branch in check.

Taxes

The Congress shall have Power To lay and collect Taxes, Duties, Imposts and Excises, to pay the Debts and provide for the common Defence and general Welfare of the United States...

(Article I, Section 8, United States Constitution)

The Congress shall have power to lay and collect taxes on incomes, from whatever source derived, without apportionment among the several States, and without regard to any census or enumeration.

(Amendment XVI, United States Constitution)

Americans were taxed too much, according to President Treatise. As with his earlier budget presentation, Augustus developed a similarly unique approach to explaining tax reform legislation. He used a combination of filmed locations and a live appearance from the Oval Office to broadcast his message to all taxpayers.

The first video segment took place on the sidewalk at 10th Street NW, with the entrance to the Internal Revenue Service building in Washington, D.C. as background. "Welcome to the Internal Revenue Service. Next to Congress, probably the most hated of all government agencies. You know it, I know it, and the IRS knows it. Let's take a look inside."

A camera followed him throughout the agency. He stopped

periodically to say a few words. Standing next to a six-foot-high stack of current tax code: "On average each individual or family filling out their income taxes uses about one hundred pages of existing tax code, a self-employed person about one thousand pages, a small business about ten thousand pages, and a corporation about twenty-five thousand pages. Most individuals fill out their own forms, businesses hire accountants, and corporations hire tax firms—all to read, review, and interpret federal tax laws."

At an IRS employee's desk, Augustus picked up someone's tax return. "A few years ago it took me nearly three weekends in a row to complete my federal income tax return. Those were six days that the taxman robbed me of quality and quantity time with my wife and children. Even today with the help of technology, it still takes me an entire weekend to complete my federal return."

The camera panned a huge room filled with workers in cubicles. "The Americans who work here are just as patriotic as every other citizen. They are hardworking grandparents, parents, brothers, sisters, spouses, church goers, veterans, and regular folks who live day-to-day life just like the rest of us."

The camera refocused on the chief executive. "I want you to think a bit about your public servants here at the IRS and what they handle. Look at your neighbors on your block, in your mobile home park, complex of apartments, condominiums, retirement community, wherever you may reside. How many differences are there in jobs, incomes, numbers in the family, investments, tax deductions, exemptions, expenses, donations, and any number of other aspects of living?

"While each of us may deal with 100 pages of tax code, the employees here at the IRS must review, read, and interpret yours and every one of your neighbors' tax returns—using more than eighty thousand pages of existing tax code. That is more than one hundred million tax returns for every individual, business, nonprofit organization, and corporation. Adding to their challenges, every year Congress enacts new legislation that invariably changes multiple aspects of tax laws. Small wonder a percentage of the answers the IRS provides to your letters, telephone calls and e-mails are incorrect; and so too are some errors made by accountants and tax attorneys."

The second filmed segment opened in Boston harbor with "Bean Town" as background. The deck of the three-masted frigate U.S.S. Constitution—"Old Ironsides"—was Augustus' stage. "Here in this historic town the Boston Tea Party took place, in part, because of excessive taxes. The forefathers of this great nation fought and won a revolution because of taxation without representation in King George's parliament. Over the past several decades, taxpayers have come to believe elected officials who serve in Congress no longer represent the interests of the citizen where taxes are concerned. Expenditures far exceed revenues. Borrowing now, paying later is the norm. Continuing resolutions replace basic budgeting and accounting principles. The words *debt* and *deficit* are comingled to the point they have lost their distinction. National debt is spoken in terms of percentage of Gross Domestic Product. It is as if every representative of the people has a severe case of 'affluenza.' Congress is so addicted to taxpayer-financed public funding that elected officials have lost all powers of common sense and reasoning—and wholeheartedly believe they should be pardoned and reelected multiple times for their irresponsibility."

The last segment was broadcast live from the Oval Office. President Treatise closed his presentation. "With your help we are going to scale back the Internal Revenue Service, conduct a modern day tax revolution, make Congress more responsive to the taxpayer, and ultimately change America's tax system."

Augustus espoused the concept of less is more and "income should only be taxed once." His tax policy proposal was very simple: an even ten percent tax rate on the gross income of each individual, regardless of marital status, including the self-employed, and on the gross revenues of every family-owned and small business, company and corporation, coupled with the elimination of all deductions for individuals, business expenses, and tax loopholes. Once that 10% was paid, whatever else remained was entirely available to the individual, family, self-employed, small business, company, and corporation. Interest earned on savings, capital gains dividends on investments, and profit from real and personal property sales were not taxed. Social Security was neither taxed nor offset by other income sources. Estates were not taxed; the death tax was eliminated.

In addition to establishing a single fixed percentage tax rate on gross income, the tax plan eliminated the Federal Communications Commission fee on cable television, Federal Universal Fee (an average 3% of Augustus' monthly telephone bill), Federal Subscriber Line Charge (an average 9% of Augustus' monthly telephone bill), Federal Universal Service Charge (an average 3% of Angelica's monthly wireless bill), and other such "mandated" fees and charges passed on to consumers by utility, energy, telecommunications, and other federally regulated entities.

One of the chief executive's goals was to encourage Americans to save for retirement, whatever might be their needs and wants. More money deposited in banks and credit unions meant more money available for lending and investment. A second goal was to get more taxpayers investing in the markets and thus creating greater economic opportunities. New tax legislation meant individuals were taxed only on their wages/salaries. Any interest and dividends earned from savings accounts, investments, or legalized gambling was not taxed. Win the lottery; keep 100% of the winnings. He reasoned that if you wanted to stimulate the economy, create jobs, encourage entrepreneurs, and find solutions for many of the challenges that faced America and the world, you needed to have capital.

President Treatise stated, "I want the 'little guy' to have an opportunity for generating wealth like the rich. Middle and lower income taxpayers need money to invest in stocks, bonds, commodities, T-bills, or precious metals and contribute to a 401(k), 403(b), Thrift Savings Plan, Individual Retirement Account, pension, or other retirement plan. The benefit of taking such action is no taxes on any gains realized from investments. Conversely, for tax purposes, income will not be adjusted for any losses incurred."

For those with employment contracts and who received all or a majority of their income from investments, property, or other "bennies" and often avoided income tax altogether, the plan included the following provisions. Ninety percent of total gross compensation was to be in the form of wages or salaries instead of gifts, property, stocks and bonds, or other in-kind arrangements. That accomplished a couple things, not the least of which was more revenue for the Treasury. It also forced Boards of Directors to look hard at compensation packages for executives. Stockholders, too, had a greater say in executive pay as returns on their investment holdings would likely increase if exorbitant executive wages and "giveaways" were reduced.

The remaining ten percent of any total compensation package in the form of investments or other financial instruments was to be held for a minimum of ten years. After that ten-year period, they could be disposed of only at the rate of 10% per year until those assets were depleted. The intent was to ensure executives retained a stake in the company well after they departed. Also, any real or personal properties received as part of any compensation package were to be retained for a minimum of five years before disposal—no depreciation allowed. Included were such items as club memberships, furniture, vehicles, yachts, airplanes, works of art, and cabins on lakes, ski lodges, resort condominiums, or houses on golf courses. In addition, those "giveaways" were no longer allowed as business expenses. Moreover, the face value of those items was taxed at the 10% gross income tax rate, as well.

Parents want their children to have a better life. Therefore, heirs should not suffer a government-induced penalty because parents were smart enough to generate wealth. That was Augustus' reason for eliminating the "death tax." Where estates included investments or other financial instruments from business compensation packages, after probate, those assets were to be held and disposed of by the heirs in accordance with the original 10-year holdings and 10% per year withdrawal rule. The 5-year rule applied to real and personal property, also.

There were several advantages to the overall tax policy. First, an even ten percent tax rate on gross income, revenue, or profits and eliminating all deductions and loopholes meant individuals, self-employed, small businesses, and corporations planned better. The worry about a huge tax liability on April 15 each year, quarterly payments, or the anxious wait for a delayed tax refund was eliminated. Second, because 10% was taken out of a person's paycheck, up front and automatically, just like Social Security and Medicare, salaried and wage earner employees did not have to file income tax returns. Others simply determined their gross income, multiplied by 10%, completed the one-page tax form, and mailed or e-filed their payment.

Third, the number of individuals, self-employed, businesses, and corporations that did not pay income taxes or repeatedly filed for extensions was significantly reduced. The IRS was able to obtain the full income tax amount rather than spending dollars litigating and settling for a reduced tax liability amount. Fourth, the government saved money by not revising the tax code or printing changes to tax law, tax forms, tax instructions, and tax publications every year, not to mention the time and expense necessary to retrain employees. The IRS focused more on determining, arresting, and prosecuting tax cheats rather than auditing honest citizens or providing incorrect tax advice.

Fifth, members of Congress concentrated on more important issues than haggling over every little tax code item. Sixth, having a fixed idea of how much revenue was coming into the U.S. Treasury every pay period made balancing the budget, dealing with deficits, and paying off the national debt much easier. Seventh, putting more money into the hands of individuals and releasing the tax burden on businesses expanded the economy, created new ideas that generated jobs, and ultimately enhanced the country's coffers. Finally, stresses on the environment were eased as fewer trees and less hazardous materials were required for producing tax related paper products.

Augustus addressed the nation a second time.

> Regardless of party affiliation, from the founding of the country and up to and including my time in office, tax discussions focus on whether a given tax is progressive or regressive. A progressive tax is often defined as the tax rate increasing as the taxable amount increases. America's current

income tax tables and tax categories fit that definition. A regressive tax is often defined as the tax rate decreasing as the taxable amount increases; a flat fee dollar amount is an example.

Augustus used two charts to demonstrate the difference.

Progressive Income Tax

Taxable Income	Tax Rate	Income Tax	After-Tax Income
$10,000	10%	$1,000	$9,000
$100,000	22%	$22,000	$78,000
$1,000,000	32%	$320,000	$680,000
$10,000,000	37%	$3,700,000	$6,300,000

Regressive Income Tax

Taxable Income	Tax Rate	Income Tax	After-Tax Income
$10,000	10%	$1,000	$9,000
$100,000	1%	$1,000	$99,000
$1,000,000	0.1%	$1,000	$999,000
$10,000,000	0.01%	$1,000	$9,999,000

Politicians like to obfuscate the word 'fair.' Those in favor of a flat tax say it is 'fair' and helps everyone because all pay the same amount of tax and people get to retain more of their hard-earned income (regressive income tax). Those opposed say it disproportionately hurts the poor and overly favors the rich; the wealthy must pay their 'fair' share—meaning more taxes since they earn more income (progressive tax policy). Both sides use the word fair. Who is correct? In actuality, neither and both. Words matter. That is why I use the words, 'An even ten percent tax rate.'

Augustus showed the following example.

Even Percentage Income Tax Rate

Gross Income	Tax Rate	Income Tax	After Tax-Income
$10,000	10%	$1,000	$9,000
$100,000	10%	$10,000	$90,000
$1,000,000	10%	$100,000	$900,000
$10,000,000	10%	$1,000,000	$9,000,000

My plan combines both concepts. At an even, across-all-income-levels, percentage tax rate, individuals generally pay more tax than in a pure regressive tax system and less tax than in the existing progressive tax system. As my charts indicate, the poor generally pay the same taxes and keep the same take home income regardless of the tax system implemented. The middle class incurs significantly less tax liability. Higher income earners pay less tax than in the current progressive tax system, but more tax than in a regressive tax system. The bottom line overall is taxpayers keep more of their income than in the current tax laws.

Individual Income Ranges and Even Tax Rates Applicable to Each

Gross Income	Income Tax Rate
$0 – $50,000	5%
$50,000 – $100,000	10%
$100,000 – $250,000	15%
$250,000 – $1,000,000	20%
$1,000,000 – $10,000,000	25%
$10,000,000 +	30%

With citizens speaking at town halls, writing letters, making telephone calls, sending e-mails, and posting on social media, Congress and the chief executive resolved their differences, over the objections and money of lobbyists and special interests, and reached a tax plan compromise. A combined or phased system similar to England's was adopted. It retained the even percentage tax rate on gross incomes for individuals, self-employed, family-owned businesses, companies, and corporations and eliminated all deductions and loopholes. Tax tables for singles, married couples, and heads of household were eliminated. Six new even percentage tax rate categories and gross income ranges were established.

It worked like this. Earned income of $50,000 or less paid 5% of gross income. Those who earned income of $100,000 or less paid 5% on the first $50k and 10% up to $100k. Persons earning $250k or less in income paid 5% on the first 50k, 10% on $50k to $100k, and 15% up to $250k. That formula was used for every subsequent category.

Taxes on self-employed, small businesses, companies, and corporations followed the same concept and formula but had different gross income ranges.

Business Income Ranges and Even Tax Rates Applicable to Each

Gross Income	Income Tax Rate
$0 – $1,000,000	5%
$1,000,000 – $100,000,000	10%
$100 million – $500 million	15%
$500 million – $1 billion	20%
$1 billion +	25%

In the compromised legislation, income on salaries and wages in contractual compensation packages were revised to 75% cash and 25% for other investments and real and personal property. Retention for investments was set at seven years and 20% disposal per year for five years after that. Real and personal property could be disposed of after two years. Heirs could dispose of all assets at the time the estate was probated. Estate (death) taxes and taxes on Social Security income were rescinded. A proviso was included in the legislation that permitted annual adjustments to the income categories and even percentage tax rates, depending on the revenues received by the Treasury. Augustus signed the act into law.

Chapter 19

Social Security

An Act. To provide for the general welfare by
establishing a system of Federal old-age benefits,
and by enabling the several States to make more
adequate provision for aged persons, blind persons, dependent and crippled children, maternal
and child welfare, public health, and the administration of their unemployment compensation
laws; to establish a Social Security Board; to raise
revenue; and for other purposes.

(Public Law 74-271, 49 United States Statutes at
Large 620, August 14, 1935, now codified as 42
United States Code Chapter 7)

The positive news was, due to better science, medicine, diet,
and exercise, more Americans were living longer, healthier, and
productive lives. On the down side, the costs of living
continued to rise. Earlier congresses had raided the Social
Security Trust Fund to pay for other programs. Legislators
passed additional social welfare laws which otherwise never
would had been enacted had those entitlements not been placed
under the Social Security umbrella. Those actions created
massive unfunded liabilities. Thus, during Augustus'
presidency, Social Security was once again under threat of
insolvency.

Social Security (Old-Age, Survivors, and Disability Insurance–OASDI) was initially envisioned as one, if not the only,

source of income to aid senior citizens live out their "golden years." At the time of its enactment, the overwhelming majority of citizens had minimal to no savings, and very few businesses provided employee pensions. Social Security is based on a "pay now, receive later" concept. Working children and grandchildren pay for their retired parents and grandparents' benefits. Those grandchildren's future benefits are paid by subsequent working generations. Financial stability of the program is based on the major assumptions that there will always be enough employed people to fund the system, and investments of the Social Security Trust Fund will increase faster than expenditures. Unfortunately, that was not always the case, and a review of its history reflected periodic premium increases paid by taxpayers and upward age category adjustments kept the program funded.

Demographics reflected birth rate decreases in recent years. The trend was projected to continue into future years. The resulting impact was there would not be enough working young to fund anticipated expenditures. Cyclic periods of recession and high unemployment also contributed to reduced revenue for the Social Security Trust Fund. To those concerns was added the fact that more and more taxpayers retired from the work/labor force in their forties and fifties, while at the same time seniors were reentering the labor market. The net impact was an average 40% loss of projected revenue for the Social Security Trust Fund and a corresponding 25% increase in expenditures.

The president, first lady, and their parents were examples. Augustus' father began full-time employment right out of high school at age 18 and worked two years before his employment was interrupted for service during World War II. After the war, he returned to full time work and remained employed with the same company for thirty-seven more years. He retired at 63 and waited two years to draw his full Social Security benefits. The president, on the other hand, began work after college at 22 with the goal of retiring at age 55—which he did—and later began receiving Social Security at the age 62 reduced rate. Augustus worked six years less than his father did, and after leaving the labor force, did not pay into Social Security for seven years before beginning to receive benefits.

Angelica's father began working the farm after eighth grade at 14 and did so until 58, after which he continued with his second job another twelve years. Eventually, he retired with 35 years in the meat packing plant business and began drawing Social Security at the age 70 highest rate. The first lady began working full time right out of high school at 18 and worked, off and on, in various jobs—thirty-five years' total employment. She began drawing Social Security at age 65. Angelica was employed twenty-one years less than her dad was, and did not pay into Social Security for twelve years whereas her dad paid into the system for fifty-six years.

In recent years, many men and women have become millionaires in their thirties and forties after working only fifteen to twenty-five years. They not only could afford to stop working, but also often did. Leaving the work force at age 46 meant they paid no money into the Social Security Trust Fund for twenty years before they began taking full benefits at age 66. During those same years, senior citizens continued to receive Social Security, thus endangering its solvency.

To save Social Security, President Treatise incorporated program adjustments into his overall tax plan. First, the Federal Insurance Contributions Act (FICA) amount employees and employers paid was raised from 6.2% to 8%. The Self-Employed Contributions Act (SECA) fee was reduced from 13.85% to 8%.

That provided those who were self-employed a modicum of additional capital with which they could save or expand their chosen field of endeavor. Second, the income earnings cap was eliminated so high income earners making $132,900 or more paid into Social Security, thus increasing taxes on the wealthy.

Third, since Americans lived longer, ages for receiving Social Security were adjusted upward. The previous limits were Reduced Retirement age 62, Full Retirement age 66, and Delayed Retirement age 70. The new limits were set at Reduced Retirement age 66, Full Retirement age 70, and Delayed Retirement age 74. Citizens born before 2000 were not affected and were grandfathered into the old program. The new age requirements applied to persons born in 2000 and later. That group, most of whom were still in K-12 schooling, trade school, or college, had yet to find gainful employment and had plenty of time to plan for their financial future, retirement, and old age lifestyle.

To cut down on fraud or taxpayer money sent to deceased persons, Augustus directed the Social Security Administration, the Internal Revenue Service, and the Treasury Department compare and coordinate each other's records. The Social Security Administration developed computer algorithms, much like the sort program for spreadsheets, and reviewed the entire database. The first sort started with Social Security number 000-00-0000 and, in numerical sequence, ended with 999-99-9999. That checked for the same number being repeated and used by different people. A second sort listed everyone alphabetically and identified individuals who used several different Social Security numbers. The third sort compared dates of birth with the Social Security number. That weeded out numbers assigned to persons before they were born. A final sort compared numbers already issued against those available for assignment.

That methodology looked for fake and stolen numbers.

Whenever any issues arose in the sorting procedures, those files were intensively reviewed, and federal agents investigated each person associated with that particular anomaly. Internal Revenue Service files were crosschecked for Social Security number and name discrepancies. That process determined those who received Social Security checks but did not pay taxes or who received multiple payments and did not report all income. It also determined who claimed IRS tax refunds based on a false Social Security number or who received money based on one or more fake numbers. Social Security numbers of questionable files were also cross-referenced against each state's birth, marriage, divorce, adoption, court approved name change, and death records. Once the paper and electronic files were reconciled, federal agents were sent to interview persons of interest where questions still existed.

In cases where a beneficiary was legally entitled to the Social Security number and related benefits, the file was duly recorded as "Authorized" or, in the case of deceased recipients, "Closed." The files of beneficiaries who could not be found or whose status was unconfirmed were marked "Unverified." In those situations, the Treasury Department stopped payment of Social Security benefits, which also included Medicare and Medicaid coverage. That action resulted in legally authorized recipients reporting to their local offices for verification, reinstatement of benefits, and having their files annotated accordingly.

Persons who operated outside the law never showed up. That meant they were not paid, money was saved, and federal agents opened criminal investigations. Criminals who did appear were arrested, charged, tried, convicted of fraud, and ordered to pay back 100% of all illegally received Social Security benefits. If necessary, their personal assets were confiscated, as with drug dealers under Asset Forfeiture statutes, and treated as restitution. Dollars from those assets were deposited into the Social Security Trust Fund.

By adjusting Social Security tax rates and ages to receive benefits, verifying recipients, and cracking down on criminal activity, the Social Security Trust Fund was stabilized and salvaged for a projected two more generations of taxpayers.

Chapter 20

Jobs

job *n.* **1** A piece of work; regular employment, as, to have a good *job*. **4** The thing on which work is done.

Augustus outlined and presented two job creation concepts. One, proposed during the West Coast's "fire season," focused on establishing a Strategic Water Reserve similar in concept to the country's Strategic Petroleum Reserve. The other, significantly more ambitious, proposed the elimination of all nuclear waste from the planet.

As was his custom, President Treatise selected a locale relevant to his speech and introduced the Strategic Water Reserve employment plan from the drought-stricken, burned to the ground, wildfire-devastated hills outside of and overlooking San Diego. A site where once green and tan ground was covered in gray ash, charred-black chimneys represented rows of family homes, and empty-of-foliage trees had been reshaped into twisted arches, bent from their boiling sap.

Augustus and Angelica had immense empathy for the people in this area. Their youngest child Morgan, a diesel engine mechanic, and daughter-in-law Dorthy's house had burned to the ground in a northern California wildfire earlier that year. They had lost everything.

When Augustus had first proposed running for president, Morgan had been vehemently opposed to his father's candidacy, let alone becoming leader of the free world. "Dad, my issue is that you are going to open up not only your current and past life to severe scrutiny, but all of ours, as well. Given the treatment of past presidents' children by some malicious rabble—I don't want that. Nor do I want Dorthy's or our son and daughter's lives investigated, nitpicked by opposition research firms hired by your opponents looking for anything and everything negative. Or have something innocent twisted into something evil."

Morgan's concerns had come to fruition. Throughout his father's candidacy and first year of presidency, Morgan and Dorthy had been confronted by intruders wanting to know something, anything, about Augustus, Angelica, and siblings Cooper and Bailey. Intrusions did not stop with Morgan and Dorthy; their children had been approached, as well. Over the past three-year period, the constant invasions of their privacy had stressed the family's ties. Morgan had not spoken to his father for more than two years. Such was Morgan's animus and pride, that he refused all offers of fire relief assistance from Augustus. In spite of the love-hate relationship between father and son, Dorthy got along famously with Angelica and quietly accepted limited support. The suffering of his own family reinforced Augustus' efforts to establish a Strategic Water Reserve.

Water is the earth's most precious resource; without it nothing survives, neither plant nor animal life. In light of severe drought conditions of the past, such as the Dust Bowl days in the 1930s and the multiple devastating fires during the first two decades of the twenty-first century, I propose the construction of a network of water pipelines, pump stations, purification sites, and storage tank systems all across central and south-western United States.

Nearly every waterway west of Appalachia and east of the Rocky Mountains eventually flows into the Mississippi River. That river often overflows its banks as a direct result of too much water from its tributaries upstream. President Treatise's plan diverted excessive amounts of floodwaters from the Mississippi River in Missouri, Arkansas, and Louisiana, to California. Tank farms, each to store 100 million barrels of water, were to be constructed along the pipeline routes. Because stagnant water required periodic changing, the water in the storage tanks would be expended for irrigation or firefighting or drained into the regional ecosystems; then it would be replenished, as necessary.

The overarching goal of this national project is to establish and maintain a reserve supply of water with priority of use for agriculture, replenishment of lakes, reservoirs, water tables, and firefighting operations to save lives, property, wildlife, and aid the environment. A secondary function is the long-term safety, security, health, welfare, and survival of future generations.

Using a map as a visual aid, Augustus pointed to the pipelines, pumping stations, water purification plants, and storage tank sites that followed three primary routes. One traced the I-44 and I-40 interstate highway corridors from St.

Louis, Missouri, through Oklahoma, Texas, New Mexico, and Arizona, into California and terminated near Los Angeles. A spur line would feed into southern Nevada to replenish Lake Mead. The second followed I-40 to I-30 to I-20 routes from Memphis, Tennessee, through Arkansas, into Texas and connected with the third pipeline east of El Paso. System three tracked I-10 from Baton Rouge, Louisiana, across Texas, continued through New Mexico and Arizona into California, and terminated near San Diego. Over time, if future flooding made it necessary, a fourth pipeline might be added along I-20 from Vicksburg, Mississippi, across Louisiana, to connect with the first pipeline passing through Dallas-Fort Worth. Each of the named states would have one water tank farm. Texas would have two storage sites because of the joining of routes two and three near El Paso. California would have a second, as well, since two pipelines terminated in that state.

As to the labor force required for such an undertaking, Augustus envisioned a new version of the Civilian Conservation Corps or Works Progress Administration of the 1930s — updated, of course. Each state would be responsible for and have oversight of the private businesses constructing the pipelines, pump stations, treatment plants, and storage tanks within its borders. Taking a lesson from the Alaska oil pipeline, Native Americans who lived on reservations in those states were to comprise five percent of the total work force hired. In addition, other minorities in percentages equal to that state's population based on the latest census were to be employed. If employment goals were not met, affected states could hire minorities and Native Americans from other states.

The labor goal is a work force that mirrors
the population of the state. The most signif-

icant tertiary goal is to provide untrained workers with job skills they can fully utilize then and in the future. This job-generating project is designed to break the cycle of poverty among many of the nation's poorer citizens. Unemployed and underemployed persons are to be given hiring priority. The 800-mile Trans-Alaska Oil Pipeline was built in about three years. I now challenge Americans to construct and complete the 5,000-mile Strategic Water Reserve system in five years.

Congress agreed with the overall concept and authorized the funding even though resistance came from some environmentalists concerned about the terrain and species affected and from some legislators who felt additional job-creating pipelines should traverse their states. Construction was well underway by the time Augustus left office.

Even more ambitious was President Treatise's second jobs bill—the elimination of all nuclear and radioactive contaminated materials from the earth. While water is man's most precious resource, nuclear and radioactive materials are man's most hazardous waste.

Augustus had been wrestling with the idea for some time. He had a limited familiarity with nuclear power plant operations and the disposal of radioactive waste materials from his time as an emergency manager. In addition, in the midst of formulating his campaign platform and complying with Angelica's demand to talk with the children, he had asked for input at Christmas dinner. While everyone commented, it was Bailey, their adopted daughter and second child, christened after Augustus' great-

great grandmother, who provided the most useable ideas. She had taken the traditional route of high school and college to become an astrophysicist and had accepted employment at an Asian space agency. Bailey offered her experienced thoughts.

"The ideal launch site is an island in the Pacific Ocean close to the equator where rockets can be fired from west to east. That is best because the closer to the equator, the greater the earth's rotational speed, which provides rockets with an extra boost, thus reducing the amount of fuel required for launch. Only enough fuel necessary for rockets to be free of earth's gravitational pull is required. Once on course in space, rockets can be tracked all the way to their destination; possibly Sol, the earth's sun, itself a nuclear fusion reactor. Once rockets get close enough, gravity takes over, and the nuclear waste is drawn into the sun, dissolving as it enters the sun's atmosphere. A secondary option is the planet Mercury. It is uninhabitable and close enough to the sun that all deposited materials would do no harm to the sun."

After more in-depth research and consultations with NASA, space agencies of other countries, and private rocket businesses, Augustus announced his intentions. From the Yucca Mountain Nuclear Waste Repository in Nevada, in one of several below ground tunnels, he stood in front of several black-labeled, yellow radioactive waste containers stacked three high. With those as backdrop, the chief executive presented a simple-in-concept, complex-to-execute plan to the world.

> Today, burning trash is banned in favor of clean air to breathe. Refuse in landfills pollutes the earth and its decomposition by-products may seep into underground aquifers. Garbage on barges submerged in

oceans may endanger sea life and ocean food sources. After vitrification, which essentially turns liquefied radioactive waste into a more stable glass-like substance, the existing procedure is to bury hazardous nuclear materials in caves such as you see behind me now.

If we continue on our current path, ultimately the people of the earth will have run out of land, destroyed the seas, and filled underground storage sites. At that time, the planet's humans will be forced to address overflowing landfills, polluted seas, and radioactive caves. Currently, all that is being accomplished is delay of the inevitable. I, along with millions of the world's inhabitants, do not want to pass that legacy on to future generations.

As citizens of the globe, we have taken monumental steps to clean the air and water. I propose efforts be immediately undertaken to resolve a second pollution challenge — removal of all radioactive materials from the planet. Using the concept of "fire and forget," encapsulated nuclear and radioactive waste will be mounted on top of rockets and fired into outer space. Once free of earth's gravitational pull, the hazardous materials will follow a pre-charted course to their ultimate destination.

The program would reestablish old, reinvigorate existing,

and create new industries in the fields of aerospace, outer space, steel, shipbuilding, transportation, technology, security, and communications. Nearly every field of endeavor would be impacted, including construction, housing, utilities, food service, refuse management, and physical sciences. In addition, this program would involve every nuclear energy and nuclear weapons nation in the world. The U.S. would become the earth's leading—and only—nuclear waste materials eliminator.

Special ocean-going ships, designed by America's naval and marine architects, built with United States manufactured steel, assembled in America's shipyards by shipwrights, and sailed by U.S. Merchant Marines, would carry the hazardous cargo from seaports around the globe to the launch island. New trucks, trains, and rocket payload containers would also be designed and constructed to carry the nuclear waste from land-based sites to seaports.

In addition to Bailey's initial launch site factors provided to her dad that Christmas, administration officials determined the selected island had to have certain characteristics. The location had to be isolated to preclude the possibility of any debris from a malfunctioning rocket falling onto a populated area such as Hawaii or South America. It had to have a deep water harbor to facilitate the offloading of ocean-going vessels and available terrain large enough to support, maintain, and sustain the infrastructure necessary to assemble, fuel, position and launch rockets—a minimum of one launch per day with a goal of three launches per day—all year long. The island itself would be transformed into a small city-state spaceport.

Guam, American Samoa, and Northern Marianas, as U.S. territories, were first considered, followed by Christmas Island under Australian control, and then the independent Marshall Islands. All met the criteria and possessed existing infrastructure. Rota Island in the southern portion of the United States Commonwealth of Northern Mariana Islands was ultimately selected.

After initial investments, the entire project's day-to-day operational costs would be financed by fees levied against every country that desired to eliminate its nuclear waste from within their borders. It would take a public-private partnership of the international community to make this dream a reality.

The concept received nearly universal praise, and many nations signed on to the project. American businesses and unions liked the job creation aspects. The environmental community supported the overall concept but had some reservations. Many scientists expressed concern about the potential impact on Mercury and any negative effects on the earth from the possible increase in radiation caused by solar flares, were the sun to be the primary waste site.

One year after Augustus' speech, a successful test launch took place from the Kennedy Space Center at Cape Canaveral, Florida. That flight, loaded only with scientific instruments, was directed at the sun. A similar instrument-loaded rocket, launched from Vandenberg AFB in California, was sent to Mercury. A small payload of nuclear waste and instruments to measure any effects on the sun comprised a successful third mission. The fourth rocket, containing payload similar to that of the previous flight, was delayed as debates about turning Mercury into a nuclear trash site raged. Eventually, it too was launched. Program growth continued into the next decade after Augustus left office but slowed as scientists and environ-mentalists continued to question the wisdom of dumping nuclear waste into space.

President You

Chapter 21

Energy and Environment

climate *n.* The typical temperature and weather conditions of a region.

Climate, the totality of weather for a given region taken over a long period of time.

weather *n.* The state of the atmosphere with respect to cold, heat, rainfall, drought, and storms.

Weather, the general condition of the atmosphere at a given time and place as regards to temperature, precipitation, sunshine, cloudiness, humidity, atmospheric pressure, and velocity and direction of wind.

environment *n.* Surroundings, esp. the conditions and influences under which one lives.

energy *n.* Effective force; vigor; activity in physics, the capacity for doing work.

Energy. Energy is divided...into two forms, potential and kinetic, potential energy being stored in a motionless system,...Kinetic energy is energy of motion, and is contained in a moving mass, or a beam of radiation.... Modern civilization depends for its existence upon sources of available energy.

In mid-March of his third year in office, with perhaps the

most iconic fixture—Old Faithful "Eternity's Timepiece" in Yellowstone, the nation's first National Park established in March 1872—as his stage, Augustus outlined his plan for establishment of America's future Energy and Environmental policy. The predominantly clear sky was sapphire blue, dotted with cotton ball puffs of cumulus clouds. The temperature was an unseasonably mild 70 degrees Fahrenheit and the prevailing westerlies provided a slight breeze. The sun shone bright. Dark green fir trees, looking black from a distance, stood in the background—vertical columns sporadically aligned on a tapestry floor of beige, brown, and white earth. Grayish-white steam vented upwards from the mouth of the small sulfur-colored mound of soil to dissipate in the wind. President Treatise waited patiently for the famous geyser to erupt and spew its white boiling liquid more than 100 feet into the surrounding air. It was the introduction to his speech.

> Climate Change exists. As a boy, I remember every summer afternoon around four o'clock, dark, water-laden clouds would form above my neighborhood, followed by a brief, violent, refreshing downpour of rain that cooled the air and cleansed the earth. It was all over in five or ten minutes. You could set your watch by those showers. Today those regular deluges no longer soak the field where I played sandlot baseball. That may not be scientific evidence, but long-time city dwellers and generations of farmers can tell you the differences in climate between now and a half a century ago. They should be heard, and we should listen.

We cannot ignore the fact that more than one hundred twenty-five years ago, patients ill with consumption were told by their doctors to move to the hot, arid Southwestern United States. Now many of those dry areas are beset with humidity and smog after rivers have been dammed, lakes and reservoirs created, communities and large cities established, and where water inundates lush green lawns. Not very scientific, but a practical reality.

The debate is not whether earth's climate is changing or why or who is to blame—whether it is the normal cycle of earth, Mother Nature, or Man. The debate is what, if anything can or should be done.

He reminded fellow citizens that more than a century before, "Conservationist President" Theodore Roosevelt established 150 national forests, 51 federal bird preserves, 18 national monuments, 5 national parks, and 4 national game preserves. He also protected 230 million acres of land. Augustus quoted President Roosevelt:

We have become great because of the lavish use of our resources. But the time has come to inquire seriously what will happen when our forests are gone, when the coal, the iron, the oil, and the gas are exhausted, when the soils have still further impoverished and washed into streams, polluting the rivers, denuding the fields and obstructing navigation.

It is also vandalism wantonly to destroy or to permit the destruction of what is beautiful in nature, whether it be a cliff, a forest, or a species of mammal or bird. Here in the United States we turn our rivers and streams into sewers and dumping-grounds, we pollute the air, we destroy forests, and exterminate fishes, birds, and mammals—not to speak of vulgarizing charming landscapes with hideous advertisements.

Augustus stated, "I could not have said it better," and informed the people in that same spirit and vein, he would host a summit for energy and environmental leaders in May of the following year. They would be tasked with the development of America's energy and environment policy for the near-term (25 years), mid-term (50 years), and long term (100 years).

The goal was to present Congress with a single agreed upon national plan, much like our Founding Fathers did when they hashed out the Constitution and presented it to the people. Stakeholder attendance was limited to one representative per industry. This agent would have full legal and binding authority to agree to the terms of the final proposal, must bring all requisite documentation, and must be prepared and willing to stay at least one full month.

Lodging at the conference site was limited, so one final and very important factor was considered. It took more than 50 Founding Fathers to draft the Constitution. It was difficult enough dealing with 535 members of Congress. Augustus did not want to attempt to create policy with more than 3,000 energy and environment delegates. He advised everyone that before the Energy and Environment Convention next May, members of like-minded groups were to convene their own meetings, determine their common interests, develop their positions, and select one person who would represent their perspective. All expenses to, from, and at the conference would be paid by the government. Each of the following agencies, causes, clubs, groups, individuals, industries or organizations, was invited, as were others:

- Energy: Coal, gas, geothermal, nuclear, oil, solar, space, water, wind, and wood
- Environment: Clean (Air, Water, Land), endangered species, save the flora and fauna, and anti-climate and pro-climate change
- Waste disposal: Incineration, landfill, nuclear materials storage, ocean dumping, recycling, and sewage treatment
- Transportation: Airplane (passenger and cargo), automobile, bus (city, cross country, schools, tourist), helicopter, limousine, taxi and ride sharing services, motorcycle, motor and wind racing (land, sea, air), railroad (passenger and cargo), light rail and trolley, recreation (RV, ATV, off-road, boating, flying), shipping (cargo, container, oil, natural gas), aerospace, subways, tourism (ocean, river, lake cruise lines), and trucking
- Government: Bureau of Indian Affairs, Bureau of Land Management, Bureau of Ocean Energy Management, Bureau of Reclamation, Centers for Disease Control and Prevention, Chemical Safety and Hazard Investigation Board, Coast Guard, Corps of Engineers, Environmental Protection Agency, Fish and Wildlife Service, Federal Aviation Admini-

stration, Federal Railroad Administration, Forest Service, Maritime Administration, Migratory Bird Conservation Commission, National Aeronautics and Space Administration, National Railroad Passenger Corporation (AMTRAK), National Marine Fisheries Service, National Ocean Service, National Oceanic and Atmospheric Administration, National Park Service, National Science Foundation, National Weather Service, Natural Resources Conservation Service, Nuclear Regulatory Agency, Office of Fossil Energy, and Pipeline and Hazardous Materials Safety Administration

— Cabinet: Agriculture, Commerce, Defense, Education, Energy, Health and Human Services, Housing and Urban Development, Interior, Labor, State, Transportation, and Treasury departments

Fourteen months later the summit was convened in a remote Alaskan locale. To reach the facility required two hours' drive by bus on a tundra road that traversed a stunted spruce forest, forded glacier-fed streams of whitish ice-cold water, and ended in an emerald glen adjacent to a crystal blue lake.

At the facility, cars were not allowed except for those of the owners and key staff of the lodge. Everyone, including resort kitchen, cleaning, and maid service staff, was bused to the site; the exceptions were the president and vice president—who arrived by helicopter—some Secret Service, and the White House communications team, who brought equipment necessary for the head of state to maintain contact with world leaders.

The lodge for sleeping and dining was of a log cabin motif. The lobby displayed snowshoes, cross-country skis, an army akhio, an Inuit qamutiik, Eskimo artifacts, and Iditarod race paraphernalia. The floors were covered with colorful, woven area rugs. Pictures of Alaskan landscapes, the Northern Lights, and native wildlife hung on the walls. In consideration of selected attendees, all taxidermied animals, fish, and fowl had been removed and placed in storage. Each room was equipped with basic necessities and few amenities.

To replicate the circumstances of the Founding Fathers during the Constitutional Convention, the sleeping accommodations provided none of the communication conveniences, such as Internet, wireless cell phone access, and television. All electronic devices for communicating with the outside world were, in effect, useless—which was one of the reasons Augustus had selected this location. He wanted the attendees to focus on the mission at hand and not be distracted by demands from the entities they represented or by newshounds.

The first day at the lodge was consumed with routine processes associated with any event, including check-in, registration, issuing credentials, and assigning rooms.

Day two began in the nearby meeting facility at nine a.m., where President Treatise and Vice President Addums greeted and thanked everyone as each person entered the convention hall. The Cabinet secretaries in attendance were in the same receiving line. After less than two hours, all delegates had arrived and had taken their seats at assigned tables. Seating was arranged in such a fashion that representatives from different energy or environment areas of expertise commingled at each table.

Shortly after everyone was settled, Augustus began his welcoming remarks. He reiterated his comments of over a year ago and reemphasized their challenge. Throughout the day, the president traversed the summit, stopped at every table, answered questions, clarified his intent, and visited with the attendees. The opening session ended about four o'clock that afternoon, giving way to a less formal "meet and greet" social activity. President Treatise, Vice President Addums, and Cabinet secretaries remained until closing, about nine o'clock that evening.

On the third day, discussions were held in earnest, and, as expected, progressed slowly. That day began with comments from Augustus.

> Months ago, I quoted a couple of President Theodore Roosevelt's thoughts on conservation and saving the environment. I made similar remarks to open this summit. Those comments might have given you the impression I was pro-green and anti-fossil fuel. Today, my remarks and actions address the other side of the coin.
>
> Reflect on how your life, and your family's lives, might be different without energy provided from fossil fuels. Examine your communities without the means to generate electricity or power. Consider your country's processes to convert raw materials into airplanes, automobiles, a child's bicycle, or laptop computer. Contemplate your world without energy to refrigerate or cook food or boil water. Ponder how, without automation, you might turn lambs' wool into clothing, or animal skins into shoes. As you work through your tasks today, these weeks, and this month, think about the life of ancient

man before he gained the ability to harness
fire.

With those additional thoughts, the attendees began their
deliberations. Meanwhile, President Treatise put his plan into
action. That day in May, the weather was unseasonably hot and
humid, and he ordered the air conditioning to be shut off. As
the day wore on, the temperature in the facility rose to an
uncomfortable 92 degrees. Heated discussions devolved into
temper tantrums. As the day's work ended and participants left
the conference hall, they came upon their evening meal,
displayed out of doors, on row after row of tables for perusal
and consumption.

No containerized beverages were provided. To drink water,
individuals had to kneel on the shore of the lake and use their
hands to scoop the liquid into their dry mouths. Berries, fruits,
and nuts as well as raw, uncooked grains and vegetables were
available. Caged live creatures included birds, mammals, and
reptiles. If attendees wanted to eat meat, they had to select their
food of choice, kill it, skin it, clean it, and consume it raw. No
weapons were provided—bare hands and teeth were to be used.
No fires for cooking were permitted. Not one delegate accepted
that challenge and instead only availed themselves of readily
available edibles.

Augustus' morning comments were reinforced as one
participant after another discovered the electricity, gas, and
plumbing to their rooms had been turned off all day long. That
night, individual rooms were hot and humid and without water
for bathing or using the toilet. Lighting inside each room came
through the windows. Daylight hours in Alaska that time of
year ran from 1:30 a.m. to 10:30 p.m. By morning, everything
mechanical was restored to normal and a more pleasing

breakfast greeted the angry horde. After a morning of venting, cussing, and discussing on his or her own or in small groups, the assemblage reconvened on the summit's fourth day at one o'clock. Augustus stood in front of the gathered mass and withstood the vocal and verbal assaults by perturbed attendees.

> The point of yesterday's exercise was that too many individuals talk about such issues, having never experienced them.
>
> A purist environmentalist cannot exist except as Adam and Eve in the Garden of Eden. Even then, Eve disturbed Mother Nature when she plucked the apple from the tree. Without energy, almost every modern convenience would not exist or function. To enjoy many of the fruits of our labors, we must utilize energy. In using energy, some pollution is necessary, the destruction of selected environments inevitable, and the loss of creatures unfortunate. The irreparable harm to and potential destruction of our planet may be a distinct possibility.
>
> What you are trying to accomplish this month is important and may very well determine the future of America, the survival of earth, the lives of your children's, children's children, and the many generations to follow. The challenge before you is to reach an acceptable and feasible balance. We—you—must decide here and now, for the sake of the larger picture, to stop the petty and ultimately meaningless ideological turf wars.

We—you—must reach a consensus with which everyone can agree.

Our Constitution is not perfect and not everyone was happy with the final product, but overall it turned out to be a great thing. You, for the greater good, like our Founding Fathers who pledged their lives, fortunes, and sacred honor to create a new nation and a new government, must create a new energy and environment plan that will last for generations to come.

As the first week ended, some progress occurred. The opening of the second week began with each table group presenting their proposals. Groups were then realigned for week two. The president departed the convention and allowed attendees to concentrate on their mission. The vice president remained and used his effective negotiating skills to keep everyone focused on the mission at hand. As the days of May and the discussions continued, Augustus returned twice, lent his influence and support, provided guidance, and received updates. Near the summit's conclusion, with a draft proposal imminent, delegates requested an additional week to finalize some details. That extension was granted, and President Treatise received a final product for presentation to Congress. Unfortunately, as it had been with the Founding Fathers, a few agents could not accept the whole or selected parts of the document and refused to endorse it.

Augustus read the entire proposal in detail and spent a full day asking the authors questions about the agreement. He wanted a full understanding of both the pro and con issues. The chief executive needed that knowledge as a foundation for negotiations with Congress and so he could respond appropriately to media questions. The document was presented to the legislature after their August recess. Unfortunately, both the House of Representatives and Senate began nitpicking portions, depending on their allegiances to special interests. It was, after all, an election year. It took all the energy Augustus could muster, his bully pulpit, and Forrestor Addums' negotiating skills to convince Congress to keep the major tenets of the proposal intact and generate legislation eventually signed into law.

Chapter 22

Election Day Moved

The electors of President and Vice President shall
be appointed in each State on the Tuesday next
after the first Monday in the month of November
of the year in which they are to be appointed...

(Statutes at Large, 28th Congress, Second Session,
Statute II, Chapter I, An Act to establish a uniform
time for holding elections for electors of President
and Vice President in all the States of the Union,
approved January 23, 1845)

From when Augustus began voting after graduation from
high school, throughout his adult life and into his presidency,
he saw an ever-increasing number of Americans not performing
their civic duty of voting. As news media reported and polls
showed, too many voters were disenfranchised by political and
election processes. A variety of reasons underpinned public
indifference. Too many people believed candidate selection was
just a choice between the lesser of two evils. Others thought
everyone running for office was a liar, a cheat, and a snake in
the grass. Some felt it did not matter who served in the Capitol
or White House; their vote did not change anything. Party
machinery truly determined who was elected to high office, not
voters.

One often reported example was Party rules which, regardless of how participants voted or caucused during each state's

primary election procedures, allowed "special" delegates to cast a ballot for their candidate of choice. In essence, the election of the person who won by popular vote was nullified by weighted delegate votes. "Why bother to have a public and primary election whatsoever? Just let delegates sort it out at national party conventions," were feelings expressed by some. Pundits opined, "Small wonder voters no longer trust the election process and feel the system is rigged."

Another reason for disgust arose from reports of election results—declarations of winners before final ballots were cast or counted and polls were closed. Those prognostications were based on as little as ten percent of reporting precincts. There was no empirical evidence to confirm such reports kept voters from the polling stations, but there were historical cases where exit polling and media forecasts were wrong. The "Dewey Defeats Truman" headline of November 1948 being the most famous.

Additionally, many citizens identified themselves as "single candidate" or "one issue" voters. Simply, if their preferred individual was not on the ballot or no candidate supported that person's "chosen" issue, individuals saw no reason to vote. Loyal party members stayed home on Election Day if they did not like their party's nominee; the same was true about any candidate's stance on a particular issue.

Analysis of earlier elections indicated the days of choosing a president whose overall campaign platform was in line with that of the voter were passing. Voters were more likely to have a single-issue mindset; sometimes this resulted in refusing to support an overall agenda. Both those conclusions explained the increasing numbers of voters who declared themselves independent rather than join or affiliate with a particular political party. Independents became increasingly significant players in national elections and they were heavily courted.

Individuals no longer felt loyal to one party or another. There appeared to be no distinct difference between Democrats or Republicans vying for support. Or else the parties were so egregiously far left or far right that they were too radical for the vast majority of voters. Any differences espoused were often made moot by the "do as we say, not as we do" actions of those elected. That abandonment of traditional political parties led to less involvement. Plus, the "ins" of high office counted on party loyalist participation and the inaction of independent thinking or disgruntled voters.

Many other excuses for not going to the polls were offered by citizens: inconvenience was a reason often used; lack of time was another. Too often people chose to ignore, shun, or boycott voting, and by not going to the polls, they left politicians to their own devices. Failure to cast a ballot assured Legislative Branch and White House continued dysfunction and contributed to further dissatisfaction with and lack of trust in government.

Those attitudes explained why members of Congress had a 95% re-election rate, even though as an organization it had an approval rating around 15 percent or less. In other words, 85 of 100 Americans thought their elected officials were doing a lousy job. Yet those same poor performers were repeatedly reelected, primarily because disgruntled voters stayed away from the polls and party loyalists cast ballots.

Augustus believed it was shameful that in the United States, the freest democracy in the world, where citizens had the right to elect their government by voting, there was less voter participation than in other lands, his election being an anomaly.

From America's beginning, eligible voter
participation in presidential election years

235

used to be in the 70% to 80% range. Over the past few decades, it has been in the 50% to 60% range. For every off-year federal election of Congress since 1960, less than 50% (low of 36%, high of 48%) of the people voted. On average, 60 million registered voters do not cast a ballot. That means 100% of all citizens are being governed by minority rule.

American foreign policy promotes United States' democracy as the model form of government the rest of the world should adopt. Yet our participation in voting, the most democratic of all actions a citizen can take, gives a poor example to emulate. America's enemies cite that lack of voter interest as justification not to adopt the United States' "of the people, by the people, for the people" way of life.

President Treatise decided to address these challenges by proposing to declare Election Day a national holiday. He believed more voters would go to the polls if the country were, in essence, completely closed for business. In an effort to reduce the potential for people taking a four-day holiday weekend and not voting, he proposed breaking a nearly two-hundred-year-old tradition by readjusting Election Day from Tuesday to Wednesday.

Augustus felt once every four years the nation could afford a total shutdown for one day. By "totally shut down," he meant from one minute after midnight at the beginning of Election Day until one minute before midnight at the end of Election Day, every public entity, nonprofit organization, and private sector business released its employees, turned off the lights, closed and locked its doors, and ceased operations completely.

He reasoned that closing for a nationwide presidential election was not an issue. Federal, state, county, municipal agencies, the Post Office, and schools already closed during the thirteen existing federal holidays, as did banks, the stock exchange, and commodities market. Some entities even closed for designated state holidays. Many businesses routinely closed for annual inventory, and a multitude of entities closed every Saturday and Sunday and three-day weekend. Restaurants often closed one day per week. Faith-based businesses closed on their day of religious services. Many facilities periodically closed for sports team victory parades, St. Patrick's' Day, Cinco de Mayo, other ethnic celebrations, or the anniversary of a town's founding or a territory becoming a state. In addition, businesses and organizations that remained open during existing federal holidays often did so with reduced staffing; the major noticeable exceptions were retailers for holiday sales events, theme parks, tourism, and the travel industry.

Under his plan, added to entities that already shut their doors was everything else—amusement parks, casinos, communication businesses, constructors and contractors, gas stations, grocers, haulers, health-care providers, maintainers, manufacturers, repairers, restaurateurs, retailers, service industries, shippers, telemarketers, theaters, transporters, and wholesalers—every public, for-profit, and not-for-profit entity in the U.S.. Everything was to be closed to the maximum extent possible. President Treatise's plan eliminated Election Day as a reason for shopping at the next best sale. He wanted every citizen focused on his or her civic duty of voting. With everything closed, people had no option except to vote—or stay at home.

By necessity, and obviously, some places would remain open, albeit at reduced staffing as much as possible—which many already accomplished for current holidays. Those included police and fire departments, hospitals and ambulance services, nursing homes and hospice care facilities, jails and prisons, utilities, military installations, Emergency Operations Centers, selected factories, some soup kitchens and homeless shelters, and the like. Taxis, busses, subways, ride sharing, and other local modes of transportation would remain open to transport voters to and from the polls.

Even radio, television, cable, satellite, Internet broadcast networks, social media programs, and stations were to be closed except for their Emergency Alert System operations. Much of their normal, taped programming remained, as scheduled, but live broadcasts were limited. No political ads would be allowed on Election Day. Media outlets would be encouraged to broadcast educational programming all about the United States, its history, the Constitution, the election process, voting, other American topics interspersed with patriotic music and reminders to vote. The government would provide multiple Public Service Announcements tailored to and in support of those broadcasts. But there was to be no reporting on any election arrival and exit polling, no predictions or prognostications, and no results announced until the last polling station closed— at 7 p.m. Hawaii time; midnight Eastern time. Media, however, could interrupt broadcasts for an "I lost" concession speech as well as the corresponding "I won" declaration.

The chief executive's objective was to eliminate any possible misinterpretation of election information that, no matter how small, might influence a citizen to vote or not cast a ballot. Augustus did not view this action a violation of the First Amendment. It was merely a delay in reporting, an activity media voluntarily performed numerous times for reasons and circumstances, such as national security, not releasing the names of abused children or rape victims, and not showing photos of corpses or video of beheadings.

The changed statute contained tax incentives for businesses not to open. Any closed entity was allowed an average full day's income tax deduction equal to 1/365 of its annual gross revenues. Conversely, if a non-essential entity were open, it paid a fine equal to 1/365 of its annual gross revenues. All employees (salaried, wage earner, exempt, non-exempt, union, non-union, temporary, part-time, full-time, and contract) who worked on Election Day were to be paid overtime. Use of the new law as a bargaining point in labor union-management negotiations was restricted.

Also included in the proposed legislation were changes to voter registration and education. It provided for high schools and colleges to register all U.S. citizens who became eighteen years of age. Registration was to occur after children were educated on multiple aspects of their country's Constitution, government, and voting processes. All four years of this intense high school education was designed to prepare children to be better-informed citizen-voters. Mandated core subject matter was arranged by class year.

Beginning with ninth grade, civics introduced students to the Declaration of Independence as well as the basic structure and broad overview of our government, its three branches, the duties and responsibilities of each, how each entity operated, the system of checks and balances, and, from a historical perspective, how and why the Founding Fathers created such a government.

Tenth graders learned about the Constitution, its authors, and the convention that ultimately led to its creation. In addition, they were educated about the historical documents (Magna Carta, The Mayflower Compact, Articles of Con-federation, Mount Vernon and Annapolis Conventions, The Virginia and New Jersey Plans, the Connecticut Compromise, the Three-Fifths Compromise, Bill of Rights) and their relationships, which led to the final document.

Juniors were taught the history and philosophies of, and the individuals behind, the past and present political parties since the country's creation.

Seniors read and discussed the writings of Silas Dogood and all Federalist Papers to gain an appreciation of the issues of colonial times and the thoughts of the Founding Fathers as they created the Constitution—and how many of those initial concepts were settled and decided upon or are still being discussed, ignored, or bastardized today.

Augustus believed his change to the federal statute would increase voter participation through education and encourage more people to get involved in their government. However, businesses objected to being taxed and told when to close their doors and cease operations. Unions supported the additional holiday and overtime wages, but disliked the inability to include that provision in labor-management negotiations. Media totally rejected the idea based on the First Amendment. Teachers' unions felt Washington, in this particular case, had no business telling schools what to teach. His biggest opposition came from the long-established political parties, which felt voter registration was their arena.

Despite the objections, Augustus' proposed statutory change was eventually adopted with limitations. Election Day was moved to Wednesday and declared a National Holiday—but that was all. Schools continued to eliminate civics, government, and history from their curriculum in favor of more "tolerant" lessons; businesses remained open to operate and conduct sales events; workers' overtime wages remained negotiable; the press was allowed to report poll results and project winners; and political parties continued campaign advertising. Election Day would be treated no differently than any other federal holiday.

President You

Chapter 23

Political Information and Affiliation

political *adj.* Pertaining to government.

information *n.* Communicated knowledge or news.

affiliation. *n.* to join or become connected, as, to *affiliate* with a political party.

Foreign nations or wealthy citizens of other countries attempt to influence United States elections through "back door" campaign contributions, cyber-warfare and hacking, disinformation, false news, or political advertisements. As a result, accusations of collusion are levied against officials of all political persuasions. To deter foreign influence efforts, President Treatise sent to Congress the Political Information and Affiliation Act. That specifically designed legislation sought to enhance the Federal Election Commission campaign advertising statutes. It required campaigns or other entities supporting or rebuking candidates, party platforms, policies, or proposed legislation fully disclose the nature of their existence.

Public, Coordinated, and Electioneering Communications laws require candidates' advertisements to state who they are and that they approve their message, and provide a disclaimer stating who paid for the ad and who authorized—or did not authorize—the message. In many cases, party affiliation is mentioned or visible, but not always—it is not required. Entities that advertise for or against a particular candidate or policy initiative must merely state or display their name, address, or website. They, too, are required to provide a similar disclaimer. The law requires little else regarding identification.

Consequently, the voting public at large does not know in any detail who or what is really behind any supportive or derogatory message. Administrations, agencies, associations, boards, businesses, commissions, contributors, corporations, committees, clubs, donors, enemies, foreign governments, fraternities, groups, guilds, individuals, industries, leagues, lobbyists, memberships, orders, organizations, politicians, Political Action Committees, the self-employed, sororities, unions, and the like know that. Entities also know most voters will never research who or what that posts the advertisement. Individuals and organizations use public ignorance to enact or defeat legislation for their political advantage, monetary gain, or personal benefit.

When it came to electing candidates and enacting legislation that determined the fate of the American people and the United States, Augustus felt an informed voter was crucial. All too often actors or famous persons were paid to appear in advertisements, thus masking the real personality behind the message. President Treatise believed if an individual or entity was so committed for or against a politician or idea and was willing to spend thousands or millions of dollars in their efforts, then that person or organization should take full ownership, pride in, and responsibility for their position. In other words, replace "Put your money where your mouth is" with "You made a political advertisement, now back in up—in person."

From the chief executive's perspective, citizens had a right to know if a foreign government, for example, through campaign advertising and social media, attempted to influence for whom and what Americans voted. Individuals and entities should willingly and fully disclose to voters who, what, when, where, how, and why of their political advertisement. Borrowing Missouri's state motto, "'Show Me' the person behind the message," demanded Augustus.

The proposed law was simple.

> Regardless the communications medium utilized, the owner or most senior person, by whatever title held, of any entity, shall personally appear in the advertisement and that individual shall, in verbal, audible, readable and written form, provide his or her:

- Full name
- Nationality and citizenship (including dual/multiple)
- Place or places of residence (city, county, state, country)
- Voter registration status (including which state, country)
- Political party affiliation (or none)
- Job title

Additional information to be provided:
- The name of entity they represent
- Whether it is a United States or foreign entity (if foreign, the country)
- The location of that entity's headquarters (city, county, state, country)
- Its political party affiliation or the party it primarily supports (or none)

    – As a member of said entity, they authorized the message in the advertisement

    – And, who or what entity paid for the advertisement.

    When all the above is properly included in the advertisement, the owner or most senior person of the entity can broadcast and/or publish his or her message.

Augustus told citizens, "If this legislation is enacted, at least the voter will have more information to conduct their own research into the person and organization and their relationship to the candidate, political party, legislation, policy, or cause being promoted or opposed."

Every year he was in office, President Treatise's proposal was rejected; even though in the not-too-distant and historical past, collusion was alleged to have taken place between the two major parties and a foreign government. In addition, foreign individuals and governments had purchased, through shadow organizations, advertising on multiple social media sites. The first year the legislation was thrown out—not even reviewed. In the second year, when all representatives and one third of senators came up for re-election, Augustus used the bully pulpit and took his case directly to the people. That generated some interest—enough for Congress to address the legislation. However, their speeches were merely theater, as many congressional mutterings so often were. Another year went by, and it never made it out of any committees.

The influences of forces on legislators were too significant to warrant serious consideration for helping the U.S. voters determine, in an advertisement, what may be a valid argument for or against a particular candidate or proposed legislation, as opposed to a personal vendetta or efforts by foreign agents to influence America's election results. Those external pressures on members of Congress proved the chief executive's point why citizens needed the law. Up to the point he left office, Augustus promoted passage of this simple act of transparency to no avail.

President You

Chapter 24

Fraud

fraud *n.* Deliberate deceit; deception planned and
executed with intent to deprive another of property or rights.

Fraud, a willful misrepresentation of facts either
by conduct, false assertion, or such suppression of
part of the truth as makes the rest positively false,
with the result that the innocent party acts upon it
and suffers harm.

Our nation's legal basis for existence, the Constitution, is
mute regarding political party association by citizens running
for elected office. As our system of government began, the first
few congresses were composed of pro-administration and anti-
administration representatives, senators, and vice presidents;
even President Washington was unaffiliated with any political
party.

The Founding Fathers well understood that as the former
individual colonies got used to being a single group of united
states, the nation grew, new territories became states, and times
changed, so would citizens' beliefs, politicians, and the ideas
they represented. Throughout America's history, new concepts
allowed for and led to the creation and demise of a variety of
political parties.

Over time, parties took the name of their candidates or
presidents: Adams, Adams-Clay Federalist, Adams-Clay

Republican, Crawford Republican, Jacksonian, and Jackson Republican. Some candidates declared political affiliation based on his or her individual or their constituents' beliefs: Farmer Alliance Party, Farmer-Labor, Free Soil, Law and Order, Re-Adjuster, Silver, and Unionist. There were even American (Know-Nothing), Conservative, Democratic-Republican, Federalist, Independent Democratic, Independent Republican, Liberal Republican, Populist, Progressive, and Whig parties. Gradually, political perspectives were narrowed and focused into the two major parties of today: Democratic and Republican. Still several other named and lesser-known parties in the 2016 presidential election existed, as well: American Delta Party, Constitution, Green, Libertarian, Party for Socialism and Liberation, Reform Party, and about ten others.

Regardless of political association, it was generally expected and mostly believed that individuals elected to high office would serve in that position and dutifully perform their responsibilities on behalf of all the people. Politicians would not shirk their obligations to all, even though their views leaned more towards those who got them elected. They would, according to House Concurrent Resolution 175, "Put loyalty to the highest moral principles and to country above loyalty to persons, party, or Government departments" and "Never use any information coming to him confidentially in the performance of govern-mental duties as a means for making private profit." However, since the beginning of the twenty-first century, the public widely believed politicians regarded serving in Congress as a mere stepping stone—a ticket to be punched for greater individual wealth and power.

President Treatise was concerned about many aspects of politicians' actions. Campaigning and fund raising, for example, was not illegal, certainly was not immoral, most likely was not unethical, and probably did not meet the criminal definition of fraud. Nevertheless, Augustus felt politicians who left the Capitol halls to campaign and raise money for either re-election to their existing post or election to another office, committed fraud, as campaigning and fund raising took them away from their official duties and responsibilities. He also believed once any politician accepted campaign contributions, a written financial contract existed with the donors in addition to the many "Get me elected and I'll do this and that for you" verbal contracts made daily.

The chief executive thought while Congress was in session, politicians who were away from Washington making speeches, attending fundraisers, eating state fair food, marching in parades, kissing babies, and appearing on talk shows instead of working in the Capitol committed fraud—they were not fulfilling their contract with the people of their district or state. Too many politicians did not vote on legislation, failed to attend important hearings, missed meetings on relevant issues, and otherwise ignored constituents because they campaigned during their 125 congressional workdays. As examples, he highlighted the "number of missed votes" campaign strategy used by one challenger against a serving Senate rival in 2016, and news reports of the percentage of missed votes by several 2020 candidates for president.

As Augustus saw it, each member of Congress was paid an annual base salary of around $174,000 per year, which equated to $1,392 per day given they only worked 125 days per year, computed as $174 per hour for an eight-hour day. By contrast, federal minimum wage was $7.25 per hour, several states' minimum wage was $10.20 per hour, and nationally the average hourly wage was $22.60. Being paid for not showing up at work, while campaigning in another city, district, state, or across America to become a governor, representative, senator, vice president, or president, was fraudulent. For the average wage-earning American, employers frowned on employees who were paid while missing work for visiting career fairs, attending job interviews, and seeking employment elsewhere. If found out, the person could be fired for cheating the business out of a day's wages for work not performed (a mere $58 at minimum wage for 8 hours). When a senator or representative received $1,392 for failing to show up for work because of a job search (campaign), nothing happened. Augustus believed something should.

"How many senators or representatives promise voters they will serve the entire term in office, only to change their minds and run for president before their terms are finished?" Augustus asked. To rectify these situations, President Treatise proposed new legislation. If approved, the statute required members of Congress to serve their full elected term in office; exceptions were allowed for appointment to the Cabinet, selection to the Supreme Court, acceptance of an ambassadorship, military service, terminal illness, and, obviously, death. Campaigning for a different elected office, while still serving, was banned. Resigning or departing early to seek election to any federal, state, or local office was forbidden. That aspect of the law was designed to ensure members met their full term obligation to the electorate.

In addition, after leaving office, each former member of Congress had to wait a minimum period of two years before announcing their candidacy for another elected position in government. That two-year wait rule applied, as well, to all political appointees seeking any federal elected position. The two calendar year window of non-elected office participation would begin in January effective the date each new Congress convened.

The proposed changes to existing public election law addressed three important goals. First, politicians fulfilled their contract with the people and remained at work during the 125 days or more Congress was in session. Second, politicians could not campaign, often across the country, for a different elected office during the 240-day congressional recess when they ostensibly were in their home states meeting with constituents. Third, politicians got a minimum two-year taste of the "real world" outside of and away from the influences of Washington. Despite support from the populace, the proposed changes to election law failed.

A second concern for President Treatise: Not only was the Constitution silent on the subject of political party association, it said nothing regarding individuals, candidates for office, or those already elected to office changing party affiliation. People were free to change party membership as they wished. What was becoming increasingly habitual, however, was elected officials changing alliances during the election cycle or after being elected to public office.

Such chameleon acts had occurred several times in the past. In one case, a serving member of Congress affiliated with one party to run for president, and after defeat, returned to Congress in his original party. Even a governor and state legislators, after being elected to office under the banner of one party, changed factions once sworn in. It seemed odd to President Treatise that a person who was a member of one political party, professed that philosophy, served in elected office as a member of that bloc, all of a sudden had an epiphany and changed association. Odder still was that voters seemed not to be bothered by such antics.

Augustus believed anyone elected to office as a member of

one political party and who, once in office, changed the proverbial "horse in mid-stream" to another political party committed an act of fraud. Voters identified with a party because that organization's vision, mission, platform, and reasons for existence espoused beliefs identical or similar to their own. Candidates for elected office and those elected to office represented a political party's tenets. That philosophy was validated when candidates and office holders spoke, wrote, advertised, and referred to party morals and values in order to garner monetary contributions and secure votes.

Any elected officials who changed political affiliation deprived constituents of their right to have their principles represented. Such officials abandoned a party's fundamental precepts and adopted the canons and conventions of another. A legal case should be made available on behalf of donors who acted upon an elected official's "misrepresentation of facts by conduct or false assertions"—claiming to be a Democrat, then becoming a Republican, for example. If voters contributed money to a candidate or official who failed to maintain political party core values, affiliation, association, or obligation, they suffered financial harm because the politician took money (property) under false pretenses.

Based on that rationale, the chief executive proposed another change to existing election law.

> Citizens serving in any federal elected public office or elected capacity shall immediately resign once they make the decision to change political party affiliation. Persons serving or seeking federal elected public office or elected capacity who decide to change political party affiliation shall

publicly announce that change and shall not seek federal elected office or elected capacity until two years after the date of their announcement. These same laws shall apply to all political appointees to federal office or capacity. Violation of these tenets and this statute shall be grounds for removal, recall, or impeachment.

"Currently," Augustus argued, "there is no law preventing any member of Congress, the vice president, or even the president from changing party affiliation once elected and sworn into office. That scenario may be considered ridiculous, but given the past attempts by foreign governments to influence our elections, the theory I just posited is entirely possible or, at least, plausible."

Augustus' second proposed statute, as written, also failed. The legislators, agreeing with the premise, however, changed the verbiage to read:

No elected or serving President or Vice President shall change political party affiliation. No person seeking the office of President or Vice President shall change political party affiliation less than four calendar years prior to announcing his or her candidacy seeking the office of President or Vice President. Violation of these tenets and this statute shall constitute a high Crime and Misdemeanor.

President Treatise vetoed that legislation, wanting to include all elected federal positions, but Congress overrode his veto and it became the law of the land.

The chief executive's separate attempt to prevent potential fraudulent or undue foreign influence by any future occupant of Congress or the White House was a more challenging piece of legislation—a constitutional amendment that would apply simultaneously to Article I, Section 2 and Article I, Section 3, and Article II, Section 1. It was designed to clarify the Fourteenth Amendment as it applied to persons seeking federal elected public office as representative, senator, vice president, or president. The proposed amendment read:

> A Citizen of the United States is any human being born in any of these United States, or an Incorporated Organized Territory of these United States that later became or becomes a State, or any State as defined by International Law, who was sired by parents, both of whom are United States citizens.

The basis for Augustus' concern was that there are thousands of Americans raised in foreign nations as citizens of that country. Their parents came to the U.S., gave birth to a child, and then returned to their native land. That child, since 1868 by common practice and publicly understood, is legally eligible to become a member of Congress, vice president, or president. Augustus wanted to clarify the Constitution and limit any future potential estoppel by silence or acquiescence litigation (i.e., the government is prevented from asserting a person, sired by one or more foreign parents, and who was born under the Fourteenth Amendment, cannot be a member of Congress, vice president or president since the government had the right and opportunity to do so earlier).

"It is within the realm of possibility," argued Augustus, "that a 'natural born Citizen,' raised in another country, could run for office as a traditional Democrat or Republican. Then, once in office, change to the Adalet ve Kalkinma Partisi (Islamist based on the conservative traditions of the Ottoman Empire), Communist (in the mold of China, Cuba, Russia, and Vietnam), Indian National Congress (secular party and social democratic platform), Pakistan Tehreek-e-Insaf (a welfare state, where the government is responsible for education, health and employ-ability of citizens), or Worker's Party (PT) of Brazil (a long-term strategy to construct an alternative to capitalism)."

Those opposed to the proposed amendment often referenced the foreign father of a former president and a parent of others who sought the highest office in the land. Service members who served America with honor and distinction and brought back "war spouses"—their children would be denied a chance to lead this great nation. The children of diplomats and business-persons in similar circumstances would also be denied the opportunity, it was argued. So too would be Americans' off-spring born in foreign lands.

Many in favor of the proposed amendment countered that existing law already provided for foreign spouses, as well as children of Americans born in other countries, to become citizens; if they did, there was no issue. They also cited that marriages between U.S. citizens and citizens of other countries many times ended in divorce. All too often, American children were taken by kidnapping or awarded by a court to the foreign parent, ended up in a foreign culture, and were raised as citizens of that land. In addition, some foreign parents in America illegally had no intention or desire to become citizens. Many non-citizens living in America denounced the U.S. at every turn and taught their American-born children hatred for the country. It was argued that those children should not be allowed elected federal office.

When the president left office, the amendment was still being processed through the stages of adoption or rejection by the states and their citizens; no definitive decision had been reached.

Chapter 25

Immigration

The term "alien" means any person not a citizen or national of the United States.

The term "immigrant" means every alien except an alien who is within one of the following classes of non immigrant aliens.

The term "immigration laws" includes this Act and all laws, conventions, and treaties of the United States relating to immigration, exclusion, deportation, expulsion, or removal of aliens.

(Section 101, Title 8, United States Code, §1101 (a) Immigration and Nationality Act)

Oath of Renunciation and Allegiance

I hereby declare, on oath, that I absolutely and entirely renounce and abjure all allegiance and fidelity to any foreign prince, potentate, state, or sovereignty, of whom or which I have heretofore been a subject or citizen;

that I will support and defend the Constitution and laws of the United States of America against all enemies, foreign and domestic;

that I will bear true faith and allegiance to the same;

that I will bear arms on behalf of the United States when required by law; that I will perform non-combatant service in the Armed Forces of the United States when required by the law; that I will perform work of national importance under civilian direction when required by law;

and that I take this obligation freely, without any mental reservation or purpose of evasion;

so help me God.

(Section 337, Title 8, United States Code, Chapter 12, Subchapter III, Part II, §1448, Immigration and Nationality Act)

Reforming America's immigration system was one of President Treatise's major achievements. Implemented piecemeal, the reformation took his entire presidency. Augustus used nearly every opportunity to tell the people,

All tallied, the United States' current Immigration and Nationality Act and its accompanying amendments, statutes, regulations, and rules for implementation have created hundreds of exceptions to granting green cards, work permits, and visas; as well as allowing aliens in the country illegally temporary legal or protective status. It has reached the point any foreigner can enter the U.S. illegally, reside in a sanctuary city, obtain a state drivers' license, receive a tuition-free college education, obtain food, acquire health care, and be granted temporary citizenship just for being a person from another country.

It had always perturbed Augustus that the decades-long immigration debate was couched in terms of "We versus They": politically, Democratic versus Republican; racially, white versus brown; linguistically, American versus Hispanic; financially, poor versus rich; economically, haves versus have nots; philosophically, capitalism versus socialism. Any person who attempted to conduct meaningful discussions about illegal aliens, undocumented workers, migrants, or immigration reform, immediately and systemically was labeled racist, bigot, and anti-immigrant; the words "illegal" and "alien" were conveniently removed by detractors.

The immigration debate seemed formulated as if it were 1840 and the United States was at war with Mexico—and commentary came only from the pro-Latino alien perspective. Some Americans who openly expressed strict enforcement of existing immigration laws experienced attacks on their children, their spouses were fired from jobs, employers were picketed or boycotted, cars were smashed, and their homes were set on fire.

Rarely, if ever, did national news media report on groups or interview individuals who represented thousands of citizens from other than Hispanic lands. Potential terrorist threats by aliens from predominately-Muslim Middle Eastern countries were discounted. The flags of Communist China, Ethiopia, India, Jamaica, The Philippines, or South Korea were not seen flying at America's public schools in celebration of that country's battle victory over some enemy or as a protest replacement for the Stars and Stripes. Other nationalities were not boycotting a city because the mayor appointed someone to a town commission to whom they objected. Illegal immigrant groups from other nations were not shown protesting in front of the White House or the Supreme Court. Those who believed in collusion between one president's campaign and Russia were mute when it came to undocumented Russians, some of whom may have voted in local elections. What was repeatedly broadcast and reported were Hispanics, many of whom lived in America illegally, vehemently voicing the mantra that deportation was a violation of human rights.

Other attempted debates in terms of legal versus illegal, right versus wrong, or fair versus unfair were often disrupted and foiled, as well. To the president it was simple. Card games, board games, sports games, even children's games had rules. Playing by the rules was right. Cheating was wrong. Children who violated rules were subject to expulsion or banishment from their group of friends. Many consumers sat in chairs, pitched a tent, slept overnight, and waited for their chance to purchase the latest gizmo or see that year's blockbuster movie. It was fair, upon arrival, to take a place at the back of that line and wait, allowing those in front to go first. To cut in line ahead of everyone else who had patiently waited was blatantly unfair. Not playing by the immigration rules and cutting in front of waiting legal immigrants was cheating. Obeying the law was legal. Disregarding the U.S. Constitution and federal statutes was illegal. It was as simple as that.

Augustus provided Americans a larger perspective of illegal immigration. He referred to Homeland Security, and Customs and Border Protection numbers that estimated the nationalities of the 11 to 12 million aliens who were in the county illegally.

Another 1,760,000 aliens were from other countries: Afghanistan, Algeria, Australia, a few other African countries, Belize, Canada, Egypt, some European nations, Indonesia, Iran, Iraq, Jordan, Libya, Lebanon, other Middle Eastern and Persian Gulf states, Palestine, Russia, Sudan, Syria, Turkey, United Arab Emirates, and Qatar.

AFRICA

Ethiopia......................35,000

Ghana.........................36,000

Kenya 24,000

Nigeria 45,000

ASIA

China.........................285,000

India 284,000

Pakistan 55,000

The Philippines.......197,000

South Korea.............192,000

Vietnam 116,000

CARIBBEAN

Dominican Rep.......123,000

Jamaica......................77,000

NORTH AMERICA

Mexico...................6,200,000

CENTRAL AMERICA

El Salvador 436,000

Guatemala 704,000

Honduras.................317,000

Nicaragua 68,000

SOUTH AMERICA

Argentina..................35,000

Brazil 117,000

Columbia 137,000

Ecuador...................146,000

Peru 105,000

Venezuela 44,000

The chief executive considered former presidents, Cabinet secretaries, administration officials, Congress members, and some heads of government entities analogous to "zebras" at sporting events; they refereed immigration issues and made too many bad calls. The people knew it and booed the "stripes" at every opportunity. Moreover, like fans in the stands or at home, citizens felt there was nothing they could do about it. As such, President Treatise decided he would be the official in the instant replay review booth—the ultimate decision-maker.

Augustus' thoughts on immigration emanated from his ancestors who had legally entered the colonies through the port cities of New Amsterdam and Philadelphia decades before there was a United States. He had more than 330 years of American history and heritage, family customs, and public education as a foundation upon which to build his beliefs—years enough to forget the plight and struggles of earlier immigrants.

The first lady had a more recent family experience perspective. Angelica was of Czechoslovakian descent. Her ancestors, the Mluvnice family, departed war-ravaged Europe soon after World War I decimated millions of families, dissolved empires, and created new nations. She recounted stories of her grandparents' odyssey from the Moravian District of what is known as Slovakia today, across the ocean by steamship, to New York City. There were deaths and burials at sea. Passengers were unanimously jubilant at the first sighting of the Statue of Liberty. Hopeful immigrants were patiently waiting aboard ship before being allowed onto Ellis Island. Hours standing in line being processed, examined, and interviewed. Overwhelming joy when granted entry. Sorrowful tears of disappointment by those denied and turned away.

Angelica's forebears had crossed America by train, boat, wagon, and foot to farm. As immigrants often did, her grandparents read, wrote and spoke their native tongue in their newly adopted community and at home and sent their foreign-born children to public schools to become true Americans. By necessity, children communicated in Czech by night and American by day. There were no English as a Second Language classes. Her parents succeeded because they had to, learned from classmates, practiced in stores as translators for their parents, and took advantage of teachers' willingness to assist after school. The first lady's parents grew up in that old-new world.

Angelica provided Augustus perspective as she gave him one of her "looks." "You are a hard man, a principled man—which is why I love you. Descendants of the Pilgrims, the grand-children of people who arrived with my grandparents, families of the Mariel Boat Lift, and even immigrants who arrived by Boeing 777 yesterday may agree with you. Nevertheless, on this, you need a reality check. What you feel and believe at home is one thing. As president, you must think differently. There is no way you can deport ten to twenty million people. First of all, some countries from where illegals came no longer exist. Second, even though government estimates are 10 to 11 million, others estimate 20 million. Your opponents will use that greater number, as I will now.

"You're talking about depleting the population in the U.S. by 6%. The Spanish Flu Pandemic in the last century killed 0.6% of Americans. What havoc did that cause? Remember what happened to the towns around Fort Hood, Texas, when ten thousand troops and their families were reassigned to Germany in 1979 and 1980. Now imagine twenty million used cars flooding the market, twenty million vacant homes for sale, twenty million bank accounts emptied, and twenty million employees no longer working in agriculture or business. What

265

is the impact?"

Augustus responded, "Angelica, I have greater concerns. None of those ten, twelve, or twenty million people has taken the oath of citizenship. They have not renounced their allegiance to other countries. They have not sworn to support and defend the Constitution. That, to me, is a national security challenge."

She countered, "In six decades, how many have tried to overthrow the government? Moreover, for the minor few who attempted or want to still, is an oath or a piece of paper really going to make any difference? Naturalization did not stop some people from joining ISIS. Look, whatever your decision, I think your plan should include asking many to leave voluntarily, deport who you can, and accommodate the remainder."

Contemplating Angelica's words, Augustus reminded Americans why citizens of other countries came, and continued to come, to the United States. "For the same reasons my ancestors came to America—to escape religious persecution and famine. For the same reasons the first lady's ancestors came to America—to flee war-torn countries and dictatorships. For the opportunity for a better life, to obtain an education, to learn to read and write, for freedom of speech, political expression, a chance to vote, to earn a decent wage, to flee ethnic intolerance, and many other reasons as different as the cultures they left behind. They came to experience 'unalienable rights of life, liberty, and the pursuit of happiness,' as written by Thomas Jefferson in the Declaration of Independence. Ultimately, they continue to come because the governments of their native lands are not meeting the political, economic, education, religious, social, and cultural needs of its people." Augustus believed those factors were the root causes of global, international migration as a whole and illegal immigration into the U.S. in particular, and why he needed to take action.

My comprehensive plan for reformation of America's immigration system has several parts. It uses existing and new resources to secure the border, deport alien criminals, temporarily suspend new visas, maintain employment, reunite families, limit legal immigrant entry points, clean the environment, and change statutes. Parts of this proposed legislation will enact a review and reissue of outdated visas, work permits, or green cards, as appropriate, and grant citizenship to those who qualify. Much of the plan will be financed and paid for by the United Nations and specific applicable countries. To be effective and fully successful, my Immigration and Alien Naturalization Reform Act requires total enactment and implementation of all parts and phases.

Base Re-Alignment Commission

As commander in chief of Armed Forces, Augustus directed the Department of Defense identify vacant installations capable of supporting the implementation of his Reform Act.

Since the late 1980s, under congressionally mandated reductions to DoD operational costs, military installations across the U.S. have been systematically combined, their missions realigned, and geographic footprints lessened or eliminated. Those actions were directed by the Base Re-Alignment Commission (BRAC). Many bases were partly or fully closed and put up for sale. Universities, colleges, and technical and trade schools purchased facilities for classrooms and dormitories. Recreation businesses bought golf courses, bowling alleys, tennis courts, swimming pools, and gymnasiums. Officers', non-commissioned officers', and enlisted clubs were modernized into restaurants, nightclubs, or entertainment centers. Quarters became housing for civilian families or single men and women. Temporary lodging complexes were managed as hotels. Airfields and fire stations retained their function, but under local city or county control. Some Uniformed Services Military Police, Provost Marshals, Masters-at-Arms, and Security Forces stations and accompanying jails and brigs became branch offices for community policing efforts. Base hospitals, dental clinics, Military Treatment Facilities, and dispensaries transitioned to private or public health or urgent care centers.

Many mothballed bases, forts, and posts were self-contained communities in and of themselves. Several that were closed remained under Defense Department control. Regardless of any financial savings in the overall national budget, many communities where installations were shut down suffered greatly from the negative economic snowball effects through loss of jobs, businesses, and revenue. Area housing prices collapsed; a direct result of Armed Forces personnel moving away and the resultant glut of vacant homes for sale. In addition to the closed but not sold military installations maintained at caretaker levels, the General Services Administration managed thousands more government owned buildings that were also vacant.

In order to accommodate President Treatise's directive, selected sites were identified as Visa Processing Centers, Employment Verification Centers, Family Reunification Centers, or Deportation Facilities. Many members of Congress publicly objected to the commander in chief's overall concept, all the while privately intensively lobbying the Defense Department to designate and reopen a closed installation in their district. Come re-election, politicians wanted to be viewed as bringing prosperity back to their constituents.

Aliens and immigrants temporarily housed in military quarters created jobs in the hotel, apartment management, and service industries. Mess halls and dining facilities opened for restaurant and food service workers to prepare and serve meals. Health-care professionals and associated providers treated patients in reopened hospitals and clinics. Drivers transported people from place to place. Day care, childcare, and youth activities workers monitored children while alien parents were being interviewed. A variety of skilled workers (carpenters, electricians, HVAC (heating, ventilation, and air conditioning), plumbers, and roofers) maintained facilities. Many installations were fenced and had entry gates where security forces protected undocumented workers and controlled access to the areas. Needed police, fire, and ambulance services were reestablished on bases or contracted with local communities. Courtrooms once used for courts martial became facilities where judges and attorneys conducted citizenship or deportation hearings. Airfields reopened for aircraft to bring aliens to the centers and transport those deported to their home countries. Many other individuals were hired in a variety of fields to process the migrant population and to support the overall operation. Those actions reinvigorated the affected communities.

After installations were operational, a series of public service announcements were broadcast. Advertisements identified the nature of each center or facility and asked aliens who had overstayed their visas, entered the country without proper authority, were hired as undocumented workers, were considered illegal immigrants, or otherwise in the United States improperly, to voluntarily report to the appropriate location for processing. At the same time, instructions were sent to employers, education institutions, law enforcement, housing authorities, and any appropriate entity that may have contact with aliens regarding the forms to complete, advice to be provided, directions to be given, and actions to take.

Secure the Border

During an early twenty-first century Middle East conflict and resulting refugee migration, Hungary, in 2015, constructed a 110-mile-long fence in two weeks. The United States border with Mexico was 2,000 miles long. Augustus calculated that America would be able to construct a similar fence in 40 weeks, or 10 months—at any rate, in less than one year since nearly one-third of the border was already fenced.

Whether it was to be called a wall or a fence, it was a device to mark a boundary. History has repeatedly shown that walls or fences created by either Mother Nature or Man were eventually breached. Hannibal crossed the Alps to invade Rome. Columbus sailed the flat ocean, discovered the "New World," did not fall off the edge of the earth, and proved the world was round. Magellan circumnavigated the globe. Lindbergh flew solo across the Atlantic Ocean. Yeager traveled faster than the speed of sound. Gagarin was the first human in space. Armstrong stepped on the moon first. Each exemplified nature's obstacles overcome by the ingenuity and willpower of Man.

Man-made barriers have suffered the same fate. The Romans took less than one year to break down the gates of Masada. The Walls of Jericho, Great Wall of China, Berlin Wall, and Iron Curtain were all destroyed or compromised. Daily news reported on prisoners who escaped from walled and fenced jails or prisons. A wall or fence alone would not stop illegal entry into America; humans, as they have demonstrated throughout history, will eventually find a way to go over, under, around or through it.

Augustus, who did not like either the terms wall or fence, was not deterred. He preferred the word barrier. Barriers took many forms and were constructed to stifle illegal activities as part of the national plan to obstruct passage, hinder advance, and channelize the movement of people in efforts to stem the migration of citizens from other countries, deter human and drug trafficking, prevent the spread of disease, and lessen the possibility of a terrorist attack on American soil.

The commander in chief convened a combined meeting with his Cabinet and the Joint Chiefs of Staff of the military services. One of the most basic skills Augustus had learned as a soldier was to erect barriers that used concertina or razor wire in strands of three; one strand placed upon two strands and held in place with metal poles staked to the ground. The president ordered, as part of Armed Forces training, that such a barrier be constructed immediately on military installations that shared the United States international border with Mexico. Next, he directed such barriers be constructed on all other federal property that directly bordered Mexico: national parks; lands for grazing, agricultural, and mineral use; and waterways— including Indian nations under the Department of the Interior. Active-duty and Reserve personnel from all services (Army, Navy, Marines, Air Force, and Coast Guard) were deployed for barrier training.

From the time of the Pilgrims, America's militias, National Guard, and Active-duty military trained its personnel on private property. As part of Augustus' plan to secure the border his first year in office, he met with the governors of Texas, New Mexico, Arizona, Nevada, and California, their Adjutants General, and the Chief of the National Guard Bureau. The commander in chief explained his barrier erection plan and extended it to those states. They trained their National Guard in a similar fashion and installed barriers on all state-owned property. The National Guard from other states were similarly deployed and trained. Barrier construction took place simultaneously along the entire border. Only the governor of California refused to use his National Guard in such a fashion.

Seeking additional support for training the military, the administration contacted property owners all along the Mexican border and obtained permission for the Armed Forces to practice erecting barriers on private land. Owners were also approached about the sale of that small portion of their property along the border to the government. Many individuals and businesses were receptive and allowed the erection of barriers or sold the requested portions of ground as a sign of policy support.

The second aspect of the overall barrier plan involved observation. A barrier could not be erected but then abandoned, or not be observed for routine maintenance, breaches, and illegal activity. A second skillset the commander in chief learned while in the Army's Ranger School involved patrolling techniques designed to conduct reconnaissance, gather intelligence, and intercept those who attempt to infiltrate controlled areas. The acronym SALUTE (Size, Activity, Location, Unit, Time, and Equipment) was utilized. He had legal and historical precedent for ordering military along the border. From 1916 until 1943, the Army routinely patrolled America's southern border to prevent unauthorized incursions—including on privately owned land. In 1981, Congress enacted and President

Reagan signed into law the Military Cooperation with Civilian Law Enforcement Agencies Act. Since then a whole range of military technologies were available to and used by federal, state, county, and municipal civilian law enforcement. Former commanders in chief federalized some National Guard air and army assets under Title 10 to aid in border security. During and after construction of the barrier, Active-duty, Reserve, and National Guard patrolled the entire southern border as part of their skills training.

A third element of border security was the humane handling and treatment of aliens, illegal immigrants, undocumented workers, migrants, citizens, and others who ventured into military training areas. Armed Forces personnel were already trained in the capture and processing of Prisoners of War. While the U.S. was not at war with any nations, the military's Seize, Secure, Search, Segregate, Ship (5-S) method was readily modified to the proper techniques for use with civilians. Persons were detained (not arrested), checked for weapons or drugs, asked for identification and other documents, and separated from "coyotes" or guides. For safety reasons, single men were separated from single women; families were separated from single individuals, and children were separated from non-related adults. Immediate medical aid was rendered by medics and corpsmen, as necessary. All were turned over to civilian law enforcement for proper adjudication. Citizens and identified authorized individuals were escorted from the training zones and released.

An additional part of border security involved protection: Protection of military personnel training along the border, protection of civilian law enforcement in the performance of their duties, protection of contractors hired to construct additional barriers more elaborate than the triple-strand concertina, protection of detained aliens, and protection of Americans. Armed Forces and law enforcement members were all trained on the use of deadly force with special emphasis on defending oneself when one's own life or the lives of innocent civilians was threatened. That training was deemed a necessity given the nature of the armed coyote and drug, human, and sex trafficker threat.

Simultaneously with the construction of the concertina barrier by members of the Armed Forces, a more elaborate barrier was installed. Where possible, Active-duty, Reserve, and National Guard engineer and construction units were used. Barrier construction on Indian reservations employed Native Americans to the maximum extent possible. For those sections of the barrier that required civilian contractors, effort was made to hire local businesses and employ residents of the states involved. The concertina barrier was installed in less than sixty days, and the more substantial barrier was erected within nine months.

Two months after starting the barrier operation, America published in Mexican, Central American, and South American newspapers and broadcast on their radios and televisions that the United States border with Mexico was closed to persons attempting to enter illegally. U.S. ambassadors and consuls general around the world provided their host nations the same message, as did our United Nations ambassador. Migrants from other countries attempting to enter the U.S. illegally were told to stay at home or return to their homeland. They were further told if they were detained by military personnel, apprehended by Border Patrol agents, or arrested by civilian law enforcement, they would be immediately sent back into Mexico or deported.

Aliens caught before crossing the border were given a map annotated with their exact position and the location of the closest Mexican community. They were provided with the address of the nearest Policía Federal or "Federales" office, local district police and city police stations, churches, and charitable organizations. They also received food and water and were told to go home. Drug smugglers were arrested, drugs and weapons were confiscated, and offenders were transported to the nearest Deportation Center, where they were photographed, finger-printed, processed, and immediately turned over to Mexican or appropriate country authorities. Human traffickers met a similar fate; their prey, individuals designated for use as drug mules, sex workers, or slave laborers, were taken to Family Reunification Centers.

Environmental Cleanup

Several locations along the border were discovered as dumping grounds for trash, used clothing, feces, dead animals, and, occasionally, bodies—making them potential crime scenes necessitating civilian law enforcement, forensics, and coroner investigations. Human remains were recovered and taken to one of several reopened GSA facilities for safekeeping, to determine cause of death, and for possible identification. Bodies identified were reported to their home country for family notification. A DNA and forensics database was established so foreign family members seeking their loved ones could provide their own DNA for comparison. Arrangements were made for the return of identified and claimed remains. If remains were not identified or claimed within one year, they were cremated and their forensic file and any possessions were placed in storage with their urn for another four years. At the end of those four years, the remains, possessions, forensic file, and case number were relocated to a permanent columbarium located below ground inside an abandoned salt mine.

Small trash dumping sites were cleaned up by either the military or contractors as part of their routine operational training or barrier construction duties. To keep taxpayer costs as low as possible, agencies, businesses, organizations, schools, and local jurisdictions were asked for volunteers. From those entities came individuals and groups seeking community service recognition, academic extra credit, merit badges, and fundraising opportunities. Others sought to work off court ordered punishments in lieu of jail or took part in prisoner work release programs.

For larger sites, a list of local and national not-for-profit environmental organizations was utilized. Each was contacted and given an opportunity to return the land to its natural state. Many accepted. For those that opted out, the organization's mission was compared with the type of environmental cleanup needed. If there was a match, the reason for its refusal was annotated for future consideration regarding requests for federal grants and government policy changes. As a last resort, companies experienced in environmental cleanup were hired.

Every contaminated site 250 yards north of and along the entire 2,000-mile Mexican-American border was returned to its natural state, as much as possible, by the time barrier construction was completed. Drones were used to locate any refuse-polluted terrain up to one mile north of the border, and those sites were cleaned, as well.

Deport Alien Criminals

Roughly, 168,000 criminal aliens were deported the year before Augustus assumed the presidency. Ninety-seven percent went to Mexico and Central America. That same year, about

380,000 criminal aliens remained in America's multiple incarceration systems—4% of the estimated total illegal alien population. After the border was secured, approximately 100,000 criminal aliens per year were transferred from local jails, state penitentiaries, or federal prisons and taken to the nearest Deportation Facility, processed, and returned to their native country. Any alien convicted of a new criminal offense was automatically deported and that conviction reported to his or her nation's authorities. No time was wasted processing them into and out of jails, penitentiaries, or prisons. Over four years, these procedures removed nearly all criminal foreign nationals from detention and reduced incarceration overcrowding in many locales.

Aspects of criminal aliens' lives not already on file were documented prior to their deportation, and these documents were provided to his or her country of origin's police. By realigning Department of Homeland Security and Justice Department budgets, communities or detention facilities were reimbursed for expenses incurred for each criminal alien turned over for deportation.

Temporary Suspension of New Visas

According to the *Department of Homeland Security Yearbooks of Immigration Statistics,* the average number of Non-Immigrant Admissions (foreigners temporarily allowed entry) into the U.S. approached 75 million each year. These included roughly 60 million tourists, eight million business travelers, two million students, two million temporary workers, and a half million diplomats. The remaining two-and-a-half million fell into other categories. President Treatise wanted to place a temporary suspension on all new visa applications. That was not feasible given the number of foreigners entering annually, and it would be economically detrimental to the country.

In addition, government estimates reported that roughly 40% (4,800,000) of all illegal aliens currently in the U.S. remained on expired visas. That equated to less than 100,000 per year since America restarted legal immigration in the 1960s, a comparatively insignificant annual number to warrant suspension of all future visas. He did, however, seek recommendations on which nations should have visas suspended. Student and work visas were denied to people from countries deemed to be enemies — China, Russia, North Korea. Nations on the State Department's list of sponsors of terrorism were included.

Augustus' second year phase of immigration reforms included soliciting assistance from the education, employment, housing, and related industries, as well as local jurisdictions in an effort to determine the whereabouts of those who had overstayed their welcome. A visa tracking task force was established which consisted of a representative from nearly every federal agency. As a starting point, the task force was provided a list with the name of each visa holder, the type of visa, and the last known location of that alien.

The State Department verified foreign dignitaries who were ambassadors, embassy and consulate staff, spies, and United Nations employees. Internationally, each country was asked for the status and location of their citizens named on the visa list. Health and Human Services searched the records and files of Medicare, Medicaid, Health Insurance Marketplace, and Social Security. The Department of Housing and Urban Development reviewed lists of Section 8 housing tenants. The Department of Education looked at university, college, trade and on-line school enrollment records, student loans, research grants, and applications. The Defense Department checked enlistment files.

The Justice Department reviewed cases of known or alleged criminals and those bound over for trial or already incarcerated and deported. Cabinet departments reviewed their databases of government assistance enrollees. The Internal Revenue Service reviewed tax filings. The Office of Personnel Management scrubbed federal employee hiring records. Homeland Security cross-referenced terrorist watch lists—both at home and abroad—and the Transportation Security Administration's No Fly list. Other federal agencies performed similar tasks in banking, investment, lending, and mortgages including credit reports from credit bureaus. States were contacted and searches of birth, death, marriage, divorce records as well as driver's licenses and voter registration rolls were conducted. Political parties were asked to review their lists of campaign contributors.

As those efforts took place, public service announcements requested those with expired visas, work permits, and Temporary Protected Status to report to the nearest Visa Processing Center for a review of their situation. They were advised to bring all related documents which may aid in their case such as their passport, old visa, marriage or divorce papers, birth records for themselves and any children, driver's license, utility bills showing current address, apartment rental agreement, mortgage, any paperwork related to loans, credit cards, or other pertinent papers. Married persons were to bring their spouse and children as well. If they were approved to remain, new visas, work permits, or even green cards were provided. Many who took the Oath of Renunciation and Allegiance were granted citizenship. Others were bound over for deportation. This procedure was still in progress when the president left office.

Maintain Employment

A second aspect of year two's phase of the Immigration and Alien Naturalization Reform Act was strongly supported by businesses and pro-immigrant forces. Many citizens, however, were against the legislation. Before its enactment, the government fined, penalized, or took to court employers that hired illegal aliens. This legislation modified that procedure and rewarded companies identifying undocumented workers in their employ and took—not sent—alien employees to Employment Verification Centers.

Employers were provided a standard paper or e-form that required as much of an illegal alien's personal information as possible, including details on family or relatives currently in the U.S. and their contact information. A section of the form provided a place for an embedded digital or hard copy color photo. The employer generated a second document on its business letterhead to be signed by the company's President/Chief Executive Officer that provided the nature and length of employment, as well as the undocumented worker's performance. A duplicate of the photograph provided on the form was embedded or attached to the letter.

The business kept the original of both forms. The undocumented worker was provided a copy of the two forms to take to the Employment Verification Center. Well ahead of the alien's arrival, the company sent a copy of the two forms to the center. Duplication of both the federal form and business letter requiring an illegal alien's personal and family information and photograph reduced the possibility of error or misuse in case the two documents were separated.

As with other portions of the new law, employed aliens were advised to bring all related documents that may aid in their case. They were required to take their spouse and children to the center, as well.

The intent of this part of Augustus' revised immigration program was to allow employers to retain the services of the now documented worker. The business had already invested time, effort, and training in the illegal alien, and that employee had acquired necessary skills to perform the job. To avoid shutting down operations, employers were strongly encouraged to divide their alien labor force into twelve groups and bring only one-twelfth to the center each month for employment verification.

Companies and businesses that complied with this procedure were not fined, but were granted a one-time tax deduction for each undocumented worker brought to the processing center. Illegal aliens allowed to remain were issued the requisite documents, work permits, appropriate visa, or green card and were provided with a valid employee ID, federal tax ID, or Social Security number and placed into the appropriate database. Many who qualified were granted citizenship. Businesses were required to retain that immigrant as an employee for at least one year or return the tax deduction. Any current and newly documented alien who left the employment of the business was to be immediately reported to the government for appropriate disposition. Finally, each employee's wages were garnished and every business assessed a monthly levy to pay any past due income taxes, FICA, and Medicare premiums. This requirement had been added to the legislation in order to placate many who disagreed with the granting of citizenship to these illegal aliens.

Reunite Families

The third phase of immigration reform took place in the third year of Augustus' term. It included a provision to reunite families of illegal aliens with their families in their home country. Illegal aliens had a 12-month grace period to voluntarily leave the U.S. or report to one of the Family Reunification Centers. After that time, any undocumented worker, regardless of how long they had been in America, could be detained by law enforcement and taken to a center for determination of family reunification eligibility. Detained individuals were allowed, under escort, to gather from his or her residence all records pertinent to their case. Participating law enforcement departments received a monetary grant for every illegal alien brought to the Family Reunification Center.

Individuals and families received an onsite hearing. If the decision was deportation, their home country was notified, and they were placed on an airplane and flown back to their native land for reunification with their families. Deportees who voluntarily reported to one of the centers and had no criminal record were provided instructions on how to apply for legal immigration to the United States from their country of origin. In addition, they were given a letter stating how long they had been in America, where they had resided, and any jobs they had held. That letter, with photograph embedded, was attached to their immigration application.

A special identifier was assigned to illegal aliens who took their American born children with them or had children who remained, thus giving them priority immigration processing status for reentry into the United States. Their information was provided to the State Department and forwarded to the appropriate embassy or consulate in anticipation of an immediate application for legal immigration. In addition, all American born children taken to a foreign country with their illegal alien parents received a passport. A copy of their file was retained for future use should their parents' immigration papers reach the appropriate office for legal processing back into the U.S. or should the children wish to return to America on their own. When aliens were allowed to remain, as was the case in the Visa Processing and Employment Verification Centers, appropriate documents were issued.

Legal Immigration

From the time of the first established provinces and colonies until the 1800s, Philadelphia was the primary city to which immigrants came to America. As the United States grew and more states were added to the Union, the port and piers of New York City became the central site of immigrant debarkation, so much so that in 1892, Ellis Island was established as the designated place for immigrants to enter the U.S. and remained so until 1954. Since then, immigrants enter at multiple locations. Every year approximately one million foreigners follow the legal procedures of both their home country and America to become Lawful Permanent Residents (Green Card Holders).

President Treatise did not stop that process. However, he did modify how, when, and where immigrants entered the country. His review of *Department of Homeland Security Yearbooks of Immigration Statistics* aided his decision. Those reports revealed, since the beginning of the twenty-first century, the average annual number of legal immigrants by continent or region: Africa – 100,000; Asia (including Mid-East, Persian Gulf, sub-Asian countries) – 430,000; Europe (including Ukraine) – 85,000; North America (including Canada, Mexico, Central America, Caribbean Islands) – 325,000; South America – 75,000; and Oceania (Australia and Pacific Islands) – 5,000.

To enable the government to have better entry control and easier processing of immigrants, the chief executive's revised Immigration and Alien Naturalization Reform Act limited the number of aerial ports of entry. There were just over 150 airports in the U.S. authorized for international aircraft travel. Larger passenger airliners transported approximately 250 people in each aircraft. Basic math revealed that the number of annual legal immigrants could be transported in twelve flights per day.

To account for legal immigrants arriving in the calculated numbers from the identified continents and regions, Augustus had his Cabinet search for fifteen regional international airports for designation as Lawful Permanent Resident sites. Major airports were not to be used for immigration. With the cooperation of the Federal Aviation Administration, the passenger airline industry, airport authorities, governors, and mayors, smaller international airports capable of handling large commercial aircraft and connecting flights to regional hubs were identified. They were designated the only airports into which citizens of other nations who were legally immigrating could fly. The strategically positioned airports welcomed one "Immigration Flight" per day. At each airport, officials processed the 250 foreigners and sent them on their way to their final destination elsewhere in the U.S.

The number of airports required per region was based upon the number of immigrants who entered the U.S. every year from a particular part of the globe. Designated airports were located as follows: One in a Mid-Atlantic state received Africans, one in the Northeast accepted Europeans, one Gulf Coast state welcomed South Americans, four Southern states guided Mexicans and Central Americans, five West Coast or Rocky Mountain States accommodated Asians, and Hawaii handled

Pacific Region (Oceania) countries. One airport in America's Mid-west/Great Lakes region and one airport in the Central Plains were identified as alternates should one of the primary airfields be unavailable. Each daily flight originated from preselected airports within those six continents and one region. All legal immigrants made their way to designated foreign airports where U.S. Immigration officials processed them before boarding.

A major advantage for Americans, especially in those communities designated to receive planeloads of immigrants, involved jobs creation in government and the airline, hotel, food service, restaurant, transportation, retail, and currency exchange industries. As a whole, there was tighter control, accountability, and identity verification of legal immigrants. The program could be expanded so refugees could be similarly processed and transported.

Immigration sites located at America's seaports were not closed or altered. Border crossing by ground transportation, however, was altered. Southern and Northern border towns already dealt with masses of tourists, day workers, farm laborers, and others who routinely and legally crossed the U.S.-Mexico or U.S.-Canada border multiple times daily, weekly, monthly, and annually. Vehicular traffic and human congestion was often the norm. Thrown into that morass were legal immigrants seeking entry into the U.S. To alleviate that situation, separate legal immigration-only points of entry were established in the same border towns, but away from the existing border crossing locations used daily by workers, tourists, and those seeking asylum.

Negotiations with Congress, states, cities, airline industry, airport authorities, and foreign nations took skill, tenacity, "horse trading," and three years of hard work. This phase of

Augustus' plan was passed by the legislature and signed into law at the beginning of his fourth year in office. It was October before all airports, airlines, communities, and foreign cities were ready and the first flights began.

Change the Statutes

President Treatise ordered a review of the plethora of immigration statutes and their accompanying regulations. Subsequent to that review, Augustus' Immigration and Alien Naturalization Reform Act proposed to Congress changes that reduced the number of exceptions to immigration law, streamlined processes for those in the country illegally who were apprehended, and added a few new restrictions. Some proposed wording included:

> Any female alien who is in her third trimester of pregnancy shall not be granted entry into the United States. Any female alien granted Non-Immigrant Admission entry into the United States under any of the exceptions shall have such authorization revoked once she becomes pregnant and reaches her third trimester of pregnancy, and she shall subsequently be immediately deported.

More importantly, the chief executive wanted to clarify and codify that portion of the Fourteenth Amendment to the Constitution that stated, "All persons born...in the United States and subject to the jurisdiction thereof, are citizens of the United States..." He proposed:

> Any child born in the United States to
> aliens known to be in the country legally (not
> immigrating for citizenship) or illegally shall
> be deemed not a United States citizen and
> that child's birth certificate shall reflect the
> nationality of its alien parents and the child's
> nationality shall be recorded as the same as
> one of the nations of its alien parents.

These proposed changes were designed to keep foreigners from traveling to the U.S. as tourists, students, workers, and in other categories with the motive or the explicit purpose of having a baby and the child becoming an American citizen. Augustus' wording and efforts regarding pregnant females was considered discriminatory against women and was not adopted. Congress, however, did agree with clarifying citizenship by birth and accepted, with minimal modification to ensure proper legal language, his birth certificate annotation proposal. That modification to the Fourteenth Amendment, combined with the chief executive's earlier proposal, was sent to the states for ratification.

Paying for It All

Taking a page from commercialized Christmas at one shopping mall where children had to pay a fee to see Saint Nicholas, sit on Kris Kringle's knee, and tell Santa what they wanted, the head of state decided the best way to finance immigration reform was to have the United Nations or individual countries pay the costs America incurred. Many expenses of the U.S. government, local authorities, the judicial and penal systems, and businesses to secure the border, clean the environment, deport alien criminals, temporarily suspend visas, maintain employment, reunite families, limit legal entry points, and change statutes programs were to be paid by others and not by the taxpayer.

Simply, for every foreigner found in America without proper or current documentation or authority, the United States billed either the United Nations or that illegal alien's country for costs associated with dealing with that foreign national. Foreign aid, UN membership dues, loans to countries and loan guarantees to the World Bank, or International Monetary Fund financial support were reduced accordingly and retained in the U.S. Treasury. Since his administration's policy was to stop illegal immigration and reduce forced population migration across the globe, he agreed that the United States must help effect political, economic, education, religious, and social change in selected countries. One step was charging for services rendered to those homelands' citizens.

Challenges

In researching, developing, and implementing the Immigration and Alien Naturalization Reform Act, President Treatise, his Cabinet, and the heads of government agencies and departments had to identify challenges and present solutions.

The biggest remonstrations came from individuals, businesses, and organizations that owned land and favored open borders, supported sanctuary cities, and provided aid and comfort to aliens. They habitually denied access to their property by the military, law enforcement, contractors, and anyone else they deemed interfering with their rights and the rights of illegal immigrants and undocumented workers. Many provided safe passage across their terrain, distributed food and water, and gave shelter to the handful of migrants entering illegally. For most of those detractors, however, the situation resolved itself. One purpose of a barrier was to channelize the movement of people. With barriers and patrols covering nearly the entire border, thousands of illegal aliens began crossing those same private lands where years before only a few hundred ventured. The unprotected ground was trampled, trash was dropped in the open, property was damaged, drugs were left behind, crimes were committed, and provided resources were expended—the reality of rising and significant cost soon outweighed many a moral stance.

In another respect, the channelization of migrants made it easier for border patrol agents to arrest and detain illegal aliens. Officials needed only wait at public thoroughfares, on public lands, and on private property whose owners authorized Customs and Border Protection and Immigration and Customs Enforcement personnel access, for immigrants to walk into their locations. Chasing people over rough terrain was curtailed. For those few obstinate, wealthier, or heavily financed property owners, the government attempted to purchase a strip of land along the border at fair market value. Some sold. Others did not—at which point the federal government employed its Eminent Domain policy to procure the terrain. Buildings abutting the border were razed to enable new barrier construction.

Under the Posse Comitatus Act, which was signed into law by President Rutherford B. Hayes in June of 1878, members of the active Armed Forces are forbidden from conducting civilian law enforcement activities. That Act stemmed from the Reconstruction Era in the aftermath of the Civil War, when military personnel were used to enforce national policies and local laws. The statute does not apply to National Guard in their state law enforcement role or to the Coast Guard, as it has a maritime law enforcement function. There are other exceptions, as well. Department of Defense police are allowed to detain individuals who gain access to military reservations until their identity or the nature of their business is determined. Afterwards those persons are escorted off the installation and released or turned over to the appropriate civilian authorities.

To lessen restraints on Armed Forces personnel who erected barriers and conducted patrols along the border, strips of land extending from the Mexico border north were turned over to the Defense Department and designated as military installations or training areas. Included in that classification were existing federal lands formerly under the auspices of other federal departments and agencies, property purchased from land-owners, and terrain or structures acquired under Eminent Domain. Fences were erected on all sides of the newly created training areas, and signs in many languages were attached advising trespassers of the military reservation and of their immediate detention or deportation if they were found on the property.

Another difficulty concerned refugee camps that were springing up in northern Mexico, just south of the U.S. border. It became international news, and the United Nations denounced America for creating the problem. Augustus' response was fivefold.

First, Mexican government leaders and officials repeatedly stated they sealed their own southern border with Belize and Guatemala. If that were true, how did they explain the presence of Central and South American refugees along the U.S.-Mexico border? Moreover, where was the corresponding humanitarian crisis along the Mexico-Guatemala-Belize border? Second, Mexico had very strict immigration laws regarding the arrest and imprisonment of persons who enter Mexico without proper authority or documentation. One had to ask, "Why hasn't Mexico entered the camps and arrested and imprisoned all those foreigners?" Third, Mexico now had its own illegal immigration situation that was up to its leaders to solve. Fourth, since the vast majority of the migrants are Mexican citizens, what was Mexico doing to take care of its own residents? Fifth, he asserted, "The refugee situation, the migration of people, is exactly the challenge I addressed to the UN. Right now, it is up to the United Nations and Mexico to deal with the political, economic, educational, religious, cultural, and social issues within the member countries whose people fled into Mexico. The UN must take action in regards to the world's population migration challenges."

There was an emotional component to immigration reform. Many citizens, be they pro-legal immigration or supportive of illegal immigrants, espoused the idea that it was cruel to break up families. They especially focused on undocumented workers with American born children or whose children were very young when they were brought to America through no fault of their own. Many were raised as Americans, educated in American schools, and have known only America. Another emotional aspect presented was that it was wrong to take American children to a foreign country to be raised as other than Americans—arguments that tugged at individuals' heartstrings.

The president, however, maintained clarity on three seldom mentioned points in that regard. "Many south-of-the-border parents who could not afford the financial burden to legally immigrate to the U.S., voluntarily broke up their own family by handing their underage daughters and sons to multiple male adults for days or weeks, and paid thousands of dollars to coyotes to take their children to America. Tens of thousands of children, unaccompanied by their parents, illegally entered the United States.

"America's legal system breaks up families every day. Children are often removed from homes where parents sexually or physically abuse their children, endanger children by leaving them in a closed and locked car in the summer, allow children to play outside or walk to school unattended, or expose children to drugs such as meth, crack cocaine, or heroin. Single parents sent to jail for criminal acts such as theft, robbery, forgery, battery, drunk driving, embezzlement, manslaughter, and murder break up their families. In divorce cases, where the parent given custody is a foreign national, American born children are sometimes taken to live and be raised in that other country's culture.

"I am labeled cruel and denounced for enforcing federal immigration law. Child endangerment and child neglect are also violations of the law. Yet I have not seen massive nation-wide protests denouncing the police, the courts, judges, child protective services, child advocate attorneys, and claiming unwarranted cruelty for their rulings breaking up families by enforcing existing local laws and adhering to court decisions.

"Entering the United States illegally is a violation of the law. In criminal, civil, administrative, and divorce cases, children become wards of the state, are sent to group homes, are assigned foster parents, and are temporarily given to or adopted by a close relative—most often the child's grandparents or a sibling of the child's parents. Under my Immigration and Alien Naturalization Reform Act, all those avenues for parents and children are made available to those illegal aliens being deported."

Currently, twenty-three nations refuse to take back their

deported citizens who enter or remain in the U.S. illegally. Some of those recalcitrant and uncooperative countries are Afghanistan, Algeria, China, Cuba, Iran, Iraq, Libya, Somalia, and Zimbabwe. In order to deport illegal aliens, two basic procedures are required: an administrative final order of removal by a judge and a travel document issued by that foreign government. Many countries refuse to issue the requisite travel documents that allow their citizens to return home.

Under the United States Supreme Court ruling in *Zadvydas v. Davis*, deportees are generally not to be detained beyond 180 days. Other court rulings reduced that time to twenty days for some migrants. In concert with his immigration reforms and use of America's economic instrument of national power to levy a fee against the United Nations and reduce foreign aid to countries whose citizens were found to be illegal aliens, President Treatise added more financial penalties to recalcitrant countries. For every deportee refused reentry into their homeland, that nation was charged for services rendered to every one of their citizens for every year that illegal alien lived or remained in the United States. The fee was recompense for U.S. programs and services from which undocumented workers benefited while in America. If necessary, those fees were charged against any debt the United States may have had with an illegal alien's home country.

Final Thoughts

The overarching goal of the Immigration and Alien Naturalization Reform Act was to identify, locate, account for, and determine a proper disposition for all illegal aliens in the U.S. In order to accomplish that task, the border was secured. Criminal aliens were deported. At Visa Processing Centers, thousands had their visas renewed, work permits granted, or applications for green cards generated. Businesses were provided the voluntary option to take their undocumented workers to an Employment Verification Center for retention as employees. Illegal immigrants were given the opportunity to voluntarily return to their native country or report to one of the Family Reunification Centers for disposition. Not automatically granting citizenship to those born in the United States of foreign parents was another deterrent to illegal entry.

It took less than a year to construct the entire barrier, establish the alien immigration centers, prepare public service announcements, and subsequently notify the public and private sectors. Deportation of the more than 380,000 alien criminals in jails, prisons, or penitentiaries continued, although at a higher rate than under former administrations, especially after the border was secured. The employment verification aspect took about eighteen months to accomplish. Both the business and the employee were very receptive, as both were rewarded rather than punished. Businesses received a financial stipend, and the undocumented worker received papers to remain legally.

Family reunification efforts were less successful; most of the time, it meant deportation—some penalty had to be imposed. For that reason, illegal aliens did not use the program even though the major benefit was creation of a file that gave the deportee priority when applying for legal immigration into the U.S., especially if they had American born children either with them or who remained in America.

Researching, finding, and determining the status of nearly 5 million people who remained in the country beyond their visa-authorized period of stay went well beyond Augustus' term in office, primarily because it was such a massive undertaking and involved so many government and private agencies. The processes implemented identified a large number of them. Many, especially those who had come to the country on college or work visas, had married U.S. citizens, sired families, obtained jobs, or served in the Armed Forces, were granted immediate citizenship. Over 1.5 million adults who were brought to America as children were also granted citizenship. More than 250,000 illegals had already voluntarily returned to their native homelands. Roughly, 133,000 aliens had perished in accidents, from illnesses, or murders.

As was the case with prior administrations, Augustus's administration faced the potential of multiple lawsuits from organizations, cities, and states.

Many Americans were not enthusiastic about aspects of the new law that provided an eventual path to citizenship. But their ire was tempered with the facts that the border was secured, illegal entry was mostly stopped, drug and human trafficking were significantly reduced, criminal aliens were deported, nearly two million illegal aliens were deported, and those who remained paid back taxes and reimbursed Social Security and Medicare.

President You

Chapter 26

Repeal the Twenty-Second Amendment

The executive Power shall be vested in a President of the United States of America. He shall hold his Office during the Term of four years.

(Article II, Section 1, United States Constitution)

No person shall be elected to the office of the President more than twice

(Amendment XXII, Section 1, the United States Constitution)

Frustrated with political stalemates in Washington, many of the president's friends and associates often spoke of placing term limits on members of Congress. Augustus disagreed and offered another approach; repeal the Twenty-Second Amendment to the Constitution. His reasons for turning back the clock, which seemed common sense and obvious and were not supported by the machines of the political parties, followed two basic premises.

Over the last several decades, functionaries in the Legislative Branch had become too divisive. They could not, would not, conduct the people's business. Gridlock occurred, with each party entrenched in its far left and far right ideological beliefs. It was common practice for both parties to effect political strategies designed to thwart the opposing party's White House agenda. As far as members of Congress were concerned, every chief executive elected to the Oval Office was a lame duck.

That attitude was also prevalent in the minds of United States' adversaries and allies. The leaders of those nations need only delay, impede, postpone, or stall foreign policy initiatives with which they disagreed in the hopes a different head of state would view their position in a more favorable light. Reelecting America's leader as often as the citizenry wanted provided an additional and important presidential tool in the world of geopolitical negotiations.

The Twenty-second Amendment violated the checks and balances system established by the Founding Fathers to ensure one branch of government did not have too much power over the other, to the detriment of the people and the country. In essence, it restricted citizens from electing a chief executive who could serve multiple terms in office as a check on and counterbalance to multiple term, careerist-minded legislators.

To get any Congress to work for the people, as its members were hired to do, required lifting the restrictions on the two terms in office of a president. Repealing the Twenty-Second Amendment, Augustus reasoned, would force legislators not only to work together but with the chief executive, as well. The citizens would once again have the power of electing a president as many times as they wanted. Political parties would no longer be guaranteed a two-term lame duck.

Although noble in cause, Augustus' multi-year efforts were rejected. Members of Congress would not give up any of their power either individually or as a legislative body. In addition, President Treatise could not convince voters in large enough numbers that repeal of the Twenty-second Amendment was in their best interests. Consequently, citizens continued to enjoy the benefits and drawbacks of their dysfunctional government.

President You

Chapter 27

Vice President

...the Congress may by Law provide for the Case of Removal, Death, Resignation or Inability, both of the President and Vice President...

(Article II, Section 1, United States Constitution)

...the Congress may by law provide for the case wherein neither a President elect nor a Vice President elect shall have qualified, declaring who shall then act...and such person shall act accordingly until a President or Vice President shall have qualified.

(Amendment XX, Section 3, United States Constitution)

(a)(1) If, by reason of death, resignation, removal from office, inability, or failure to qualify, there is neither a President nor Vice President to discharge the powers and duties of the office of President, then the Speaker of the House of Representatives shall,...act as President.

(b) If...the Speaker fails to qualify as Acting President, then the President pro tempore of the Senate shall ... act as President.

(Presidential Succession Act of 1947. United States Code, Title 3, Chapter 1, Section 19 – Vacancy in offices of both President and Vice President – 3 U.S.C. § 19)

It happened in December that third year of his administration. Long-time friend Vice President Forrestor Addums suffered a severe stroke and died unexpectedly. An autopsy revealed Moyamoya disease had had an indirect effect on his passing years before his time. Flags across the nation were flown at half-staff. Christmas and New Year's functions at the White House were significantly curtailed or cancelled. For the first time in many years, portraits, hearths, doors, and windows were adorned with black drapery instead of evergreen branches, red and green ribbons and bows, shiny ornaments, and colorful lights. The mood was subdued. Forrestor's passing hit Augustus hard.

He and Augustus met in graduate school and had become fast friends. While Augustus remained in the Army, Forrestor had pursued a career in politics and business. He had been a city mayor, a member of a state legislature, and had served four terms in Congress as a representative. Along with his political service, Forrestor had continued to manage his growing business, which expanded to the point that he took it public on the New York Stock Exchange. He had been surprised when Augustus approached him to become his vice presidential candidate. After first declining, Forrestor joined the cause. A sharp contrast to Augustus, after his time in the Capitol he was less idealistic and certainly more experienced with the Washington establishment. An affable man, the vice president dealt with the legislature; Augustus had the vision, policy initiatives, and focus on change while Forrestor negotiated the details. Many in Congress openly considered him to be—or behind closed doors, wished he were—the president.

After Forrestor's funeral, the immediate question arose, "Who will be your new vice president?"

"At this point in my presidency, I don't need one," Augustus angrily declared.

Vice President Addums had barely been laid to rest, and President Treatise was still mourning his friend.

Regardless his personal feelings, calls began in earnest from members of Congress, political opponents, and the media for names of a potential replacement.

Over the Martin Luther King weekend, the White House returned to some sense of normalcy. Augustus used the Friday immediately after the holiday to address the vacancy and questions of a constitutional crisis.

> The passing of Vice President Addums was a blow to all Americans. Forrestor's sudden death dealt me a personal kick in the gut. He was an unwavering friend, a man of integrity, and an honorable vice president who cannot be replaced. Therefore, I do not intend to select a substitute for the remainder of this term, or my next term, in office.
>
> This is nothing new. At various times, for a variety of reasons, America did not have a vice president, the latest during President Gerald Ford's administration. Prior to Ford, as many as eight presidents had no vice president during an entire term in office. No constitutional crisis occurred in those situations.
>
> The Founding Fathers created a document and subsequent leaders amended it and enacted statutes that made allowances for such situations. I trust their judgment, the current

statutes, and the Constitution of the United States.

Opponents, media pundits, and many of those who believed they had any influence whatsoever, continued to harp on his refusal to identify a vice president. True, there was a downturn in the markets, geo-political issues with allies and foes, concerns about the economy, and other national considerations, but those, as with past administrations, were temporary.

Over his objections, Congress labored through the process of finding, nominating, and voting their choice for vice president. Augustus countered,

> In the first few of America's elections, the vice president was a member of a different political outlook than the president. He was often ignored and left out of any governing processes. George Washington and John Adams offer the most obvious example. In some cases, the vice president worked directly against the efforts of the president— as was the case of Adams and Jefferson.
>
> Just because both were eventually placed on the same ballot as running mates of the same party did not mean the VP was a governing participant. Roosevelt kept Truman in the dark about the Manhattan Project during World War II, and northerner Kennedy selected Johnson for the main purpose of getting southern votes. Hence, the creation of such phrases as "The vice president is to be seen and not heard" and

"The vice presidency is probably the most important job that nobody wants."

As with Lyndon Johnson, Harry Truman, Theodore Roosevelt, 10 other presidents, and even Founding Father James Madison, I am perfectly capable of leading America without a vice president.

As happened all too often, gridlock prevented any one legislature-favored candidate from being selected—neither party wanted the other party to provide the next in line for chief executive and potentially run the country. By law, without a vice president, the successor to the presidency was the Speaker of the House of Representatives. Next in line was the President pro tempore of the Senate. Neither individual saw any reason why they should give up their powerful status to become a de facto vice president, who in all likelihood would be ignored by Augustus.

No vice president was ever investitured.

President You

Chapter 28

The White House

White House, the Executive Mansion and official residence of the Pres. of the U.S., situated on Pennsylvania Ave., Washington, D.C.

What was it like living in a two-hundred-year-old museum—the President's House, as it was originally called? Augustus said it was, "daunting and haunting." He wrote in his diary that first night in office, "Celebration over. Burden begins."

A month later an entry read,

> The pressure of responsibility as the free world's leader feels as if I am a modern day Atlas with the weight of the earth upon my shoulders. Adding to that stress are the eyes from oil paintings of every predecessor that seem to follow me in and out of rooms, along hallways, and up and down staircases, as if constantly asking, "are you good enough?"

The Treatises' years in the White House were decidedly different from those of many administrations. Previous chief executives, while in office, retained their original residences and stayed there periodically. To do so cost the taxpayers millions of dollars in upgrades. The houses were renovated with bullet-

307

proof glass, rocket- and explosive-deterrent siding, bombproof roofs, and safe rooms. Multiple and redundant security systems, alarms, video cameras, and high intensity lighting were added. Secure Internet and telephones were installed. Electrified and passive sensor fences or walls were built around property perimeters—all modifications to support the "Hometown White House."

Added to those residential enhancements were office structures or mobile homes for Secret Service agents, weapons caches for immediate response, and communications centers for contacting anyone, anywhere, anytime across the world. When land area did not support the number of facilities necessary, houses next door were purchased and modified or razed to construct garages for limousines, SUVs, motorcycles, all-terrain vehicles, snowmobiles, or a helipad. All these taxpayer-funded expenses were unnecessary under his presidency.

Keeping a campaign promise to cut government spending, Augustus and Angelica did not reside outside the White House. They sold all three of their automobiles, as well as their home. After moving furniture, clothing, and selected personal items into the White House, their remaining household goods were placed in storage.

Both the president and first lady dressed appropriately but not ostentatiously for official occasions. The days of $5,000 suits and $10,000 designer dresses were gone. All Cabinet secretaries, ambassadors, judges, political appointees, and Executive Branch personnel were expected to follow suit—to use a military term, "lead by example"—when it came to clothing. Appropriate yet moderate became watchwords for attire.

During their occupancy, Augustus and Angelica met every White House employee whose duty it was to maintain and keep that icon of power operating to perfection. They roamed halls, rooms, attic, basement, nooks, and crannies to find the people behind the scenes. It was common to find either of them visiting graveyard shift workers. Exhibiting their inquisitive natures, the president and first lady often accompanied and occasionally assisted individual staff members as they performed their duties. Both kept that personal contact approach during their entire time in office, greeting and welcoming new employees as well as bidding a fond farewell to those who departed for other opportunities. They arranged for employees' families to meet the senior representatives of the U.S. in a less formal atmosphere.

Augustus and Angelica's interactions were not limited to the White House. Their personal touch carried over to Camp David, Joint Base Andrews, and Naval Support Facility Anacostia. Often either the commander in chief or first lady would show up after midnight—what Armed Forces members referred to as o-dark-thirty—to converse with military personnel inside Hangar 1 who were busily preparing Air Force One for flight. The rest of the 89th Airlift Wing, whose responsibility it was to transport senior government officials across the globe, was not excluded from those visits; neither were the air traffic controllers nor ground and maintenance crews and security teams. Similar visitations occurred with flight crews and support teams of Marine One under the command of Marine Helicopter Squadron One.

Angelica would write of those excursions,

> Those dark-of-night or before dawn visits with White House, Camp David, Joint Base Andrews, and Anacostia civilian workers and military personnel were some of the best times of my life. They were breaths of fresh

air, away from the polluted atmosphere of Washington. Oh, how conversing with those wonderful people comforted me!

The Treatises attempted to keep to their pre-White House daily routine as much as possible. At 5 a.m., Angelica would slide from beneath the bedcovers, careful not to disturb her mate. In the bedroom closet she would remove her pajamas and don a "been there, done that" t-shirt from a long ago vacation adventure, sweatpants, ankle socks, and athletic shoes. Walking softly across the floor, she would depart the residence. Along the well-travelled route to the basement workout room, her Secret Service detail in tow, she offered "Good morning" to fellow early risers preparing for the day's scheduled events. The wall-mounted television had been activated and tuned to her favorite morning news program before she arrived. After a forty-minute workout, the first lady would head back upstairs, stop at her office, check her calendar and e-mails, gather work materials, and mull over thoughts for the day. By six o'clock, she would return to the bedroom. Once inside the Residence, Angelica would wake her husband of many years and proceed into the master bath to complete her morning ritual.

Augustus eased slowly into the day. He would lie naked in bed another fifteen minutes. Then, unhurriedly, he would crawl out of bed, put on socks, underwear, sweat suit, and sneakers and head downstairs to the mini-gym. Turning on the TV and selecting a movie channel, he would perform a series of pre-scribed physical therapy exercises designed to strengthen his core muscles to relieve the stress on his back caused by a bulging disc. Working out with his security detail, he alternated treadmill and heavy weight-lifting days with the more difficult elliptical and less strenuous weight routines. Two hours later, skin beaded and clothes soaked in sweat, the president would return to the residence for a well-deserved shower and chuckle to himself as he recalled the three S's (shit, shower, shave) from his army days. After a breakfast of oatmeal with sliced strawberries and a glass of orange juice in the Family Dining Room, Augustus would dress and walk to the Oval Office via the West Colonnade adjacent to the Rose Garden.

In the evenings, they would watch an old movie on DVD or television, and then off to bed by 9:30 p.m. Augustus would read aloud to Angelica from one of his many biographies of historical figures or spy novels until she fell asleep. He often continued reading until he dozed off or eventually turned out the light around 11:30.

Under Augustus' presidency, the White House was no longer a tourist stop exclusively for the rich and famous. Gone were private visits and entertainment by A-list actors and actresses of film and stage, recording star singers and musicians, renowned dancers and dance troupes, comedians, icons of television, and other notable talents. The Lincoln bedroom, so often notoriously linked to favors as if it were rented by the hour, remained idle. Selected annual events were no longer held. The President's House returned to what Augustus and Angelica believed it was always supposed to be: a residence first; a private office second; the People's House third; a symbol of the greatest nation on the face of the earth fourth; and lastly, the identified locale of the most temporarily powerful person in the world.

Championship teams, Olympians, and individual sports winners were congratulated at their home arena, center, course, court, diamond, field, gym, pool, ring, rink, stadium, track, training camp, or turf; trips to the White House became passé. Medals of Honor and Medals of Freedom were awarded to recipients at public venues in that person's hometown. In that way the president and first lady mingled among the champions and heroes, their families and friends, support groups, fellow competitors, and fans, rather than commanding the victors and awardees come to them for an exclusive audience as if they were king and queen.

Eventually, as required by the Constitution and America's voters, Augustus and Angelica prepared to leave their temporary home after what felt like a century of service. Their White House moment had prematurely aged them both; Father Time had accelerated the wear and tear. Over the course of his presidency, in his loneliest hours and before any major decision, Augustus had often asked the structure of white:

> If only your hallowed walls could talk. What hidden stories might you tell of bold decisions and wimpy initiatives, of quiet reflection and lively parties, of intimate intercourse and scandalous sex, of promising engagements and mournful sadness? What advice might you provide? What wisdom might you impart?

The untimely passing of their dear friend Forrestor Addums weighed heavily and was a significant factor in Augustus' decision not to seek a second term. Their lofty titles, privileges, honors, and albatrosses drew to a close—as they must.

In the midst of changing administrations, Augustus and Angelica spoke to close associates of their now completed bucket list and their desire to see less of the world. Their hours upon hours airborne on Air Force One had finally ended. Each was looking forward to years of terra firma contentment with their children and grandchildren and periods of joint solitude.

President and First Lady Treatise discussed their enduring faith in the future of the nation—their country and its citizens. They contemplated examples set by former Associate Justice Oliver Wendell Holmes and several other Americans who left the bulk of their estates to the treasured land so loved and in which they believed. However, in the decades since those earlier times, many things had changed.

Augustus explained, "The self-serving, sanctimonious vultures who occupy the halls of Congress will only borrow against any money I leave the treasury—as many times as they can get away with it. In the near term, I will be hailed as a great and patriotic philanthropist only to have my good name later associated with numerous bills for nonsensical programs touted as the next best thing since sliced bread. All designed for each drunk-with-power political hack to garner enough votes to retain his or her fiefdom. Ultimately, the scallywags will replace actual resources with a worthless I.O.U. as they have done so many times before with various federal program trust funds."

Angelica knew "self-righteous government princes" would continue circumventing laws. Presidents, members of Congress, even America had a poor track record when it came to honoring legal and binding agreements. Depending on the predilections of those in power and oxen to be gored, statutes were ignored or enforced. Treaties with Indian nations and agreements with other countries were broken time after time. Like an alcoholic, drug addict, or kleptomaniac, the malingerers in government wanted their next drink, fix, or item—in this case, the next dollar. The Treatises would put their personal resources to better use.

A monument to vanity in the form of a presidential library was instantly rejected and never established. All gifts Augustus and Angelica received while occupying the White House

313

remained in government hands—by donation to the Smith-
sonian, as they already had too many favorite possessions from
their private lives of which to dispose.

At the time of their departure, they had not decided on a
community in which to reside and live out their years. The
ultimate location would be their final move; except to a
nondescript, away from the limelight, community cemetery like
Presidents Martin Van Buren, James Buchanan, Chester Arthur,
and Calvin Coolidge, and the world beyond darkness into
eternal light. There would be no mausoleum, family crypt, or
statuary. Simple headstones, some years from now, would
eventually confirm and mark they once existed on earth.

Chapter 29

Home

home *n.* One's place of residence; the dwelling place of a family

Up to and including their departure from the White House, there had been several years, all seven continents, eighty-three countries, every state and territory in the union, twenty-three Indian nations, one district, three apartments, four military quarters, seven houses, and fifteen moves. However, it took three more disruptions over two years before Angelica finally got her wish: to retire and dote on grandchildren, enjoy life, reduce stress, and make time for each other.

First, they rented a house in Washington, D.C. into which they placed their possessions from the White House and where they temporarily resided. After ninety days, they made a more permanent move to a condominium overlooking Kansas City's Country Club Plaza. Nine months later, they acquired an apartment in a local senior living, continuing care retirement community and began to downsize in earnest. They gave their children those items they desired and relocated selected possessions into the apartment. Nearly everything else was auctioned to support several local charities. An estate agent was hired to dispose of whatever remained.

In the twilight of their years they were back almost where they started as a newly wedded couple decades before — owning little in the way of things, but possessing many special mementoes and extraordinary memories. They considered themselves lucky. Life had been good. "Not too bad for a couple of kids from the boondocks," they would say. A president and first lady returned to their roots, just two average people who lived uncommon lives and now resided with ordinary citizens.

"Angelica."

"Yes?"

"How about..."

"Are you out of your ever lovin' mind?!"

A Call to Action

Our Founding Fathers established a constitutional republic based on the representative democracy concept. Core to its creation is a government answerable to the people through citizen participation. Its genius is a flexibility that responds to the will of its citizenry.

In *President You*, independent of circumstance, every citizen has the opportunity to change national policy. It is my hope that fictional President Augustus Lincoln Treatise, the issues he confronted, and the solutions he developed, encourages you, in your own fashion, to greater involvement in America. Each of us has a voice and in our own way is a **President YOU.**

Questions for Contemplation

and Discussion

The following questions follow up on some of the key issues, moments, and situations in the story. Reflect on them alone or with a group to help connect the story with your own experiences, opinions, and possible future choices. Note that these queries are intended to be open-ended: there are no right (or wrong) answers to any of them, and you need not agree with any positions taken in the book to benefit from the story or these questions.

๛๛๛

The family of Augustus Treatise has strong reactions to his idea of running for president. How might your own family and friends react if you shared that same ambition? Do you think their concerns or opposition would stop you from running?

What might your reaction be if a granddaughter or grandson decided to run for president?

How, if at all, do you believe the inconvenience suffered by candidates' inner circles affects our ability to get high-quality candidates for elected office?

Politicians, including President Treatise, use national land-marks and monuments as settings for major announcements and speeches. What locale would you choose were you to speak on matters of national concern? How does that place reflect your vision of America, its future, or its ideals?

In our history's presidents, we see our citizens' hopes, fears, beliefs, and questions not just reflected but magnified. Do you have a favorite commander in chief from our history? What do you think that head of state expressed about what is best and most powerful about the American dream, character, and community?

Paradoxically, the presidents we most emphatically dislike or criticize also reflect our sense of America's greatness. Think about a president you disliked or disagreed with. Focusing on leadership, how do you think he let America, its ideals or its potential down? In what way do you believe his actions, beliefs, or styles reflected flaws in the American character?

Which of the issues President Treatise attempts to solve felt most urgent and important to you? Why?

How might you help support what you see as necessary change on the issue you identified? Donations? Volunteerism? Social media or other advocacy? A run for elected office?

Were one or more issues covered that you believe do not need policy change? Think about why you feel the status quo on that issue is viable and/or just.

Were any issues of importance to you omitted from the book's narrative? Why do you feel they are important? How would you like to see a future president address them?

The complexity of America's government makes change slow and difficult. Do you think changes to the system could facilitate solutions and improvements? Why or why not?

How well informed do you feel about the policy issues described in this book? Might you invest some time, even if a small amount, in further research and self-education on one or more of these issues? How?

The vision of America's greatest leaders from the Founding Fathers on was of active, informed, and engaged citizens. Do you see their vision more or less difficult to achieve today?

The ability of an ordinary citizen to make change in America through government service is a core theme of the book. Yet those who never hold government office can also have significant impact. What figures in that latter category come to mind? How did their role in a field other than government help them envision, enact, or encourage change?

How might the book's story as a whole, and/or its depiction of policy initiatives, be different if its fictional president were a woman? A younger person? A person with a religion not previously represented by an American president?

What one thing might you personally do within the next six months to play a more active role as a citizen? Within the next year? Five years?

Key Chapter Topics

Bibliography and Sources

America's Founding Documents

Declaration of Independence, July 4, 1776.

Constitution of the United States, September 17, 1787.

Proposed 12 Amendments to the U.S. Constitution, September 25, 1789.

The Bill of Rights, December 15, 1791 (Ratification of proposed amendments 3–12).

The Constitution of the United States of America, as amended, May 7, 1992.

Historical Speeches

House Divided Speech, Abraham Lincoln, June 16, 1858.

Gettysburg Address, Abraham Lincoln, November 19, 1863.

Published Works

Bradley, Sculley (University of Pennsylvania) and Beatty, Richmond Croom (Vanderbilt University) and Long, E. Hudson (Baylor University), Editors, *The American Tradition in Literature*, Third Edition, Shorter Edition in One Volume, Pages 728-747, W. W. Norton & Company, Inc., New York, 1967, 1961, 1957 ꞌ͠Ꞌ

Bibliography and Sources

Franklin, Benjamin. "Protection of Towns from Fire," *Pennsylvania Gazette,* Newspaper, February 4, 1735 edition, writing as "Old Citizen."

Holiday and Patriotic Song Book, Disabled American Veterans, Cincinnati, Ohio, undated.

Huxley, Aldous. "The Arts of Selling," in *Brave New World Revisited,* Harper & Row, Publishers, New York, NY, 1958 and Chatto and Windus, Ltd., London, England, 1959.

Kinglake, Alexander William. *EOTHEN,* written 1830, J. Ollivier, London, 1844.

Kowet, Don. "Inside Story," in *A Matter of Honor: General William C. Westmorland versus CBS News,* Page 263, Macmillan Publishing Company, New York, 1984, and Collier Macmillan Publishers, London, 1984.

Lazarus, Emma. "The New Colossus," Original Manuscript, November 2, 1883, written for the Art Loan Fund Exhibition in Aid of the Bartholdi Pedestal Fund for the Statue of Liberty, currently held by the National Park Service, Statue of Liberty, Liberty Island, New York, New York.

Muscatine, Charles (University of California, Berkeley) and Griffith, Marlene (Laney College), Editors, Copyright 1966, *The Borzoi College Reader, Shorter Edition,* Fourth Printing, Pages 74-85, 101-107, 162-179, Alfred A. Knopf, Inc., Publisher, New York, 1968, published simultaneously by Random House of Canada Limited, Toronto, Canada, 1968.

Orwell, George. "Politics and the English Language," *Horizon,* London monthly, Volume 13, Issue 76, pages 252-265, April 1946.

Risch, Erna. *Supplying Washington's Army,* Center for Military History, ' States Army, Washington, D.C., 1981.

Sherman, William T. Personal Letter dated February 17, 1863, published in *American Heritage,* Volume 38, Issue 5, July/August 1987, entitled "The New Sherman Letters," written by Joseph H. Ewing.

Swift, Jonathan. *Gulliver's Travels and other Writings,* with an Introduction and Commentaries by Ricardo Quintana, Professor of English, University of Wisconsin, The Modern Library, New York. Pages 57-116, 415-418, Copyright Random House, Inc., New York, NY, 1958.

Swift, Jonathan. "A Voyage to Brobdingnag," *Travels into Several Remote Nations of the World (a.k.a. Gulliver's Travels),* Volume III of Swift's works containing Four Parts, Printed by and for George Faulkner, Printer and Bookseller, Essex Street, Dublin, Ireland, 1735.

Swift, Jonathan. *Various Thoughts, Moral and Diverting (a.k.a. Thoughts on Various Subjects),* Written October 1, 1706; included in his *Miscellanies in Prose and Verse,* The First Edition, Printed for John Morphew, near Stationer's-Hall, 1711.

The Official Rules of Card Games, Hoyle Up-to-Date, Publisher's 48th Edition, Pages 3-5, Whitman Publishing Company, Racine, Wisconsin, 1952.

Thoreau, Henry David. *Civil Disobedience, A Yankee in Canada with Anti-Slavery and Reform Papers,* Ticknor and Fields, Boston, 1866; originally titled *"Resistance to Civil Government," Aesthetic Papers,* edited by Elizabeth Palmer Peabody, The Editor, Boston, 1849.

Webster's Unified Dictionary and Encyclopedia, H.S. Stuttman Company, Inc., New York 16, N.Y., 1960.

Wheat, Clayton E. "The Cadet Prayer," *Bugle Notes,* pages 42-43, Chaplain (Lieutenant Colonel), United States Army, United States Military Academy, West Point, New York, 1921.

Legal Background

Code of Ethics, 72 Statutes at Large B12, House Concurrent Resolution 175, 85th Congress, 2nd Session, January 7, 1958–August 24, 1958, Enacted July 11, 1958.

Feres v. United States, 340 U.S. 135 (1950).

The President, 3 U.S.C. §15. Title 3 *The President*, United States Code, Chapter 1, *Presidential Elections and Vacancies*, Section 15, *Counting Electoral Votes in Congress*, 2011 Edition. This title was enacted by act June 25, 1948, ch. 644, §1, 62 Stat. 672. (Originally enacted 3 February 1887, it has gone through several revisions and replacements until currently as written).

The Federal Register, as amended, 2016.

The Posse Comitatus Act, 18 U.S.C. § 1385, original at 20 Stat. 152, signed on June 18, 1878.

United States Code, as amended, 2016.

Zadvydas v. Davis, 533 U.S. 678 (2001).

Websites

Many websites were consulted to compare or confirm information as well as gather historical and numerical details. Below are those found to be useful.

An Official website of the United States Government – www.usa.gov, 2019.

Centers for Disease Control and Prevention – www.cdc.gov, 2018.

Centers for Medicare and Medicaid Services – www.cms.gov, 2019.

Central Intelligence Agency – www.cia.gov, 2018.

Defense Health Agency & the Military Health System – https://health.mil/, 2019.

Federal Communications Commission – www.fcc.gov, 2016.

Federal Election Commission – www.fec.gov, 2019.

Federal Emergency Management Agency – www.fema.gov, 2016.

Federal Government of Germany – www.bundesregierung.de, 2016.

Federal Trade Commission – www.ftc.gov, 2016.

Federalist Papers – www.congress.gov/resources, 2018.

Government of Canada – www.canada.ca/en.html, 2016.

Government of England – www.gov.uk, 2016.

Government of Netherlands – www.government.nl, 2016.

Internal Revenue Service – www.irs.gov, 2016.

Merriam-Webster – www.merriam-webster.com, 2019.

Military Health System & the Defense Health Agency –
    https://health.mil/, 2019.

National Aeronautics and Space Administration – www.nasa.gov,
    2016.

National Archives – www.archives.gov, 2019.

National Association of Secretaries of State – www.nass.org, 2019.

National Congress of American Indians – www.ncai.org, 2019.

National Organization for Rare Disorders – www.rarediseases.org,
    2018.

National Park Service – www.nps.gov, 2019.

National Park Service – www.nps.gov/thro/learn/historyculture/
    theodore-roosevelt-and-conservation.htm, 2018.

Office of the Assistant Secretary for Planning and Evaluation, U.S.
    Department of Health and Human Services –
    https://aspe.hhs.gov/basic-report/medicaid-estate-recovery, 2019.

Official U.S. Government Site for Medicare – www.medicare.gov,
    2019.

Public Health Law Center – www.publichealthlawcenter.org, 2018.

Russian Government – www.government.ru, 2018.

Social Security Administration – www.ssa.gov, 2019.

Statistics Portal – www.statista.com, 2017.

Supreme Court of the United States – www.supremecourt.gov, 2016.

Surgeon General – www.surgeongeneral.gov, 2018.

Thomas Paine Cottage Museum – www.thomaspainecottage.org, 2017.

Thomas Paine's Cottage, Sandwich, Kent, England – www.thomaspaineshouse.co.uk, 2017.

United Nations – www.un.org, 2016.

United States Army – www.army.mil, 2016.

United States Census Bureau – www.census.gov, 2019.

United States Coast Guard – www.usgc.gov, 2016.

United States Environmental Protection Agency – www.epa.gov, 2016.

United States Government Publishing Office – www.gpo.gov, 2019, and www.govinfo.gov, 2019.

United States House of Representatives – www.house.gov, 2018.

United States House of Representatives, Art and Archives History – www.history.house.gov, 2019.

United States Senate – www.senate.gov, 2018.

U.S. Customs and Border Protection – www.cbp.gov, 2016.

U.S. Department of Defense – www.defense.gov, 2018.

U.S. Department of Health and Human Services – www.hhs.gov, 2019.

U.S. Department of Homeland Security – www.dhs.gov, 2016.

U.S. Department of Housing and Urban Development – www.hud.gov, 2017.

U.S. Department of Housing and Urban Development, Office of Policy Development and Research – www.huduser.gov, 2017.

U.S. Department of Labor – www.dol.gov, 2018.

U.S. Department of Veterans Affairs – www.va.gov, 2018.

Utah Legislature, Senate Joint Resolution 002, calling for Repeal of the Seventeenth Amendment – https://le.utah.gov/, 2016.

Veterans Health Administration – https://www.va.gov/health, 2019.

Website of the Hungarian Government – www.kormany.hu, 2016.

White House – www.whitehouse.gov, 2018.

Wikipedia The Free Encyclopedia – www.en.wikipedia.org, 2015–2019.

World Health Organization – www.who.int/gho/, 2018.

Acknowledgements

It is my distinct privilege to recognize the following individuals for their gracious support and assistance leading to the successful publication of *President You*.

Judy, my bride of many years, who endured reading the first, third, fifth and eighth version of my manuscript, and she provided sensitive, compassionate, direct advice and correction. My close friends who offered challenging assessment, claiming they probably caused me enough grief, and neighbors who liked the concept. Amy Woods Butler (The Story Scribe, LLC, www.thestoryscribe.com), she was the first person from the professional literary community outside my close circle of confidants to provide positive observation. Suzanne "Suz" Fox (www.bookstrategy.com) publisher, author, and developmental editor, whose insights and advice were both encouraging and humbling, nudging me in the direction I really needed to go. Julie Tenenbaum (Final Draft Secretarial Service) whose copy-editing skills added sorely needed polish to what was surely a grammatical nightmare. Kelly Ludden (Kelly Ludden Design, LLC, www.kellyluddendesign.com), her creative talents, and artwork of the book cover.

To the Founding Fathers, whose foresight and wisdom codified for all Americans the authority to write and speak in freedom. Last, but not least, all courageous authors and writers who wrote before me and to those who have yet to put pen to paper.

About the Author

Tom Williams was born in the Sandhills area of western Nebraska. He attended public K-12 schools and was a Cub, Boy, and Explorer Scout. In his youth and into adulthood, he played a wide variety of sports. He earned a Bachelor of Science from the United States Military Academy, West Point, New York, and commissioning as a Second Lieutenant, United States Army. Tom achieved Cum Laude honors obtaining a Masters of Public Administration from the Martin School, University of Kentucky, Lexington, Kentucky.

Throughout his life, Tom worked in the Executive Branch of federal, state, and county governments, in corporate America, small businesses, internationally renowned charitable organizations, and as a government contractor. He is a disabled veteran who lived, served, traveled, and vacationed on six continents through nearly three dozen countries. Tom has appeared on local morning television and noontime radio talk shows and has conducted crisis management seminars in Asia, Europe, and the United States.

Since his retirement in 2011, he has focused on writing. His first work, completed in 2015 and given to his family, was a 600-page, four-year effort tracing his family genealogy from their arrival in the New World in the late 1600s until today.

Tom and his wife Judy now reside in Kansas.

Made in the
USA
Middletown, DE